GOOD HOUSEKEEPING

400
HEART HEALTHY
RECIPES & TIPS

GOOD HOUSEKEEPING

400
HEART HEALTHY
RECIPES & TIPS

HEARST BOOKS
New York

HEARST BOOKS
New York

An Imprint of Sterling Publishing
1166 Avenue of the Americas
New York, NY 10036

ISBN 978-1-61837-198-0

Distributed in Canada by Sterling Publishing
c/o Canadian Manda Group, 664 Annette Street
Toronto, Ontario, Canada M6S 2C8
Distributed in Australia by Capricorn Link (Australia) Pty. Ltd.
P.O. Box 704, Windsor, NSW 2756, Australia

For information about custom editions, special sales, and premium and corporate purchases, please contact Sterling Special Sales at 800-805-5489 or specialsales@sterlingpublishing.com.

Manufactured in China

2 4 6 8 10 9 7 5 3 1

www.sterlingpublishing.com

CONTENTS

Grilled Ratatouille Pasta (page 130)

FOREWORD

Eat well, live longer. How many times have you heard that? Of course you want to eat healthfully, limit saturated fats, add more vegetables and grains, and not overdo the salt . . . but if this equation doesn't add up to delicious food, your family won't get onboard. So how to do it? There are so many options—and on many days, so little time. In this book, we've gathered our favorite good-for-you recipes that are easy and quick to prepare, and will pass the family's deliciousness test.

Filled with smart dietary tips and great-tasting recipes—all low in calories, saturated fat, and sodium, *Good Housekeeping 400 Heart Healthy Recipes & Tips* is our solution. We open with simple heart-healthy changes you can make right now. These include suggestions like "eat more vegetables and fruits" (our antioxidant-rich fruit smoothies and vegetarian mains like Broccoli Pesto Pasta make this easy). Dinners like Five-Spice Pork with Gingered Vegetables (and a side of bulgur) will help you reduce the role of meat from star to supporting player. To help your family get their omega-3s, serve oily fish like salmon twice a week (try our Ginger-Crusted Salmon with Melon Salsa).

Blueberries, avocados, nuts, and, yes, dark chocolate, are among the superfoods we discuss on page 15. Enjoy them in Whole-Grain Blueberry Muffins and Sweet Chipotle Chicken, which stacks spicy chicken cutlets with avocado and tomato slices. We also offer ideas on how to trade "bad" fats for "good" ones and reduce sodium (for starters, look for reduced-sodium canned foods and condiments).

Throughout the book, you'll find scrumptious recipes from our Cook Your Heart Out contests. They were all developed by readers just like you, who want to eat well and deliciously, and live longer.

SUSAN WESTMORELAND
Food Director, *Good Housekeeping*

INTRODUCTION

We've all heard the sobering statistics: Cardiovascular disease affects more than one in every three American adults—and heart disease is the leading cause of death. But there's a flip side to this bad news: A healthy diet is one of the best weapons in the fight against cardiovascular disease. So, in 400 *Heart Healthy Recipes & Tips*, Good Housekeeping serves up tasty, heart-healthy recipes and cooking tips selected by our food director, Susan Westmoreland, along with nutritional information and recommendations from our nutrition director, Jaclyn London.

Whether your focus is prevention or you or a family member have already been diagnosed with heart disease (or a disease like diabetes or obesity that puts one at high risk), these satisfying recipes and real-world dietary tips will help set you and them on course. Included are great-tasting breakfasts, snacks, main dishes, sides, and even heart-smart desserts your whole family will love. In addition, we share outstanding heart-healthy recipes from the winners of our Cook Your Heart Out contests. These home cooks were inspired to create delicious recipes that meet our heart-healthy guidelines, and we hope their efforts will inspire you to cook good food for your heart, too. Think of healthy cooking and eating as an opportunity to sample new recipes and reinvent old favorites: the great-tasting recipes in this cookbook should keep you busy for a while! Just be sure to consult your physician before embarking on a new dietary regimen if you are already being treated for a cardiovascular disease.

Nutrition Guidelines for a Healthy Heart

To help keep important heart-health indicators like blood pressure, cholesterol, and blood sugar (glucose) at the right levels, the American Heart Association recommends eating a wide, balanced variety of nutritious foods. Mix nutrient-rich foods that are lower in calories, saturated fat, and sodium into your meal planning, and you and your family members will not only get a full complement of vitamins, minerals, fiber, and other essentials, but also a dazzling array of colors, tastes, and textures every day of the week.

DIETARY GUIDELINES

The recipes in this book were specially selected so that you don't have to worry about calculating nutritional totals for every meal—we do the job for you. Here is the breakdown of calories and nutrients we look for:

- All main dishes are 500 calories or fewer per serving. Side dishes and snacks contain 150 calories or fewer per serving; for desserts, we've allowed a little wiggle room on the calories because they are meant to be a treat—not part of every meal.

- Each main dish contains 5 grams or fewer per serving of saturated fat. For each side dish, snack, or dessert, that's 2 grams or fewer of saturated fat.

- Each entrée contains 480 milligrams or fewer of sodium; each side dish, snack, or dessert has 360 milligrams or fewer.

To help you keep on target, all the recipes in this book are low in calories, saturated fat, and sodium. Complete nutritional information is provided at the end of every recipe. Because we know that quick and do-ahead meals make it easier to keep on the heart-smart eating track, most of the recipes can be made in 30 minutes or less.

Saturated fat and sodium are the most important numbers to watch for a heart-smart diet, but since obesity and heart disease often go hand in hand, keeping calories in check is important, too. And remember, both a heart-healthy diet and exercise improve cholesterol and lower blood pressure and blood sugar—all factors that play a role in heart disease. So, work at least 30 minutes of exercise into your routine every day; even vigorous cleaning, yard chores, or a few laps around your office or up and down the stairs can make a difference.

NOTE: If you have been diagnosed with heart disease, high blood pressure, diabetes, or obesity, you should consult your physician before making any changes to your diet or exercise routine.

Heart-Healthy Changes
You Can Make Right Now

Eating smarter and keeping your heart in peak shape is about more than munching on a celery stick now and then. It's about the bigger picture—the pattern of decisions you make every day for yourself and the family members you cook for.

Ultimately, a heart-smart diet brims with vegetables and fruit, moderate portions of whole grains and lean protein (skinless poultry, lean beef, pork tenderloin), two servings of fish a week, and a couple of fat-free dairy servings a day (milk, yogurt). Focus on healthy fats like nuts, nut butters, and olive oil. Have a glass of wine if you like. But even small, simple changes can make a big difference. For starters, make a commitment to cooking with fresh, natural ingredients whenever possible. Then follow these ideas for additional changes you can tackle, one at a time.

- **EAT MORE VEGETABLES AND FRUIT.** These colorful beauties are loaded with vitamins, minerals, and heart-protective antioxidants. To get started, try adding a fruit or vegetable to each meal. For breakfast, sprinkle berries on your oatmeal or have a sliced banana and peanut butter on toast; at lunch, enjoy carrot sticks or cherry tomatoes with your hummus; for dinner, make a big salad or a vegetable stir-fry. Even drinking a glass of (low-sodium) vegetable juice every day can help, researchers from the University of California, Davis, recently found. In their study, more than half of the participants who drank one glass of vegetable juice a day got five daily veggie servings (meeting the guidelines of a heart-healthy eating plan), compared with less than a quarter of those who had no juice (everyone who had two glasses daily met the vegetable goals). For maximum benefits, choose fresh produce whenever possible. When cooking with frozen or canned vegetables and fruit, select those without added salt and sugars or sauces.

- **REDUCE THE ROLE OF MEAT FROM STAR TO SUPPORTING PLAYER.** To help decrease your family's intake of saturated fat, try filling two-thirds of their plates with veggies, legumes, and grains and the remaining third with lean meat or poultry—then make it

Greek-Style Tilapia (page 201)

a habit. And why not mix things up by serving two or more vegetarian-style meals each week? In Chapter 3: Veggie & Whole-Grain Mains (page 114), we provide lots of satisfying vegetarian options that may just become family favorites.

When cooking with red meat, choose leaner cuts like loin or round, as these usually have the least fat. When selecting poultry, take advantage of lean, quick-cooking cuts like skinless chicken breast halves or cutlets and tenderloins, or chicken tenders. Poultry skin gets 80 percent of its calories from fat, so it makes sense to serve chicken and turkey without it. But feel free to leave the skin on during cooking for added flavor. According to the USDA, it makes little nutritional difference in the fat content whether the skin is removed before cooking or not. Grilling, baking, and broiling are heart-smart cooking methods when it comes to both red meat and poultry.

- **TWICE A WEEK, SERVE FISH.** The fish with the highest levels of EPA and DHA—the omega-3 fatty acids that lower inflammation and help protect against heart arrhythmias—is salmon. Choose farmed, wild, or canned (which is usually wild). Or try sardines, herring, mackerel, or tuna. If you typically only order fish at restaurants, check out Chapter 4: Fish & Shellfish (page 168) for recipes, including several dishes featuring salmon that are not only delicious, but easy to prepare, too. If you're not a fan of seafood, take fish-oil capsules (you want 1,000 milligrams of DHA plus EPA daily). Vegetarians can use a plant-based omega-3 supplement.

- **GO FOR AN OIL CHANGE.** Put away the butter, and start cooking with olive or canola oil, both of which are rich in monounsaturated fats. In one Norwegian study, eating more unsaturated (and less saturated) fats yielded healthier levels of LDL and heart-boosting HDL. And if you haven't already banished trans fats from your menu, there's no better time than the present. Reviled by cardiologists as "Frankenfats" because they clog and inflame arteries, trans fats still show up in many processed foods, especially baked goods. You can't go by the product label, since foods that deliver under 0.5 gram of trans fats per serving are legally permitted to claim they contain no trans fats. It can be hard to find trans fats on the ingredients list, so it's best to avoid any food product that contains shortening or partially hydrogenated oil. See also "Five Simple Ways to Trade Bad Fats for Good," on page 15.

- **SWITCH TO REDUCED-FAT, LOW-FAT, OR FAT-FREE DAIRY PRODUCTS.** You'll be amazed by how easy it is to downsize from whole to fat-free milk and yogurt if you make the change gradually. Go to 2-percent for a few weeks, then 1-percent for a while, and you are there. (Note that calcium-fortified soy milk can meet your dairy requirements, as well.) Reduced-fat or part-skim cheeses will work well in many of your favorite recipes, too, including Grandma's lasagna.

- **MAKE AT LEAST HALF YOUR GRAINS WHOLE GRAINS.** Their high soluble-fiber content can help lower blood cholesterol levels, reducing your risk of heart disease and stroke. There are now more whole-grain choices than ever. In addition to readily available bulk grains—from brown rice to bulgur to oats—try swapping in whole-wheat or whole-grain pasta and whole-grain breads. Just be sure to read the label carefully: Look for the word "whole" in the ingredients list, and note where the whole grain falls in the list. Ingredients are listed in order of weight; if a whole grain is listed first and is the only grain, there is a lot of whole grain in the product. When baking, you can often swap up to half of the all-purpose flour in a recipe for whole-wheat flour.

- **NIBBLE A FEW NUTS.** Munching on walnuts, almonds, pistachios, or peanuts several times a week can make you 35 percent less prone to heart trouble. But the monounsaturated fats that make nuts heart-healthy can also pack on the calories. Have a half-ounce with your breakfast cereal. You're less likely to overeat nuts then. Or eat some with a piece of fruit or sliced veggies for a snack. Their fat increases the absorption of nutrients in produce up to eighteen times.

- **FINALLY, TAKE CONTROL OF SALT.** The American Heart Association recommends that you choose and prepare foods that are naturally low in sodium, with a goal of eating less than 1,500 milligrams (mg) of sodium per day. You and your loved ones will get to savor an array of wonderful new tastes, and your heart will return the favor. Because so much of the food we eat today contains high levels of sodium, it's admittedly difficult to go cold turkey and cut your daily intake that drastically. A good approach is to start by limiting yourself to 2,300 mg of sodium a day, then gradually lowering that figure over the course of several weeks until you reach the goal of 1,500 mg. One effective way to do it: Avoid eating processed or packaged foods, which tend to be high in sodium, and start cooking simple foods from scratch. You'll begin to appreciate foods for their true flavor, and your taste buds will happily adapt. For more tips, see "Shake the Salt Habit," below.

Shake the Salt Habit

Sodium—the main component of salt—is an essential nutrient. But the average American takes in far more than the 1,500 to 2,300 mg daily that's considered to be the healthy range. Increased sodium puts us at greater risk for high blood pressure, which can lead to heart attacks or strokes. Because nearly 90 percent of middle-aged Americans will develop high blood pressure at some point in their lives, now is the time to shake the salt habit. Begin your journey toward lower sodium with these simple steps:

- Choose fresh, frozen, or canned food items without added salts.
- Select unsalted nuts or seeds, dried beans, peas, and lentils.
- Avoid using salt and canned vegetables with added sodium in homemade dishes.
- Choose unsalted, lower-sodium, fat-free broths, bouillons, and soups.
- Add fresh lemon juice instead of salt to fish and vegetables.
- Use vinegar or citrus juice as a flavor enhancer for greens and other vegetables, adding them at the last moment.
- For more "bite" in your meals, add a small amount of fresh hot peppers. Remove the membrane and seeds first, then finely chop them.
- Use high-sodium ingredients like olives and cheese sparingly, as a garnish rather than a main ingredient.
- If cooking from scratch is too time-consuming to do daily, cook several dishes on Sunday night, and freeze the meals for later in the week.

FIVE SIMPLE WAYS TO TRADE BAD FATS FOR GOOD

To get more heart-healthy fats into your diet, start by making these easy substitutions.

1. Eat salmon instead of steaks or burgers. Try canned salmon in salads or sandwiches, cook salmon fillets on the grill, or whip up some salmon burgers.

2. Pass on the fried-fish sandwich at your fast-food hangout. The fish is usually cod, Pollock, or flounder—lean varieties of fish that are all low in good fat—and may be fried in partially hydrogenated vegetable oil, a source of bad fat. (Plus, frying depletes the omega-3s that are there.) Order the grilled chicken sandwich instead.

3. Instead of topping off your salad bowl with bacon bits and croutons, lightly sprinkle it with olives, avocado, and nuts. These salad toppers are all high in healthy monounsaturated fats. But don't overdo it: They are also high in calories.

4. Dip bread in some olive oil—a healthy monounsaturated fat—instead of slathering on butter.

5. Choose convenience and packaged foods that are made with healthful canola oil. Just be sure to limit your snacking to the serving size specified on the package. (You'll usually find these foods in your grocery's natural foods section.)

Heart-Healthy Superfoods You'll Love

Here's a delicious list of foods you'd eat even if they weren't good for you. We take advantage of them all in the recipes that follow, so stock up. Blueberries, nuts, dark chocolate, and avocados also make wholesome snacks. Just be sure to limit yourself to the snack sizes indicated below. As for the blueberries—eat as many as your heart desires!

- **AVOCADOS:** True, they're high in fat, but it's the healthy monounsaturated kind. Chemicals in avocados also protect against hypertension. For a snack, enjoy up to one quarter of an avocado, drizzled with fresh lemon juice or spread on whole-grain crackers.

PROS AND CONS OF ALCOHOL CONSUMPTION FOR YOUR TICKER

When it comes to keeping your heart healthy, one drink is good, but two could be too many, say Canadian researchers who studied the effect of alcoholic beverages on blood vessels. In their tests on a group of healthy adults, one drink produced relaxation of the blood vessels, pumping up blood flow. But two made the heart work harder, and also blunted the normal dilation of vessels. As for type of beverage, you can take your pick, the researchers concluded. Though red wine is a reputed heart aid, when it came to this blood vessel boost, it was no more effective than plain ethanol (similar to the kind of alcohol used in cocktails). So raise a glass of white wine, beer, vodka, or another favorite, but stop at one a day.

- **CHOCOLATE:** Dark (semisweet or bittersweet) is rich in nutrients called flavonols, which lower both LDL cholesterol and blood pressure by dilating the arteries. In an analysis of fifteen studies that compared eating cocoa-rich products with nibbling on other treats (such as cocoa-free white chocolate), the real thing lowered systolic pressure 3.2 points and diastolic, 2. To stay low via this treat, enjoy up to one ounce a day of chocolate with a high (70-percent) cocoa content.

- **BLUEBERRIES:** These top the list of fruits and veggies with antioxidants—natural ingredients that neutralize certain destructive substances that contribute to heart disease. Blueberries also prevent blood clots and reduce artery inflammation. Close runner-up: strawberries.

- **NUTS:** Almonds, walnuts, macadamias, and hazelnuts are high in monounsaturated fat, which lowers LDL ("bad") cholesterol without reducing HDL. They are also a rich source of vitamin E (a powerful antioxidant) and the amino acid arginine, which helps keep artery walls healthy. Walnuts also protect against clotting and arrhythmia. But keep nuts to an ounce a day: They're high in calories; for snacks, nibble on no more than two tablespoons.

- **OLIVE OIL:** As a monounsaturated fat, it's good for your cholesterol numbers. In addition, dressing your salad with a little olive oil or using it to sauté leafy greens will help you absorb the nutrients in those veggies.

- **RED WINE:** Grape skins contain the antioxidant resveratrol, which helps prevent blood clots and the stiffening of heart tissue. In addition, alcohol raises HDL ("good") cholesterol. For more about wine and other alcoholic beverages, see "Pros and Cons of Alcohol Consumption for Your Ticker" opposite.

Encouraging Heart-Healthy Habits in Your Kids

At one time or another, you've surely heard this cry from the backseat as you're driving past a familiar fast-food outlet: "Mom, can we stop here? Please?" Or as you're passing the bakery department in your local supermarket: "Mom, can we get chocolate cake? Please?"

Your instinct is to make your children happy, but you also know about consequences. Obesity and poor nutrition, after all, are an alarming trend among children, causing a broad range of health issues that previously weren't seen until adulthood. More and more young people get a large portion of their calories from fast food and sugary soft drinks, while neglecting nutrient-rich foods that aid in healthy development. Based on current trends, today's children could be the first generation to live shorter lives than their parents.

It's not too late to change. The American Heart Association recommends taking a positive approach that gets your children more involved and invested in their food choices, so that the decision to eat healthier comes from them, not you.

- **BE A GOOD ROLE MODEL.** "Do as I say" won't work. If, for example, your child catches you polishing off a box of doughnuts, any rule you attempt to impose about healthy eating will only confuse and frustrate her. "Do as I do," however, works. If that same child sees you eating nutritious snacks like an apple, carrots, or fat-free yogurt, she will be more likely to do the same.

- **GET THEM INVOLVED.** Let children play an active role in planning and cooking meals. Engage them in conversation about what makes certain ingredients better for them than others. Let younger children perform simple, low-risk tasks around the kitchen, gradually increasing their responsibilities as they get older. If they cook it, they're more likely to eat it.

- **COOK SMARTER.** Show your children how their favorite foods can be prepared more healthfully. For example, chicken nuggets can be made with chicken breasts trimmed of fat, seasoned, and coated in whole-grain breadcrumbs and cornflakes, then baked instead of fried.

- **SET THE PARAMETERS, BUT OFFER CHOICES.** Choose the time and place for meals and snacks. Tell children about the types of foods and beverages to be served, giving them a few options within that menu. Let them choose how much they'd like to eat, within an acceptable range of portion sizes appropriate for their age.

- **BRING EVERYONE TO THE TABLE.** When the entire family dines together, there's less chance of children eating unhealthy foods for dinner or snacking too much.

- **MAKE A GAME OF READING FOOD LABELS.** If your children join you while food shopping, test and reward their skill in identifying the appropriate levels of saturated fats, sodium, added sugar, and other important nutrition information on food product labels.

- **SPEAK UP.** Contact your child's school and insist on smart food choices. Let day-care providers and babysitters know what you want your child to eat.

- **KEEP IT POSITIVE.** Children don't like to hear what they can't do. Instead, let them know what they *can* do, in terms of looking and feeling their best. When they make good food choices, offer praise and healthy rewards like extra playtime—not video games, extra TV time, or candy.

HEART-SMART COOKING TIPS FOR THE LITTLEST HEARTS

When it comes to cooking for children, the guidelines are in line with the suggestions we offer for adults (see "Heart Healthy Changes You Can Make Right Now" on page 10). But here are some pointers about feeding kids that will benefit not only them, but the entire family!

- Serve vegetables and fruits—ideally fresh, but frozen or canned is fine, too—at every meal. Make it a family rule that your kids must eat at least a portion of the fruit and veggies on their plates—and set a good example by finishing all of yours!

- Use only lean cuts of meat and reduced-fat meat products; remove the skin from poultry before eating. And regularly serve fish as an entrée—in the "Fish & Shellfish" chapter on page 168, we've included fish recipes with kid appeal.

- In place of meat, eat legumes (beans) or tofu for dinner a couple of times a week. In the "Veggie & Whole-Grain Mains" chapter on page 114, we share vegetarian tips that'll help get your children on board.

- Cook with olive, canola, soybean, corn, safflower, or other unsaturated oils.

- Buy whole-grain breads and cereals—look for "whole grain" as the first ingredient on the food label of these products. And when choosing breads, breakfast cereals, or prepared foods such as peanut butter, apple sauce, pasta sauce, soups, and condiments, choose high-fiber, low-salt, and low-sugar versions.

- Serve water, low-fat or fat-free nonflavored milk, and no-sugar-added fruit juices at meals and with snacks. The average American consumes 22 teaspoons of added sugar (sugars and syrups added during processing, preparation, or at the table), and sugary fruit beverages and soda are key culprits for kids.

Note: Keep in mind that exercise is as important as a healthy diet when it comes to heart health. So, turn off the TV, confiscate the cell phones, and send your kids outside to play.

Granola-Yogurt Parfait (page 31)

1 | ENERGIZING BREAKFASTS

You've heard it before but we'll say it again: Breakfast is the foundation of any healthy diet. Lucky for you and your family, this chapter is brimming with high-energy morning meals that taste great and are good for your tickers. Many are loaded with fill-you-up fiber, a great way to kickstart your day.

If mornings are hectic at your house, begin the day with our multigrain cereal—it takes just five minutes to prepare. Or make a bowl of steel-cut oatmeal topped with apples and cinnamon, blueberries and almonds, or other heart-smart garnishes. A single serving of blueberries per week can cut your odds of developing high blood pressure by 10 percent, and a generous sprinkling of cinnamon on your hot cereal every day could improve your cholesterol profile (see pages 23 and 34 for details).

For breakfast on the run, blend up one of our luscious fruit smoothies—from pomegranate and berry to our Jump-Start Smoothie that features two kinds of berries, orange juice, and yogurt, these "meals in a cup" are loaded with heart-protective antioxidants. Or grab one of our high-fiber muffins: Whole-Grain Blueberry Muffins and Healthy Makeover Morning Glory Muffins are as good tasting as they are good for you.

On the weekends, treat your family to a hearty breakfast like our California Frittata or Healthy Makeover Spinach Quiche. Both are loaded with veggies and combine eggs with egg whites to keep cholesterol in check. You can even treat them to pancakes: Our recipes include healthy grains like buckwheat and oatmeal, which have proven to be effective in reducing cholesterol levels.

ORANGE SUNRISE SMOOTHIE

Make this once, and you'll want it every morning. It's just as good made with low-fat milk, if you don't have soy milk.

TOTAL TIME: 5 minutes
MAKES: about 1¾ cups or 1 serving

1	cup vanilla soy milk
¼	cup frozen orange juice concentrate
2	tablespoons orange marmalade
2	ice cubes

In blender, combine soy milk, orange juice, marmalade, and ice. Blend until mixture is smooth and frothy. Pour into tall glass.

EACH SERVING: About 360 calories, 8g protein, 73g carbohydrate, 5g fat (0g saturated), 2g fiber, 0mg cholesterol, 144mg sodium

NUTRITIONAL NOTE

With 8 grams of protein per cup and 45% of your daily calcium requirement, soy milk is an excellent replacement for cow's milk for those who are dairy or lactose intolerant. The rich body and flavor make soy milk a nice option for smoothies.

JUMP-START SMOOTHIE

This smoothie would be tasty with a variety of other fruits. Try substituting the same quantity of fresh or frozen blackberries, raspberries, or even chopped mango.

TOTAL TIME: 5 minutes

MAKES: about 2 cups or 2 servings

1	cup frozen strawberries
½	cup fresh blueberries
½	cup fresh orange juice
2	teaspoons peeled, chopped fresh ginger
¼	cup plain low-fat yogurt
2	ice cubes

In blender, combine strawberries, blueberries, orange juice, ginger, yogurt, and ice cubes. Blend until smooth, scraping down side of container occasionally. Pour into tall glasses.

EACH SERVING: About 90 calories, 3g protein, 21g carbohydrate, 1g total fat (0g saturated), 3g fiber, 2mg cholesterol, 25mg sodium

HEART-SMART INGREDIENT: BLUEBERRIES

Eating one serving (½ cup) of blueberries per week can cut your odds of developing high blood pressure by 10%, suggests research involving 157,000 women and men who were tracked for 14 years. True, 10% isn't a mega-reduction, but when we can get it from a favorite oatmeal topper, smoothie add-in, and snack, we're happy to take it.

MANGO-STRAWBERRY SMOOTHIE

Whether you pair the strawberries with mango or apricot nectar, you'll get an irresistible flavor combination.

TOTAL TIME: 5 minutes

MAKES: about 2½ cups or 2 servings

1 cup fresh or frozen strawberries
1 cup mango or apricot nectar, chilled
½ cup plain or vanilla low-fat yogurt
4 ice cubes, if needed

In blender, combine strawberries, nectar, and yogurt. If using fresh berries, add ice. Blend until smooth and frothy. Pour into tall glasses.

EACH SERVING: About 130 calories, 4g protein, 27g carbohydrate, 1g total fat (1g saturated), 3g fiber, 3mg cholesterol, 44mg sodium

DOUBLE-PEACH SMOOTHIE

Substitute **peeled, pitted, and sliced peaches** for the strawberries and **peach juice or nectar** for the mango or apricot nectar. Use **vanilla low-fat yogurt** and **3 ice cubes.**

EACH SERVING: About 160 calories, 3g protein, 36g carbohydrate, 1g total fat (1g saturated), 2g fiber, 3mg cholesterol, 45mg sodium

PEANUT BUTTER AND BANANA SMOOTHIE

Kids love the combo of peanut butter and bananas. Plus, this breakfast drink is so easy to make, they can do it with minimal help.

TOTAL TIME: 5 minutes

MAKES: about 1½ cups or 1 serving

1	small ripe banana, cut into chunks (see Tip)
½	cup soy milk
1	teaspoon creamy peanut butter
3	ice cubes

In blender, combine banana, soy milk, peanut butter, and ice cubes. Blend until mixture is smooth and frothy. Pour into tall glass.

EACH SERVING: About 165 calories, 6g protein, 28g carbohydrate, 4g total fat (2g saturated), 2g fiber, 5mg cholesterol, 85mg sodium

TIP

For a thicker, colder smoothie, use frozen bananas. You can prepare several days' worth ahead of time. Just peel and cut the bananas into chunks, place them in a resealable plastic bag, and freeze. They'll keep for up to one week.

CHOCOLATE-BANANA SMOOTHIE

Another favorite kid combo: chocolate and bananas. And it's so simple to whip up!

TOTAL TIME: 5 minutes

MAKES: 2 cups or 1 serving

1	frozen banana, peeled and sliced
¾	cup milk
3	tablespoons (or to taste) chocolate syrup
3	ice cubes

In blender, combine banana, milk, chocolate syrup, and ice, and blend until mixture is smooth and frothy. Pour into a tall glass.

EACH SERVING: About 430 calories, 9g protein, 85g carbohydrate, 8g total fat (4g saturated), 4g fiber, 25mg cholesterol, 145mg sodium

NUTRITIONAL NOTE:
BANANAS DELIVER A BOOST

A single serving of bananas is high in vitamin B_6, which is important to the health of our nervous system, as well as key to the synthesis of most of the essential molecules in our bodies. Bananas are also a good source of vitamin C, bone-building manganese, potassium, and dietary fiber.

If you want to eat bananas right away, buy solid yellow fruit with some brown spots. Bananas that are somewhat green will ripen within a few days at room temperature.

BREAKFAST SMOOTHIE

Store a can of concentrated orange juice in your freezer (it will last up to a year) and you can make this breakfast smoothie anytime you please.

TOTAL TIME: 5 minutes

MAKES: 2 cups or 1 serving

4	ice cubes
2/3	cup low-fat (1%) milk
1/4	cup concentrated orange juice
1	tablespoon honey
1/8	tablespoon vanilla extract
1	small ripe banana

Combine all ingredients in a blender, and blend until smooth.

EACH SERVING: About 320 calories, 8g protein, 71g carbohydrate, 2g total fat (1g saturated), 0g fiber, 8mg cholesterol, 78mg sodium

SUPER-HEALTHY SMOOTHIE

Great tasting and good for you, too. In addition to vitamin-rich blueberries and apples, this elixir contains flaxseed, a rich source of omega-3 fatty acids, fiber, minerals, and amino acids.

TOTAL TIME: 10 minutes

MAKES: about 2 cups or 2 servings

1	navel orange
½	cup plain low-fat yogurt
⅔	cup frozen blueberries
½	cup chopped apple
3	ice cubes

1 to 2 tablespoons honey

1 to 2 tablespoons ground flaxseed (see Tip)

Granola, such as Heart-Healthy Granola (page 30), for garnish

1. From orange, grate ½ teaspoon peel. Remove remaining peel and white pith from orange and discard. Section orange.

2. In blender, combine orange peel, orange sections, yogurt, blueberries, apple, ice, honey, and flaxseed, and blend until mixture is smooth. Pour into tall glasses. Sprinkle with granola.

EACH SERVING: About 210 calories, 6g protein, 42g carbohydrate, 4g total fat (1g saturated), 6g fiber, 4mg cholesterol, 53mg sodium

TIP

To release their heart-healthy nutrients, flaxseeds must be ground before you consume them. You can buy preground seeds, but for optimum freshness, it's best to get them whole and grind them yourself. Use a powerful blender (such as a Vitamix) or a nut or coffee grinder.

POMEGRANATE-BERRY SMOOTHIE

What a delicious and healthful way to start the day! Berries and pomegranates are loaded with heart-healthy antioxidants. If you prefer, substitute nondairy yogurt.

TOTAL TIME: 5 minutes

MAKES: about 2 cups or 1 serving

½   cup chilled pomegranate juice
½   cup vanilla low-fat yogurt
1   cup frozen mixed berries

In blender, combine juice, yogurt, and berries, and blend until mixture is smooth. Pour into tall glass and serve.

EACH SERVING: About 250 calories, 6g protein, 52g carbohydrate, 2g total fat (1g saturated), 5g fiber, 8mg cholesterol, 110mg sodium

HEART-SMART INGREDIENT: POMEGRANATES

Toast your ticker with a glass of pomegranate juice. In addition to being delicious, the flavonoid- and polyphenol-rich beverage may make your blood vessels healthier, which can mean lower blood pressure. In an Iranian study, drinking five ounces of the juice daily (about 85 calories) helped a group of adults with hypertension significantly lower their numbers— by about 6.4 points systolic (the upper number) and 3.6 points diastolic (the lower one)—in just two weeks.

HEART-HEALTHY GRANOLA

We baked oats, almonds, quinoa, wheat germ, and sesame seeds with apple juice instead of oil and butter. It still has all that crunchy granola goodness but with just a fraction of the fat.

ACTIVE TIME: 10 minutes **TOTAL TIME:** 45 minutes

MAKES: about 6 cups or 24 servings

4	cups old-fashioned oats, uncooked
½	cup honey
½	cup apple juice
1½	teaspoons vanilla extract
¾	teaspoon ground cinnamon
½	cup natural almonds
½	cup quinoa
¼	cup toasted wheat germ
2	tablespoons sesame seeds
½	cup dried apricots, cut into ¼-inch cubes
½	cup dark seedless raisins

1. Preheat oven to 350°F. Place oats in two 15½" by 10½" jelly-roll pans. Bake until lightly toasted, about 15 minutes, stirring twice.

2. In large bowl, with wire whisk, mix honey, apple juice, vanilla, and cinnamon until blended. Add toasted oats, almonds, quinoa, wheat germ, and sesame seeds; stir well to coat. Spread oat mixture evenly in same two jelly-roll pans; bake until golden brown, 20 to 25 minutes, stirring frequently. Cool in pans on wire rack.

3. When cool, transfer granola to large bowl and stir in apricots and raisins. Store in airtight container up to 1 month.

EACH SERVING: About 175 calories, 6g protein, 32g carbohydrate, 4g total fat (1g saturated), 4g fiber, 0mg cholesterol, 5mg sodium

GRANOLA-YOGURT PARFAIT

A healthy breakfast doesn't get any easier (or more delicious) than this. Substitute any berry that you like and use nondairy yogurt, if you prefer. (See photograph on page 20.)

TOTAL TIME: 5 minutes

MAKES: 1 serving

½   cup fresh or partially thawed frozen raspberries
¾   cup vanilla low-fat yogurt
2   tablespoons Heart-Healthy Granola (see recipe opposite)

Into parfait glass or wineglass, spoon some of the raspberries, yogurt, and granola. Repeat layering until all ingredients are used.

EACH SERVING: About 255 calories, 10g protein, 47g carbohydrate, 3g total fat (2g saturated), 5g fiber, 12mg cholesterol, 160mg sodium

HEART-SMART INGREDIENT: OATS

This pantry staple contains a type of fiber, beta-glucan, that studies have shown to be effective in reducing cholesterol levels. Oats are also a good source of thiamin and protein, and their regular inclusion in a diet can help regulate blood sugar. Rolled or old-fashioned oats are whole oats that have been toasted, hulled, steamed, and flattened with rollers. Steel-cut oats are the whole-grain oat kernels, with only the edible outer chaff removed, cut into pieces. They are chewy with a wonderful nutty-sweet flavor.

STEEL-CUT OATMEAL

If you haven't tried steel-cut oats, you're in for a deliciously chewy, full-flavored treat. The fruit and nut topping options keep things interesting, and the fiber helps you feel full throughout your morning activities.

ACTIVE TIME: 5 minutes **TOTAL TIME:** 30 minutes
MAKES: 4 servings

3   cups water
1   cup steel-cut oats
Pinch salt

In medium saucepan, combine water, oats, and salt. Bring to a boil over high heat. Reduce heat and cover. Simmer until water is absorbed and oats are tender¼ but still chewy, 20 to 25 minutes, stirring occasionally.

EACH SERVING: About 75 calories, 3g protein, 14g carbohydrate, 1g total fat (0g saturated), 2g fiber, 0mg cholesterol, 35mg sodium

BLUEBERRY-ALMOND OATMEAL

In small bowl, mix ¼ **cup fresh blueberries, 1 tablespoon chopped toasted almonds,** and **1 teaspoon honey.** Divide topping among servings of oatmeal.

EACH SERVING: About 95 calories, 3g protein, 17g carbohydrate, 2g total fat (0g saturated), 2g fiber, 0mg cholesterol, 35mg sodium

CRANBERRY-WALNUT OATMEAL

In small bowl, mix ¼ **cup dried cranberries,** ¼ **cup chopped walnuts,** and **4 teaspoons maple syrup.** Divide topping among servings of oatmeal.

EACH SERVING: About 165 calories, 4g protein, 25g carbohydrate, 6g total fat (1g saturated), 3g fiber, 0mg cholesterol, 36mg sodium

HAZELNUT AND FRUIT GRANOLA

Get your day off to a good start with a scrumptious combination of toasty nuts and sweetly chewy dried fruit. Enjoy this granola straight from the container, spooned over yogurt, or with a splash of milk.

ACTIVE TIME: 10 minutes **TOTAL TIME:** 55 minutes

MAKES: 10 cups or 20 servings

½   cup honey
⅓   cup vegetable oil
1½ teaspoons vanilla extract
½   teaspoon ground cinnamon
4   cups old-fashioned oats
1   cup sweetened flaked coconut
1   cup sliced almonds
1   cup hazelnuts, chopped
1   cup dried tart cherries
1   cup dried Calimyrna figs, stems removed and chopped
1   cup dried apricots, chopped

1. Preheat oven to 300°F.

2. In large bowl, whisk honey, oil, vanilla, and cinnamon until blended. Add oats, coconut, and nuts; stir until coated.

3. Divide mixture between two 15½" by 10½" jelly-roll pans; spread evenly.

4. Bake oat mixture until golden brown, 45 to 50 minutes, stirring twice during baking. Cool completely in pans on wire racks.

5. In large bowl, toss cooled oat mixture with cherries, figs, and apricots. Store in tightly covered container at room temperature for up to 1 week. For storage up to 3 weeks, and to keep granola crunchy, spoon oat mixture into one container and cherries, figs, and apricots into another. Mix together when ready to use.

EACH SERVING: About 270 calories, 5g protein, 37g carbohydrate, 13g total fat (2g saturated), 5g fiber, 0mg cholesterol, 5mg sodium

SEVEN-MINUTE MULTIGRAIN CEREAL

Get a great-grains start to your day with a hot and tasty bowl of three kinds of grains. If you like, serve it with your choice of regular or nondairy milk.

ACTIVE TIME: 2 minutes **TOTAL TIME:** 7 minutes

MAKES: 1 serving

2	tablespoons quick-cooking barley
2	tablespoons bulgur
2	tablespoons old-fashioned oats, uncooked
2/3	cup water
2	tablespoons dark seedless raisins

Pinch ground cinnamon

1	tablespoon chopped walnuts or pecans

In microwave-safe 1-quart bowl, combine barley, bulgur, oats, and water. Microwave on High, 2 minutes. Stir in raisins and cinnamon; microwave 3 minutes longer. Stir, then top with walnuts and serve.

EACH SERVING: About 265 calories, 8g protein, 50g carbohydrate, 6g total fat (1g saturated), 7g fiber, 0mg cholesterol, 5mg sodium

HEART-SMART INGREDIENT: CINNAMON

Cinnamon may have benefits beyond jazzing up your favorite hot cereal. A new scientific review found that regular users of the aromatic spice experienced declines in total and LDL cholesterol and triglycerides, along with a slight boost in HDL levels. The daily "dose"? As little as a small sprinkling (less than 1/8 teaspoon) could be enough for some people; for others, it takes up to 2 1/2 teaspoons. For the higher amounts, you may want to reach for a supplement, not the spice jar.

WHOLE-GRAIN BLUEBERRY MUFFINS

Deliciously dense, these muffins are made with a combination of regular all-purpose flour, whole-wheat flour, and old-fashioned oats for an optimum blend of taste and health.

ACTIVE TIME: 20 minutes **TOTAL TIME:** 40 minutes

MAKES: 12 muffins

1   cup old-fashioned oats, uncooked
1   cup whole-wheat flour
½   cup all-purpose flour
2   teaspoons baking powder
½   teaspoon baking soda
½   teaspoon salt
¼   cup plus 1 tablespoon packed brown sugar
1   cup low-fat buttermilk
¼   cup fresh orange juice
2   tablespoons canola oil
1   large egg
1   teaspoon vanilla extract
2   cups fresh blueberries
¼   cup natural almonds, chopped

1. Preheat oven to 400°F. Line 12-cup standard muffin pan with paper liners.

2. Grind oats in blender. In bowl, whisk together oats, both flours, baking powder and soda, salt, and ¼ cup sugar. In small bowl, whisk together buttermilk, juice, oil, egg, and vanilla. Stir into flour mixture; fold in blueberries.

3. Combine almonds and remaining 1 tablespoon sugar. Spoon batter into pan; sprinkle with almond sugar. Bake 22 minutes or until toothpick inserted in center of muffin comes out clean. Cool in pan on wire rack 5 minutes. Remove from pan; cool completely.

EACH MUFFIN: About 170 calories, 5g protein, 28g carbohydrate, 5g total fat (1g saturated), 3g fiber, 16mg cholesterol, 270mg sodium

VEGAN BLUEBERRY MUFFINS

When retooling a recipe to be egg-free, oil and/or fruit purees are often used to provide the moistness eggs typically supply. In this recipe, applesauce plays that role.

ACTIVE TIME: 20 minutes **TOTAL TIME:** 45 minutes

MAKES: 12 muffins

1	cup oats
1	cup all-purpose flour
½	cup whole-wheat flour
½	cup packed brown sugar
2	teaspoons baking powder
½	teaspoon baking soda
½	teaspoon salt
1¼	cups plain soy milk
¼	cup unsweetened applesauce
3	tablespoons canola oil
1	teaspoon vanilla extract
2	cups blueberries
1	teaspoon granulated sugar

1. Preheat oven to 400°F. Line 12-cup muffin pan with paper liners.

2. Place oats in blender and blend until finely ground.

3. In large bowl, combine oats, all-purpose flour, whole-wheat flour, brown sugar, baking powder, baking soda, and salt. In small bowl, with fork, blend soy milk, applesauce, oil, and vanilla; stir into flour mixture until flour is moistened. Fold in blueberries.

4. Spoon batter into muffin-pan cups (cups will be very full). Sprinkle with granulated sugar. Bake until toothpick inserted in center of muffins comes out clean, 23 to 25 minutes. Remove to wire rack; serve warm or cool to serve later.

EACH MUFFIN: About 180 calories, 4g protein, 31g carbohydrate, 5g total fat (0.5g saturated), 2g fiber, 0mg cholesterol, 254mg sodium

HEALTHY MAKEOVER MORNING GLORY MUFFINS

We took the ultimate breakfast muffin and reduced the calories and fat. With a tweak here and there, each lightened-up muffin has 75 fewer calories and 5.5 grams less fat than the original!

ACTIVE TIME: 20 minutes **TOTAL TIME:** 45 minutes

MAKES: 12 muffins

1¼ cups all-purpose flour
1 teaspoon baking powder
½ teaspoon baking soda
½ teaspoon salt
½ teaspoon ground cinnamon
1 cup old-fashioned or quick-cooking oats, uncooked
⅓ cup fat-free milk
⅔ cup applesauce, unsweetened
¼ cup packed brown sugar
¼ cup light (mild) molasses
2 tablespoons canola oil
1 large egg
1½ cups shredded carrots (about 3)
½ cup prunes, chopped

1. Preheat oven to 400°F. Grease 12 standard muffin-pan cups or line cups with fluted paper liners.

2. In large bowl, whisk together flour, baking powder, baking soda, salt, and cinnamon; stir in oats.

3. In medium bowl, with fork, mix milk, applesauce, brown sugar, molasses, oil, and egg until blended; stir in carrots and prunes. Add applesauce mixture to flour mixture; stir just until flour is moistened (batter will be lumpy).

4. Spoon batter into prepared muffin cups (cups will be full). Bake 23 to 25 minutes or until toothpick inserted in center of muffin comes out clean. Immediately remove muffins from pan. Serve warm, or cool on wire rack to serve later.

EACH MUFFIN: About 165 calories, 3g protein, 32g carbohydrate, 3g total fat (0g saturated), 2g fiber, 18mg cholesterol, 200mg sodium

BRAN MUFFINS

These healthful, fiber-packed muffins are sweetly flavored with a hint of molasses. Try our tasty variations: crystallized ginger and apple, shredded carrot and raisin, banana and toasted wheat germ, and date-nut.

ACTIVE TIME: 15 minutes **TOTAL TIME:** 35 minutes
MAKES: 12 muffins

1½ cups original whole-bran cereal (not bran flakes)
1   cup low-fat (1%) milk
¼   cup vegetable oil
¼   cup light (mild) molasses
1   large egg
1   cup all-purpose flour
¼   cup sugar
2   teaspoons baking powder
½   teaspoon salt
¼   teaspoon baking soda

1. Preheat oven to 400°F. Grease twelve 2½″ by 1¼″ muffin-pan cups.

2. In medium bowl, with fork, mix bran cereal with milk, oil, molasses, and egg until blended; let stand 10 minutes.

3. Meanwhile, in large bowl, combine flour, sugar, baking powder, salt, and baking soda.

4. Add liquid mixture to flour mixture; stir just until flour is evenly moistened. Spoon batter into prepared muffin-pan cups.

5. Bake muffins until toothpick inserted in centers of muffins comes out clean, 18 to 20 minutes. Immediately remove muffins from pan. Serve warm, or cool on wire rack to serve later.

EACH MUFFIN: About 140 calories, 3g protein, 22g carbohydrate, 6g total fat (1g saturated), 3g fiber, 19mg cholesterol, 205mg sodium

GINGER-APPLE BRAN MUFFINS

Prepare Bran Muffins as directed but use only ³/₄ cup milk, and fold **3 tablespoons chopped crystallized ginger**; **1 medium apple**, peeled and shredded (¹/₂ cup); and ¹/₂ **teaspoon ground ginger** into batter before spooning into muffin cups.

EACH MUFFIN: About 155 calories, 3g protein, 26g carbohydrate, 6g total fat (1g saturated), 3g fiber, 18mg cholesterol, 205mg sodium

CARROT-RAISIN BRAN MUFFINS

Prepare Bran Muffins as directed but fold **2 medium carrots**, shredded (1 cup) and ¹/₂ **cup raisins** into batter before spooning into muffin cups.

EACH MUFFIN: About 160 calories, 3g protein, 26g carbohydrate, 6g total fat (1g saturated), 4g fiber, 19mg cholesterol, 210mg sodium

BANANA–WHEAT GERM BRAN MUFFINS

Prepare Bran Muffins as directed but use only ³/₄ cup milk, and fold **1 medium banana**, mashed (about ¹/₂ cup); **2 tablespoons honey-toasted wheat germ**; and ¹/₄ **teaspoon ground cinnamon** into batter before spooning into muffin cups.

EACH MUFFIN: About 150 calories, 4g protein, 25g carbohydrate, 6g total fat (1g saturated), 4g fiber, 18mg cholesterol, 205mg sodium

DATE-NUT BRAN MUFFINS

Prepare Bran Muffins as directed but stir ¹/₂ **cup chopped pitted dates** and ¹/₂ **cup chopped toasted walnuts** into batter before spooning into muffin cups.

EACH MUFFIN: About 190 calories, 5g protein, 28g carbohydrate, 9g total fat (1g saturated), 4g fiber, 19mg cholesterol, 210mg sodium

SKINNY CARROT MUFFINS

Moist muffins studded with raisins and carrots—perfect for breakfast on the go!

ACTIVE TIME: 15 minutes **TOTAL TIME:** 45 minutes

MAKES: 12 muffins

2 ¼ cups all-purpose flour

½   cup granulated sugar

1   teaspoon ground cinnamon

1   teaspoon salt

1   teaspoon baking soda

½   teaspoon baking powder

¼   teaspoon ground ginger

3   carrots, peeled and finely shredded (1 ½ cups)

1   cup vanilla nonfat yogurt

½   cup egg substitute

½   cup unsweetened applesauce

½   cup dark seedless raisins

⅓   cup packed light brown sugar

1   teaspoon vanilla extract

1   teaspoon confectioners' sugar

1. Preheat oven to 350°F. Spray 12 standard muffin-pan cups with nonstick cooking spray.

2. In medium bowl, combine flour, granulated sugar, cinnamon, salt, baking soda, baking powder, and ginger. In large bowl, with wire whisk or fork, mix carrots, yogurt, egg substitute, applesauce, raisins, brown sugar, and vanilla until well blended. Stir flour mixture into carrot mixture just until flour is moistened.

3. Spoon batter into muffin cups. Bake until toothpick inserted in center of muffins comes out clean, about 30 minutes. Let muffins sit in pans on wire racks for 10 minutes; remove from pans and cool on wire racks. Sprinkle with confectioners' sugar while muffins are still warm.

EACH MUFFIN: About 190 calories, 5g protein, 43g carbohydrate, 1g total fat (0g saturated), 1g fiber, 1mg cholesterol, 337mg sodium

APPLE-OAT MUFFINS

These fruit-and-nut-studded muffins are wholesome and delicious.

ACTIVE TIME: 15 minutes **TOTAL TIME:** 45 minutes
MAKES: 12 muffins

2	cups old-fashioned oats, uncooked
1¼	cups all-purpose flour
½	cup packed brown sugar
2	teaspoons baking powder
¾	teaspoon baking soda
¾	teaspoon salt
½	teaspoon ground cinnamon
1	cup buttermilk
2	tablespoons vegetable oil
1	large egg, lightly beaten
1	cup shredded Golden Delicious or Granny Smith apples
½	cup walnuts, chopped

1. Preheat oven to 400°F. Grease 12 standard muffin-pan cups. In large bowl, combine oats, flour, sugar, baking powder, baking soda, salt, and cinnamon.

2. In medium bowl, with fork, beat buttermilk, oil, and egg until well blended; stir in apples. Add apple mixture to flour mixture, and stir just until flour mixture is moistened; batter will be very thick and lumpy. Stir in chopped walnuts.

3. Spoon batter into prepared muffin-pan cups. Bake 23 to 25 minutes or until muffins begin to brown and toothpick inserted in center of muffins comes out clean. Immediately remove muffins from pan. Serve warm, or cool on wire rack to serve later.

EACH MUFFIN: About 210 calories, 5g protein, 33g carbohydrate, 7g total fat (1g saturated), 3g fiber, 18mg cholesterol, 320mg sodium

HEALTHY MAKEOVER PUMPKIN BREAD

Treat family and friends to our slimmed-down quick bread. Gone are the traditional version's saturated fat and cholesterol (thanks to egg whites and a blend of low-fat yogurt and canola oil). No one will suspect you've tinkered—this bread is that good!

ACTIVE TIME: 20 minutes **TOTAL TIME:** 1 hour 10 minutes

MAKES: 1 loaf, 16 slices

1	cup packed light brown sugar
2	large egg whites
1	cup solid pack pumpkin (not pumpkin pie mix)
¼	cup canola oil
⅓	cup plain low-fat yogurt
1	teaspoon vanilla extract
1	cup all-purpose flour
¾	cup whole-wheat flour
1½	teaspoons baking powder
1	teaspoon ground cinnamon
½	teaspoon ground nutmeg
½	teaspoon baking soda
½	teaspoon salt

1. Preheat oven to 350°F. Spray 8 ½" by 4 ½" metal loaf pan with nonstick cooking spray and sprinkle with flour.

2. In large bowl, with wire whisk, combine brown sugar and egg whites. Add pumpkin, oil, yogurt, and vanilla; stir to combine.

3. In medium bowl, combine all-purpose flour, whole-wheat flour, baking powder, cinnamon, nutmeg, baking soda, and salt. Add flour mixture to pumpkin mixture; stir until just combined. Do not overmix.

4. Pour batter into prepared pan. Bake 45 to 50 minutes or until toothpick inserted in center of loaf comes out clean. Cool in pan 10 minutes. Invert pumpkin bread onto wire rack; cool completely before slicing.

EACH SLICE: About 140 calories, 2g protein, 25g carbohydrate, 4g total fat (0g saturated), 1g fiber, 0mg cholesterol, 165mg sodium

TOFU SCRAMBLE WITH CHOPPED TOMATOES AND CHIVES

Serve this nondairy scramble with whole-grain toast or roll it up in a whole-wheat tortilla.

TOTAL TIME: 15 minutes

MAKES: 4 main-dish servings

1	package (14 to 16 ounces) firm tofu
3	tablespoons extra-virgin olive oil
1	large garlic clove, finely chopped
¼	cup snipped fresh chives

Pinch cayenne (ground red) pepper

½	teaspoon ground turmeric
1	large ripe tomato, seeded and chopped
½	teaspoon salt
1	tablespoon fresh lemon juice

1. Rinse tofu and press with clean towel to absorb excess water. Place in bowl and mash into small pieces with fork.

2. In nonstick 12-inch skillet, heat oil over medium heat until hot. Stir in garlic, chives, cayenne, and turmeric; cook 2 minutes, stirring.

3. Add mashed tofu, tomato, and salt; raise heat and simmer 5 minutes. Remove from heat and stir in lemon juice. Serve immediately.

EACH SERVING: About 190 calories, 9g protein, 5g carbohydrate, 15g total fat (2g saturated), 2g fiber, 0mg cholesterol, 297mg sodium

KASHA VARNISHKES

This traditional Eastern European dish is Jewish comfort food at its best—and a delicious way to enjoy the heart-healthy benefits of buckwheat. It is made from kasha (the whole, hulled seeds of buckwheat) combined with bow-tie pasta, sautéed onion, and egg whites.

ACTIVE TIME: 30 minutes   **TOTAL TIME:** 40 minutes

MAKES: 4 main-dish servings

2	cups mini farfalle (bow-tie) pasta
1	large egg white
1	cup kasha (roasted buckwheat groats)
1	can (14½ ounces) reduced-sodium chicken broth
2	teaspoons canola or vegetable oil
2	onions, chopped
½	teaspoon salt
1	tablespoon margarine or butter
¼	teaspoon ground black pepper

1. Cook pasta according to package directions until al dente; drain.

2. Meanwhile, in medium bowl, beat egg white lightly with fork. Add kasha and stir to evenly coat with egg white.

3. Heat large nonstick skillet over medium-high heat until hot. Add kasha and reduce heat to medium-low. Cook, stirring constantly, until kasha is toasted and grains separate, about 5 minutes. Transfer to bowl and set aside.

4. Pour broth into liquid measuring cup and add *water* to equal 2 cups. In medium saucepan, bring broth, kasha, and ¼ teaspoon salt to a boil. Reduce heat to low; cover and simmer until broth is absorbed, about 10 minutes.

5. Meanwhile, in large nonstick skillet over medium heat, heat oil until hot. Add onions and cook, stirring frequently, until golden brown, about 12 minutes. Add pasta, kasha, margarine, remaining ¼ teaspoon salt, and pepper; stir to combine. Heat through and serve.

EACH SERVING: About 435 calories, 15g protein, 78g carbohydrate, 7g total fat (3g saturated), 7g fiber, 7mg cholesterol, 368mg sodium

POTATO KUGEL

A traditional side dish on Passover, this comforting and savory pudding makes a satisfying brunch dish any time of year. Pair it with a green salad like our flavorful Kale Salad with Glazed Onions and Cheddar (page 356).

ACTIVE TIME: 25 minutes **TOTAL TIME:** 1 hour 25 minutes plus cooling
MAKES: 6 main-dish servings

4	tablespoons olive oil
1	large onion (12 ounces), finely chopped
3	large eggs
1	large egg white
¼	cup packed fresh flat-leaf parsley, finely chopped
1	teaspoon salt
¼	teaspoon ground black pepper
1	teaspoon fresh thyme leaves, chopped, plus additional sprigs, for garnish
3	pounds all-purpose potatoes

1. Preheat oven to 400°F. Brush shallow 2-quart ceramic or glass baking dish with 1 tablespoon olive oil.

2. In 12-inch skillet, heat 1 tablespoon oil over medium heat until hot. Add onion and cook 9 minutes or until golden brown and tender, stirring occasionally. Meanwhile, in large bowl, whisk together eggs, egg white, parsley, salt, and pepper until eggs are blended.

3. Add thyme to skillet and cook 1 minute, stirring. Remove skillet from heat.

4. Working quickly, peel potatoes and grate in food processor with grating attachment or on large holes of box grater. Add grated potatoes directly to egg mixture to prevent shreds from turning gray. Add onions to mixture and stir until well blended. Transfer potato mixture to prepared dish and spread in even layer. Brush top of potatoes with remaining 2 tablespoons oil.

5. Bake 1 hour to 1 hour 10 minutes or until surface is browned and tip of small sharp knife pierces easily through potato mixture. Cool in pan 10 to 15 minutes. Garnish with thyme sprigs; serve warm. If making ahead, cool casserole completely, cover with foil, and refrigerate up to overnight. Reheat, covered, in 400°F oven 30 minutes or until warm.

EACH SERVING: About 280 calories, 8g protein, 37g carbohydrate, 12g total fat (3g saturated), 4g fiber, 106mg cholesterol, 440mg sodium

CALIFORNIA FRITTATA

This frittata, accompanied by salsa, crisp jicama sticks, and corn tortillas, makes for a substantial meal that's high in fiber and low in fat. An egg substitute may be used instead of eggs, if you prefer.

ACTIVE TIME: 30 minutes **TOTAL TIME:** 1 hour 5 minutes

MAKES: 4 main-dish servings

2 to 3 small potatoes (6 ½ ounces)
1   tablespoon olive oil
1½ cups thinly sliced onions
1   zucchini (6 ounces), thinly sliced
1   cup thinly sliced cremini mushrooms
2   ripe plum tomatoes (6 ½ ounces), each cored, halved, and thinly sliced
½   teaspoon kosher salt (optional)
½   teaspoon ground black pepper
1   cup shredded spinach or Swiss chard
1   tablespoon slivered fresh basil leaves (optional)
2   large eggs
3   large egg whites
½   jicama (8 ounces), peeled and cut into 2" by ¼" matchstick strips
2   teaspoons fresh lime juice
3   tablespoons crumbled feta cheese (optional)
2   tablespoons chopped fresh flat-leaf parsley
¾   cup bottled salsa
4   (6-inch) corn tortillas

1. Preheat oven to 350°F. In saucepan, bring potatoes and enough *water* to cover to a boil over high heat. Reduce heat to low; cover and simmer until potatoes are fork-tender, 15 to 20 minutes. Drain and cool. Cut into ¼-inch-thick slices.

2. In cast-iron skillet or another heavy oven-safe skillet, heat oil over medium heat. Add onions and cook until softened, about 5 minutes. Add potatoes, zucchini, mushrooms, and tomatoes and season with salt, if using, and pepper; cook, stirring gently, until zucchini begins to soften, 2 to 3 minutes. Add spinach and, if using, basil, and cook until spinach wilts, 1 to 2 minutes.

3. In bowl, with wire whisk or fork, mix eggs and egg whites. With spatula, stir vegetables while pouring eggs into skillet. Transfer skillet to oven and bake until eggs are set, 3 to 5 minutes.

4. While frittata bakes, sprinkle jicama sticks with lime juice; set aside.

5. When frittata is done, scatter feta cheese, if using, and parsley on top. Cut into 4 pieces and serve with salsa, tortillas, and jicama sticks.

EACH SERVING: About 265 calories, 11g protein, 38g carbohydrate, 7g total fat (1g saturated), 8g fiber, 106mg cholesterol, 140mg sodium

THE LEAN GREEN BREAKFAST DREAM

The whole family will enjoy these veggie-packed egg-and-sausage scrambles, created by Kim Van Dunk, finalist in the Kid Friendly category of our second Cook Your Heart Out Contest. She sautés the vegetables—including plenty of greens—with a little crumbled chicken sausage before topping with beaten eggs and baking as individual servings in a muffin tin.

ACTIVE TIME: 20 minutes **TOTAL TIME:** 30 minutes

MAKES: 6 main-dish servings

2   tablespoons extra-virgin olive oil
2   cups finely chopped broccoli flowerets
1   cup finely chopped kale leaves
1   cup shredded carrot
1   shallot, finely minced
2   garlic cloves, finely grated
1   small onion, chopped
⅛   teaspoon garlic salt
⅛   teaspoon ground black pepper
4   ounces all-natural chicken sausage
1   cup finely chopped fresh spinach
8   extra-large eggs

1. Preheat oven to 350°F. Line 12-cup standard muffin pan with silicone or foil liners.

2. Meanwhile, heat oil in large skillet over medium heat. Add broccoli, kale, carrot, shallot, garlic, onion, garlic salt, and pepper. Remove sausage from its casing and crumble meat into pan in small chunks. Sauté over medium heat, stirring frequently, about 7 minutes, until sausage is browned and cooked through and vegetables have softened. Turn off heat. Stir in spinach and allow to wilt, 2 minutes.

3. In large mixing bowl, whisk eggs until well combined and frothy. Transfer eggs to measuring cup with pouring spout.

4. Spray bottom and sides of muffin liners with nonstick cooking spray. Fill each liner two-thirds full with sautéed vegetable-and-sausage mixture. Pour enough of beaten eggs into each liner to just cover vegetable mixture. Bake 12 to 15 minutes, until center is firm to the touch. Serve immediately.

EACH SERVING: About 205 calories, 14g protein, 6g carbohydrate, 13g total fat (3g saturated), 2g fiber, 292mg cholesterol, 250mg sodium

HEALTHY MAKEOVER SPINACH QUICHE

Quiche, a French bistro classic, is a perfect one-dish meal, but it can leave you feeling less than svelte. By replacing white flour with whole wheat, and using nonfat milk instead of cream, we've bidden *adieu* to 25 grams of fat, reduced the calories by half, and quadrupled the fiber. *Bon appétit!*

ACTIVE TIME: 35 minutes **TOTAL TIME:** 1 hour 20 minutes
MAKES: 6 main-dish servings

¾   cup all-purpose flour
½   cup whole-wheat flour
⅜   teaspoon salt
4   tablespoons cold margarine, cut up
¼   cup buttermilk
3   large egg whites
1   (6- to 8-ounce) leek, white and light green parts only, cut into thin half-moons
½   teaspoon chopped fresh thyme leaves
6   ounces baby spinach (about 6 cups)
2   large eggs
1½ cups nonfat milk
1   teaspoon Dijon mustard
¼   teaspoon ground black pepper
1   ounce goat cheese, softened

1. In food processor, pulse both flours and ¼ teaspoon salt until combined. Add margarine; pulse until coarse crumbs form. Add buttermilk; pulse just until blended. If dough does not stay together when pinched, add *ice water*, 1 table-spoon at a time, pulsing after each addition, just until dough holds together. Shape into disk. Wrap in plastic; refrigerate 20 minutes or overnight. (If chilled overnight, let stand 30 minutes at room temperature before rolling.)

2. Preheat oven to 400°F. Spray 9-inch glass pie plate with cooking spray. On lightly floured surface, with floured rolling pin, roll dough into 12-inch round; place in pie plate. Gently press against bottom and up side without stretching; trim edge. Prick holes in crust with fork. Line with foil; fill with pie weights or dried beans. Bake 15 minutes or until beginning to set. Remove 1 tablespoon egg white from rest of whites; set remainder aside. Remove foil with weights; brush

bottom of crust with 1 tablespoon egg white. Bake 5 to 6 minutes or until golden brown and dry to the touch. Cool completely on wire rack.

3. Meanwhile, coat 12-inch skillet with cooking spray; heat over medium heat. Add leek, thyme, and remaining ⅛ teaspoon salt. Cook 3 to 4 minutes or until soft, stirring occasionally. Add spinach; cook 5 minutes or until mixture is very soft and dry, stirring frequently. Let cool.

4. In large bowl, whisk whole eggs, milk, and remaining egg whites. Stir in mustard, leek mixture, and pepper. Spread bottom of crust with goat cheese; place pie plate in jelly-roll pan. With strips of foil, cover crust edges to prevent overbrowning. Pour egg mixture into crust; bake 32 to 35 minutes or until knife inserted in center comes out clean. Cool on wire rack 15 minutes to serve.

EACH SERVING: About 255 calories, 11g protein, 28g carbohydrate, 11g total fat (2g saturated), 3g fiber, 66mg cholesterol, 386mg sodium

CRUSTLESS TOMATO AND RICOTTA PIE

Try this cross between a frittata and a quiche for brunch or dinner. Serve with a leafy green salad.

ACTIVE TIME: 20 minutes **TOTAL TIME:** 55 minutes

MAKES: 6 main-dish servings

1	container (15 ounces) part-skim ricotta cheese
3	large eggs plus 2 egg whites
¼	cup freshly grated Pecorino Romano cheese
½	teaspoon salt
⅛	teaspoon coarsely ground black pepper
¼	cup low-fat (1%) milk
1	tablespoon cornstarch
½	cup loosely packed fresh basil leaves, chopped
½	cup loosely packed fresh mint leaves, chopped
1	pound ripe tomatoes (about 3 medium), thinly sliced

1. Preheat oven to 375°F. In large bowl, whisk ricotta, eggs, Romano, salt, and pepper.

2. In measuring cup, stir milk and cornstarch until smooth; whisk into cheese mixture. Stir in basil and mint.

3. Pour mixture into nonstick 10-inch skillet with oven-safe handle. Arrange tomatoes on top, overlapping slices if necessary. Bake pie 35 to 40 minutes or until lightly browned on top, set around edge, and puffed at center. Let stand 5 minutes before serving.

EACH SERVING: About 190 calories, 15g protein, 10g carbohydrate, 10g total fat (5g saturated), 2g fiber, 165mg cholesterol, 380mg sodium

PUFFY APPLE PANCAKE

When you want pancakes, these skillet-browned apples topped with a light batter and then baked are a great low-cal, low-fat option. For the puffiest pancake, choose a cast-iron skillet.

ACTIVE TIME: 30 minutes **TOTAL TIME:** 45 minutes

MAKES: 6 main-dish servings

2	tablespoons margarine or butter
½	cup plus 2 tablespoons sugar
¼	cup water
2	pounds Granny Smith or Newtown Pippin apples (about 6 medium), each peeled, cored, and cut into 8 wedges
3	large eggs
¾	cup milk
¾	cup all-purpose flour
¼	teaspoon salt

1. Preheat oven to 425°F. In 12-inch skillet with oven-safe handle, bring margarine, ½ cup sugar, and water to a boil over medium-high heat. Add apple wedges; cook about 15 minutes, stirring occasionally, until apples are golden and sugar mixture begins to caramelize.

2. Meanwhile, in blender at medium speed or in food processor with knife blade attached, blend eggs, milk, flour, salt, and remaining 2 tablespoons sugar to make smooth batter.

3. When apple mixture in skillet is golden and lightly caramelized, pour batter over apples. Place skillet in oven; bake pancake 15 minutes or until puffed and golden. Serve immediately.

EACH SERVING: About 300 calories, 6g protein, 54g carbohydrate, 8g total fat (1g saturated), 2g fiber, 121mg cholesterol, 181mg sodium

BUTTERMILK PANCAKES WITH OATMEAL AND PECANS

Who doesn't love fluffy hot pancakes with warm maple syrup? To make this down-home fave healthier, we added oats to the batter and cooked the pancakes in a nonstick skillet brushed with oil.

TOTAL TIME: 25 minutes

MAKES: 16 pancakes or 8 main-dish servings

¾ cup pecans (3 ounces)
2 cups low-fat buttermilk
1½ cups quick-cooking oats, uncooked
½ cup all-purpose flour
1 teaspoon baking soda
½ teaspoon salt
2 large eggs
2 tablespoons confectioners' sugar
1 to 2 tablespoons vegetable oil
1 cup maple or maple-flavor syrup
¼ teaspoon ground cinnamon, or to taste
Fresh fruit, for garnish (optional)

1. In nonstick 12-inch skillet over medium heat, toast pecans until golden brown. Cool slightly; coarsely chop.

2. In large bowl, combine buttermilk, oats, flour, baking soda, salt, eggs, and 1 tablespoon confectioners' sugar, and stir just until flour is moistened; stir in toasted pecans.

3. Place same skillet over medium heat until hot; brush lightly with oil. Pour batter by ¼ cups into hot skillet, making 2 or 3 pancakes per batch. Cook until bubbles form on top of pancakes and then burst; edges will look dry. With wide spatula, flip pancakes and cook until undersides are golden. Transfer to platter in low oven to keep warm. Repeat until all batter is used, brushing skillet with more oil as necessary.

4. In small saucepan over medium heat, heat maple syrup until very warm. In cup, mix cinnamon with remaining 1 tablespoon confectioners' sugar. Sprinkle pancakes with cinnamon-sugar and serve with warm maple syrup and fresh fruit, if desired.

EACH SERVING (2 PANCAKES): About 330 calories, 8g protein, 50g carbohydrate, 13g total fat (2g saturated), 3g fiber, 56mg cholesterol, 388mg sodium

BUCKWHEAT PANCAKES

Buckwheat flour adds a wonderful nutty flavor to these buttermilk pancakes. The miniature blini variation, topped with smoked salmon, fresh dill, and a dollop of sour cream, makes elegant appetizers.

TOTAL TIME: 30 minutes

MAKES: 14 pancakes or 7 main-dish servings

½ cup all-purpose flour
½ cup buckwheat flour (see Tip)
1 tablespoon sugar
2 teaspoons baking powder
½ teaspoon baking soda
¼ teaspoon salt
1¼ cups low-fat buttermilk
3 tablespoons butter, melted and cooled
1 large egg, lightly beaten
Vegetable oil, for brushing pan

1. In large bowl, combine both flours, sugar, baking powder and soda, and salt. Add buttermilk, melted butter, and egg; stir just until flour is moistened.

2. Heat griddle or 12-inch skillet over medium-low heat until drop of water sizzles when sprinkled on hot surface; brush lightly with oil. Pour batter by scant ¼ cups onto hot griddle, making 2 or 3 pancakes per batch. Cook until tops are bubbly and edges look dry, 2 to 3 minutes. With wide spatula, flip pancakes and cook until undersides brown, 2 to 3 minutes longer. Transfer to platter in low oven to keep warm.

3. Repeat with remaining batter, brushing griddle with more oil as necessary.

EACH SERVING (2 PANCAKES): About 150 calories, 4g protein, 16g carbohydrate, 8g total fat (4g saturated), 2g fiber, 46mg cholesterol, 420mg sodium

TIP
It's best to store buckwheat flour in the refrigerator to keep it from going rancid.

BASIC CREPES

These delicate pancakes can be stuffed with a filling or rolled up with some jam. The crepes can be prepared up to one day ahead; wrap a stack tightly in plastic wrap and refrigerate.

TOTAL TIME: 30 minutes
MAKES: about 12 crepes

3   large eggs
1½   cups milk
4   tablespoons butter or margarine, melted
⅔   cup all-purpose flour
½   teaspoon salt

1. In blender, blend eggs, milk, 2 tablespoons butter, flour, and salt until smooth, scraping down sides of blender. Transfer batter to medium bowl; cover and refrigerate at least 1 hour or up to overnight to allow flour to absorb liquid.

2. Heat 10-inch nonstick skillet over medium-high heat. Brush bottom of skillet lightly with some of remaining butter. With wire whisk, thoroughly mix batter to blend well. Pour scant ¼ cup batter into skillet; tilt pan to coat bottom completely with batter. Cook crepe until top is set and underside is lightly browned, about 1½ minutes.

3. With heat-safe rubber spatula, loosen edge of crepe; turn. Cook until second side has browned, about 30 seconds. Slip crepe onto waxed paper. Repeat with remaining batter, brushing pan lightly with butter before cooking each crepe. Stack finished crepes between sheets of waxed paper.

EACH CREPE: About 97 calories, 3g protein, 7g carbohydrate, 6g total fat (3g saturated), 0g fiber, 68mg cholesterol, 166mg sodium

WHOLE-GRAIN PANCAKES

These pancakes not only allow you to go egg-free, they give you a double dose of whole-grain goodness (notice the whole-wheat flour and heart-healthy oats in the ingredients list). Top with fresh seasonal fruit, maple syrup, or check out our delicious pancake toppers, opposite.

ACTIVE TIME: 15 minutes **TOTAL TIME:** 30 minutes

MAKES: 12 pancakes or 4 servings

1½ cups plain soy milk
⅔ cup quick-cooking oats
½ cup all-purpose flour
½ cup whole-wheat flour
2   teaspoons baking powder
¼ teaspoon salt
3   tablespoons canola oil

1. In medium bowl, combine soy milk and oats. Let stand 10 minutes.

2. Meanwhile, in large bowl, combine all-purpose and whole-wheat flours, baking powder, and salt. Stir oil into oat mixture and add oat mixture to dry ingredients. Stir just until flour mixture is moistened (batter will be lumpy).

3. Spray nonstick 12-inch skillet with nonstick cooking spray; heat over medium until hot. Making 4 pancakes at a time, pour batter by scant ¼ cups into skillet, spreading batter into 3½-inch circles. Cook until tops are bubbly and edges look dry, 2 to 3 minutes. With a wide spatula, turn pancakes and cook until undersides are golden brown. Transfer pancakes to platter. Cover to keep warm.

4. Repeat with remaining batter, using more cooking spray as needed.

EACH SERVING: About 300 calories, 8g protein, 37g carbohydrate, 14g total fat (1g saturated), 4g fiber, 0mg cholesterol, 466mg sodium

COOK'S TIP:
DELICIOUS PANCAKE TOPPERS

Maple syrup will always be a classic, but to keep things interesting, try these yummy (and mostly nondairy) toppings.

• Fresh seasonal fruit, like the raspberries and chopped nectarines shown below, drizzled with nondairy vanilla yogurt.

• Toasted nuts (walnuts, pecans, whatever you have on hand), sweetened coconut flakes, and honey or maple syrup. Or, for a decadent treat, swap melted dark chocolate for the maple syrup.

• Dollops of homemade ricotta, plus fresh orange wedges.

PECAN WAFFLES

Crisp on the outside and fluffy on the inside, these pecan-studded waffles will wow your brunch guests. Maple syrup and pecans are a delectable match, so don't skimp.

ACTIVE TIME: 10 minutes **TOTAL TIME:** 20 minutes

MAKES: 6 waffles

1¾ cups plain unsweetened soy milk
1   teaspoon vanilla extract
2   tablespoons brown sugar
⅔   cup quick-cooking oats
½   cup all-purpose flour
½   cup whole-wheat flour
2   teaspoons baking powder
¼   teaspoon salt
½   cup pecans, toasted and very finely chopped
¼   cup vegetable oil
Fresh fruit or maple syrup (optional)

1. In medium bowl, combine soy milk, vanilla, brown sugar, and oats. Let stand for 10 minutes.

2. Meanwhile, in large bowl, combine all-purpose and whole-wheat flours, baking powder, salt, and pecans. Stir oil into oat mixture and add to dry ingredients. Stir just until flour mixture is moistened (batter will be lumpy).

3. Spray a waffle iron with nonstick cooking spray and preheat. Spoon batter into waffle iron (amount will depend on waffle iron used) and cook according to manufacturer's directions until browned and crisp. When waffle is done, lift cover and loosen waffle with fork. Serve immediately with fresh fruit or maple syrup, if desired, or keep warm in oven (place waffles directly on oven rack in 250°F oven to keep crisp). Serve while hot and repeat with remaining batter.

EACH WAFFLE: About 225 calories, 7g protein, 31g carbohydrate, 9g total fat (1g saturated), 4g fiber, 0mg cholesterol, 317mg sodium

CHERRY BRUSCHETTA

It's best to make this when sweet cherries are in season. Look for firm, plump fruit with stems attached, and a dark, almost blackberry-like color. This is a deliciously different choice for breakfast, and your guests won't complain one bit if you serve it up for dessert!

TOTAL TIME: 10 minutes plus 15 minutes standing

MAKES: 4 servings

12	ounces fresh cherries, pitted and halved
1	tablespoon sugar
1	teaspoon fresh lemon juice
4	slices (¾-inch thick) rustic bread
½	cup softened Neufchâtel or mascarpone cheese, or thick Greek yogurt

1. In medium bowl, toss cherries, sugar, and lemon juice. Let stand 15 minutes to allow juices to run.

2. Lightly toast bread; cool slightly. Spread bread with cheese. Cut slices in half and arrange on platter; spoon cherries with juices on top.

EACH SERVING: About 255 calories, 7g protein, 38g carbohydrate, 9g total fat (5g saturated), 3g fiber, 21mg cholesterol, 370mg sodium

Peanut Butter, Pear, and Cream Cheese Sandwiches (page 94)

2 | **SANDWICHES** & SNACKS

Lunchtime and snacktime can be tricky when it comes to following a heart-smart diet. When you're ready for lunch, it's all too easy to grab readily accessible–but definitely not heart-healthy–fast food. By midafternoon (or whenever the urge to snack sets in), a vending machine always seems to be right around the corner. And the opportunities for junk food are as abundant for kids as they are for adults. So, what's a family to do?

Start by packing a wholesome lunch for your kids at least three times a week, and make the same for yourself and your partner. Garden Turkey Sandwiches, Curried Chicken Pitas, or Peanut Butter, Pear, and Cream Cheese Sandwiches are not difficult to prepare for the whole family–just get an assembly line going with the kids' help and you'll all have brown-bag lunches in minutes. Throw in an apple or orange–or a baggie of our Kale Chips or Spiced Chickpea Munchies–and you're good to go. Over the weekend, prepare a big batch of Spring Pea Dip or Lemon-Cilantro Eggplant Dip; your family members can fill pitas with the dip themselves and top with veggies of their choice. Planning ahead for lunch takes discipline, but it's a routine that's good for your ticker.

This chapter also offers a selection of healthier burgers made from tuna or ground turkey; grilled-fish tacos; and even Mini Barbecued Pork Sandwiches you can serve on busy weeknights or lazy weekends. For movie night or the big game, serve our Slimmed-Down Potato Skins or Healthy Makeover Nachos Supreme–you're sure to get a thumbs up!

GARDEN TURKEY SANDWICHES WITH LEMON MAYO

Turkey, tomato, and baby spinach on whole-grain bread makes a satisfying lunch—or enjoy half a sandwich for a wholesome snack. Freshly grated lemon peel gives the low-fat mayonnaise spread a lift.

TOTAL TIME: 10 minutes

MAKES: 4 sandwiches

1	teaspoon grated lemon peel
¼	cup low-fat mayonnaise
8	slices whole-grain bread
4	cups loosely packed baby spinach leaves
8	ounces turkey breast, sliced
2	tomatoes, sliced

1. In small bowl, stir grated lemon peel into mayonnaise; spread on one side of each bread slice.

2. On 4 slices bread, layer equal amounts spinach, turkey, and tomato, starting and ending with spinach. Top with remaining bread slices.

EACH SANDWICH: About 300 calories, 26g protein, 33g carbohydrate, 7g total fat (2g saturated), 13g fiber, 57mg cholesterol, 320mg sodium

MANGO CHICKEN LETTUCE CUPS

Skip the bread and wrap these speedy, no-cook chicken wraps in crisp lettuce leaves instead. Mango, fresh mint, and jicama add a Latin-style zing.

TOTAL TIME: 20 minutes

MAKES: 4 main-dish servings

1   large ripe mango, peeled and chopped
1   cup finely chopped jicama
½   cup packed fresh mint leaves, finely chopped
¼   cup fresh lime juice
2   tablespoons extra-virgin olive oil
½   teaspoon Asian chili sauce (Sriracha), plus more to taste
¼   teaspoon salt
3   cups coarsely shredded chicken meat (about ½ rotisserie chicken)
12   Boston lettuce leaves

1. In large bowl, combine mango, jicama, mint, lime juice, oil, chili sauce, and salt. Toss to combine. If making ahead, cover bowl and refrigerate mixture up to overnight.

2. To serve, add chicken to mango mixture; toss to combine. Place ⅓ cup chicken mixture in each lettuce leaf.

EACH SERVING: About 325 calories, 32g protein, 17g carbohydrate, 15g total fat (3g saturated), 4g fiber, 94mg cholesterol, 400mg sodium

NUTRITIONAL NOTE: EAT YOUR SPINACH

Popeye had the right idea. Thanks to high levels of beta-carotene, vitamins B₂, B₆, C, and K—plus generous amounts of manganese, folate, and magnesium—spinach is possibly the healthiest vegetable in the world. To avoid the metallic taste of oxalic crystals that form when spinach is cooked, use raw spinach. We replaced the lettuce with spinach in the turkey sandwiches opposite. The acids in the lemon mayonnaise temper the spinach's bold taste.

GRILLED PORTOBELLO AND TOMATO PANINI

Crusty ciabatta, grilled veggies, and homemade basil pesto—now that's a sandwich! To keep the pesto extra heart-healthy, we've swapped in toasted almonds for the traditional pine nuts and skipped the Parmesan.

TOTAL TIME: 10 minutes

MAKES: 4 sandwiches

HEART-HEALTHY PESTO

3	cups basil leaves
1/3	cup plus 3 tablespoons extra-virgin olive oil
1/4	cup almonds, toasted (see Tip)
2	small garlic cloves
1/4	teaspoon salt
1/4	teaspoon ground black pepper

BREAD AND FILLINGS

1	loaf ciabatta (1-inch thick)
4	large portobello mushrooms, stems removed
2	ripe medium tomatoes, sliced 1/4-inch thick

1. Pulse basil, 1/3 cup oil, almonds, and garlic in food processor until very finely chopped. Sprinkle in salt and pepper and pulse to combine; pesto can be refrigerated in an airtight container up to 5 days.

2. Prepare outdoor grill for direct grilling over medium heat. Cut bread into four 4-inch square pieces, then split each horizontally in half so you have 8 pieces.

3. Brush mushrooms and tomatoes with 3 tablespoons oil and place on grill. Grill 6 to 8 minutes, turning once. Transfer to plate.

4. Brush bread with oil and place on grill until slightly toasted, about 1 minute, flipping once. Transfer to plate.

5. Spread 1 tablespoon pesto on each piece of bread. On bottom half of each bread piece, layer 1 grilled mushroom and 3 slices tomato. Set top halves of bread on filling. Cut each sandwich in half and serve hot.

EACH SERVING: About 480 calories, 11g protein, 36g carbohydrate, 35g total fat (5g saturated), 5g fiber, 2mg cholesterol, 403mg sodium

TIP

To toast whole almonds, preheat the oven to 350°F. Spread the almonds in a single layer on a cookie sheet and bake, stirring occasionally, until lightly browned, about 10 minutes. Watch the nuts carefully, because they can go quickly from well toasted to burnt.

HEALTHY CLUB SANDWICHES

This carrot, sprout, and bean spread combo will delight your palate and satisfy your hunger. To make it extra wholesome, we suggest using multigrain toast, but sourdough bread would be delicious, too.

TOTAL TIME: 25 minutes

MAKES: 4 sandwiches

2 tablespoons olive oil
2 teaspoons plus 1 tablespoon fresh lemon juice
1 teaspoon honey
⅛ teaspoon ground black pepper
1 cup shredded carrots (about 2 medium)
2 cups alfalfa sprouts
1 garlic clove, finely chopped
½ teaspoon ground cumin
Pinch cayenne (ground red) pepper
1 can (15 to 19 ounces) sodium-free garbanzo beans, rinsed and drained
1 tablespoon water
12 slices multigrain bread, lightly toasted
1 large ripe tomato (10 to 12 ounces), thinly sliced
1 bunch (4 ounces) watercress, tough stems trimmed

1. In medium bowl, whisk together 1 tablespoon oil, 2 teaspoons lemon juice, honey, and black pepper. Add carrots and alfalfa sprouts; toss until mixed and evenly coated with dressing.

2. In 2-quart saucepan, heat remaining 1 tablespoon oil over medium heat. Add garlic, cumin, and cayenne and cook until very fragrant. Stir in garbanzo beans and remove from heat. Add remaining 1 tablespoon lemon juice and water; mash to a coarse puree.

3. Spread garbanzo mixture on 8 toast slices. Place tomato slices and watercress over 4 slices of garbanzo-topped toast. Top remaining 4 garbanzo-topped slices with alfalfa-sprout mixture and place, topping side up, on watercress-topped bread. Cover with 4 remaining toast slices. Cut sandwiches in half.

EACH SANDWICH: About 380 calories, 14g protein, 57g carbohydrate, 12g total fat (2g saturated), 17g fiber, 0mg cholesterol, 270mg sodium

WATERCRESS AND RADISH TEA SANDWICHES

These tea sandwiches look demure but have a pleasant peppery kick.

TOTAL TIME: 20 minutes

MAKES: 16 tea sandwiches

3   tablespoons butter or margarine, softened
8   very thin slices white or whole-wheat bread
Pinch salt
Pinch ground black pepper
½   bunch watercress, tough stems trimmed
3   radishes, very thinly sliced

Lightly spread butter on each bread slice and sprinkle with salt and pepper. Arrange only very tender watercress sprigs on 4 buttered slices and top with radishes. Cover with remaining bread slices. Trim crusts and cut each sandwich diagonally into quarters.

EACH SANDWICH: About 39 calories, 1g protein, 4g carbohydrate, 2g total fat (1g saturated), 0.5g fiber, 6mg cholesterol, 71mg sodium

DILLED-EGG TEA SANDWICHES

Use this recipe for large-size sandwiches as well as delicate tea sandwiches. They're tasty either way.

TOTAL TIME: 15 minutes

MAKES: 18 tea sandwiches

3   large hard-cooked eggs, peeled and finely shredded
¼   cup mayonnaise
2   tablespoons chopped fresh dill
¼   teaspoon freshly grated lemon peel
¼   teaspoon ground black pepper
12   very thin slices white or whole-wheat bread

In medium bowl, stir eggs, mayonnaise, dill, lemon peel, and pepper. Spread evenly on 6 bread slices; top with remaining bread slices. Trim crusts and cut each sandwich into 3 equal rectangles.

EACH SANDWICH: About 68 calories, 2g protein, 6g carbohydrate, 4g total fat (1g saturated), 0.5g fiber, 37mg cholesterol, 95mg sodium

CHEDDAR AND CHUTNEY TEA SANDWICHES

This sweet-and-savory combination is a treat with a cup of tea or even a cocktail.

TOTAL TIME: 15 minutes

MAKES: 16 tea sandwiches

3	tablespoons butter or margarine, softened
3	tablespoons mango chutney, finely chopped
8	very thin slices white or whole-wheat bread
4	ounces Cheddar cheese, shredded (1 cup)

In small bowl, stir butter and chutney until well blended. Spread evenly on bread slices. Sprinkle Cheddar on buttered side of 4 bread slices. Top with remaining bread. Trim crusts and cut each sandwich into 4 squares or triangles.

EACH SANDWICH: About 78 calories, 2g protein, 6g carbohydrate, 5g total fat (3g saturated), 0g fiber, 13mg cholesterol, 136mg sodium

SMOKED SALMON TEA SANDWICHES

Using two different breads for these sandwiches is a nice touch but not absolutely necessary.

TOTAL TIME: 20 minutes

MAKES: 32 tea sandwiches

8   very thin slices white bread

8   very thin slices whole-wheat bread

6   tablespoons butter or margarine, softened, or whipped cream cheese

6   ounces very thinly sliced smoked salmon

Lightly spread butter on each bread slice. Arrange salmon on buttered side of white bread, trimming to fit. Top with whole-wheat bread. Trim crusts and cut each sandwich diagonally into quarters.

EACH SANDWICH: About 43 calories, 2g protein, 3g carbohydrate, 3g total fat (1g saturated), 0g fiber, 7mg cholesterol, 166mg sodium

COOK'S TIP:
MAKE-AHEAD TEA SANDWICHES

To enjoy more time with your guests, make tea sandwiches ahead of time and store them as follows: Line a jelly-roll pan with damp paper towels. Place sandwiches in the pan and cover with additional damp paper towels to keep the bread from drying out. Cover the pan tightly with plastic wrap and refrigerate up to 4 hours.

CHICKEN AND TOFU LETTUCE WRAPS

These fast and fresh Thai-style wraps from Lisa Warren of Washington, D.C., were our top pick in the family-friendly category at our first Cook Your Heart Out recipe contest. Lime juice, chiles, and soy sauce flavor the noodles. Peanuts, cilantro, and scallions add color and crunch. Eat with your hands—no utensils required.

ACTIVE TIME: 20 minutes **TOTAL TIME:** 25 minutes

MAKES: 8 main-dish servings

6	cups water
4	ounces cellophane noodles (thin rice noodles)
12	ounces reduced-fat firm tofu, drained and cut into ½-inch cubes
4	tablespoons fresh lime juice
2	tablespoons reduced-sodium soy sauce
1	tablespoon fish sauce
1	serrano pepper, seeded and minced
1	teaspoon sugar
1½	teaspoons olive oil
1	red onion, finely chopped
1	pound ground chicken breast
2	garlic cloves, minced
1	cup packed fresh cilantro leaves, coarsely chopped
½	cup unsalted dry roasted peanuts, coarsely chopped
2	green onions, finely chopped
16	large Boston lettuce leaves

Lime wedges, for serving

1. Bring water to boil in medium saucepan. Add noodles and remove pan from heat. Let stand 4 to 5 minutes or until noodles soften. Drain and rinse with cold water until cool. With kitchen scissors, cut noodles into 1-inch pieces.

2. Place tofu between layers of paper towels. In small bowl, combine lime juice, soy sauce, fish sauce, serrano, and sugar. Set aside.

3. In large deep skillet, heat oil over medium-high heat. Add red onion and sauté until softened, about 1 minute. Add chicken and garlic. Cook, stirring frequently with a wooden spoon to break up chicken, until chicken is cooked through and begins to brown. Add tofu and cook, stirring frequently, until tofu is hot, about 4 minutes. Stir noodles and sauce into chicken mixture; remove skillet from heat. Stir in cilantro, peanuts, and green onions. Serve chicken wrapped in lettuce leaves and garnished with lime wedges.

EACH SERVING: About 210 calories, 18g protein, 19g carbohydrate, 7g total fat (1g saturated), 2g fiber, 36mg cholesterol, 405mg sodium

HEART-SMART INGREDIENT: FRESH CILANTRO

When it comes to your family's health, every ingredient counts. Fresh cilantro contains phytonutrients that provide antioxidant protection as well as beta-carotene, vitamins A and K, iron, and dietary fiber.

GRILLED-FISH TACOS

Coat tilapia with a bold, Baja-style rub of cayenne and oregano and then char-crust it on the grill for taqueria-worthy tacos. Muy bueno!

ACTIVE TIME: 15 minutes **TOTAL TIME:** 20 minutes

MAKES: 4 main-dish servings

1	large lemon
2½	teaspoons vegetable oil
½	teaspoon plus 1 pinch salt
2	ears corn, husked
1	avocado, cut in half and pitted
3	garlic cloves, crushed with garlic press
½	teaspoon dried oregano
¼	teaspoon cayenne (ground red) pepper
1	pound skinless tilapia fillets (see Tip)
12	corn tortillas
1	large ripe tomato, finely chopped

Fresh cilantro leaves, for serving

Lime wedges, for serving

1. Prepare outdoor grill for direct grilling over medium-high heat. From lemon, grate 2 teaspoons peel and squeeze 2 tablespoons juice.

2. Use 1/2 teaspoon oil and pinch salt to rub all over corn and cut sides of avocado; set aside on a plate. On another plate, combine garlic, oregano, cayenne, lemon peel, 1/4 teaspoon salt, and remaining 2 teaspoons oil. Place fish on mixture and rub all over to coat.

3. Place fish, corn, and avocado, cut sides down, on hot grill grate. Cook fish 3 to 4 minutes or until opaque throughout, turning over once; cook vegetables 5 minutes or until charred, turning occasionally.

4. Transfer fish, corn, and avocado to cutting board to cool. Place tortillas on grill in single layer and cook 1 minute, turning once. Stack on large sheet of foil and wrap tightly.

5. Cut kernels from corncobs. Peel and finely chop avocado. Break fish into large chunks. In large bowl, mix together tomato, corn, avocado, reserved lemon juice, and remaining 1/4 teaspoon salt. Divide fish and tomato mixture among tortillas and serve with cilantro and lime wedges.

EACH SERVING (3 TACOS): About 420 calories, 31g protein, 49g carbohydrate, 13g total fat (2g saturated), 9g fiber, 52mg cholesterol, 425mg sodium

TIP
Flounder, catfish, or any mild white fish would be a good substitute for the tilapia. Grill fish fillets only 8 to 10 minutes per inch of thickness.

CURRIED CHICKEN PITAS

The addition of cantaloupe brings extra sweet flavor to these curry-spiced chicken salad sandwiches. They're the ideal choice for a light and casual summer meal.

TOTAL TIME: 20 minutes

MAKES: 4 sandwiches

¼ cup packed fresh cilantro leaves, finely chopped

¼ cup reduced-fat sour cream

2 tablespoons low-fat mayonnaise

1 tablespoon fresh lime juice

1 teaspoon peeled, grated fresh ginger

¼ teaspoon curry powder

¼ teaspoon ground coriander

2 cups chopped, cooked chicken breast meat

5 radishes, cut into ¼-inch-thick half-moons

1½ cups chopped cantaloupe (8 ounces)

¼ small red onion, finely chopped

3 tablespoons roasted cashews, chopped

4 pita breads, each toasted and cut into quarters

1. To make dressing, in small bowl, whisk cilantro, sour cream, mayonnaise, lime juice, ginger, curry powder, and coriander until well blended. In larger bowl, combine chicken, radishes, cantaloupe, and onion. If making ahead, cover bowls and refrigerate up to 1 day.

2. To serve, toss chicken mixture with half of dressing. Sprinkle with cashews. Spoon on top of pita pieces and serve with remaining dressing alongside.

EACH SERVING: About 380 calories, 29g protein, 45g carbohydrate, 9g total fat (3g saturated), 3g fiber, 65mg cholesterol, 465mg sodium

MINI BARBECUED PORK SANDWICHES

For a down-home meal in just half an hour, try these shredded pork tenderloin sliders. Serve with a side of Carrot and Zucchini Ribbons (page 391) to complete the menu.

ACTIVE TIME: 10 minutes **TOTAL TIME:** 30 minutes

MAKES: 6 main-dish servings

3	tablespoons light molasses
3	tablespoons ketchup
1	tablespoon Worcestershire sauce
1	teaspoon peeled, minced fresh ginger
½	teaspoon grated lemon peel
1	garlic clove, crushed with garlic press
2	whole pork tenderloins (¾ pound each)
12	small, soft dinner rolls

1. Position oven rack 5 to 7 inches from heat source and preheat broiler. In medium bowl, combine molasses, ketchup, Worcestershire, ginger, lemon peel, and garlic; add pork, turning to coat.

2. Place tenderloins on rack in broiling pan. Spoon any remaining molasses mixture on top. Broil pork, turning once, until meat is browned outside and still slightly pink in center (instant-read thermometer inserted into center should register 160°F), 15 to 20 minutes.

3. To serve, thinly slice pork. Serve on rolls with any juices from broiling pan.

EACH SERVING (2 SANDWICHES): About 390 calories, 32g protein, 35g carbohydrate, 13g total fat (4g saturated), 1g fiber, 70mg cholesterol, 360mg sodium

ASIAN TUNA BURGERS

Serve these with pickled ginger, with or without a bun. Crunchy Peanut Broccoli (page 392) would be yummy on the side.

ACTIVE TIME: 15 minutes **TOTAL TIME:** 25 minutes

MAKES: 4 patties

1	tuna steak (about 1 pound)
1	green onion, thinly sliced
2	tablespoons reduced-sodium soy sauce
1	teaspoon peeled, grated fresh ginger
¼	teaspoon coarsely ground black pepper
¼	cup plain dried breadcrumbs
2	tablespoons sesame seeds

Nonstick cooking spray

1. Prepare outdoor grill for direct grilling over medium heat.

2. With large chef's knife, finely chop tuna and place in medium bowl. Add green onion, soy sauce, ginger, and pepper; mix until combined (mixture will be very soft and moist). Shape tuna mixture into four 3-inch patties.

3. On waxed paper, combine breadcrumbs and sesame seeds. With hands, carefully press patties, one at a time, into bread-crumb mixture, turning to coat both sides. Spray both sides of tuna patties with cooking spray.

4. Place patties on hot grill rack over medium heat and grill, turning once, until browned outside and still slightly pink in center for medium-rare or until desired doneness, 6 to 7 minutes.

EACH PATTY: About 210 calories, 26g protein, 7g carbohydrate, 8g total fat (2g saturated), 1g fiber, 38mg cholesterol, 400mg sodium

TURKEY-MEATBALL LETTUCE WRAPS

Wrap it up! These lean turkey meatballs served in lettuce cups get their savory zing (but no extra fat) from garlic, mint, and Asian fish sauce. Carrots add crunch—and loads of vitamin A. No grill? Just cook the meat on a stovetop in a grill pan, and increase the cooking time to eight minutes.

TOTAL TIME: 30 minutes

MAKES: 4 main-dish servings

3	limes
3	cups shredded carrots (about 6)
½	cup packed fresh mint leaves, thinly sliced
2	garlic cloves, finely chopped
4	teaspoons reduced-sodium fish sauce
1¼	teaspoons sugar
¾	teaspoon ground black pepper
1	pound lean (93%) ground turkey
12	Boston lettuce leaves

1. If using wooden skewers, presoak in cold water at least 30 minutes to prevent burning. Prepare outdoor grill for direct grilling over medium-high heat.

2. From 2 limes, squeeze ¼ cup juice into bowl. Cut remaining lime into wedges.

3. To lime juice, add carrots, half of mint, ¼ teaspoon garlic, 1 teaspoon fish sauce, ¼ teaspoon sugar, and ¼ teaspoon pepper. Stir; let stand.

4. In large bowl, with hands, combine turkey with remaining 1 tablespoon fish sauce, 1 teaspoon sugar, ½ teaspoon pepper, mint, and garlic. Shape mixture by tablespoonfuls into meatballs. Arrange on skewers, ½ inch apart; flatten slightly.

5. Grill, turning meatballs occasionally, 4 to 5 minutes or until grill marks appear and meat loses pink color.

6. Divide meatballs and carrot mixture among lettuce leaves. Serve with lime wedges.

EACH SERVING (3 WRAPS): About 230 calories, 27g protein, 15g carbohydrate, 7g total fat (2g saturated), 4g fiber, 66mg cholesterol, 415mg sodium

TURKEY BURGERS WITH MINTED YOGURT SAUCE

Celebrate the flavors of Greece in this tasty, slimmed-down summer favorite.

ACTIVE TIME: 20 minutes **TOTAL TIME:** 35 minutes

MAKES: 4 burgers

½ cup plus 2 tablespoons plain fat-free yogurt
2 green onions, green and white parts thinly sliced and kept separate
½ cup packed fresh mint leaves, finely chopped
1 pound lean ground turkey
1½ ounces feta cheese, finely crumbled
1½ teaspoons ground coriander
⅛ teaspoon salt
⅛ teaspoon ground black pepper
2 whole-wheat pitas, cut in half
2 ripe tomatoes, thinly sliced

1. Prepare outdoor grill for covered direct grilling over medium heat.

2. In small bowl, combine ½ cup yogurt, white parts of onions, and half of chopped mint.

3. In large bowl, with hands, combine turkey, feta, coriander, salt, pepper, green parts of onions, remaining mint, and remaining 2 tablespoons yogurt. Mix well, then form into patties about 3½ inches in diameter and ¾-inch thick.

4. Place patties on hot grill grate; cover and cook 12 to 13 minutes or just until meat loses pink color throughout, turning once. (Instant-read thermometer inserted into center of burger should register 165°F.) During last 2 minutes of cooking, add pitas to grill. Cook 2 minutes or until warmed, turning once.

5. Open pitas. Divide burgers, tomato slices, and yogurt sauce among pitas.

EACH BURGER: About 310 calories, 30g protein, 24g carbohydrate, 12g total fat (4g saturated), 4g fiber, 90mg cholesterol, 460mg sodium

OPEN-FACED SMOKED SALMON SANDWICHES

Turn a breakfast treat into an elegant luncheon, swapping in premium whole-grain bread for the bagel.

TOTAL TIME: 20 minutes

MAKES: 4 open-face sandwiches

1	lemon
1/3	cup (3 ounces) reduced-fat cream cheese (Neufchâtel), softened
1	stalk celery, finely chopped
1/2	carrot, peeled and finely shredded
2	tablespoons chopped green onions
2	teaspoons chopped fresh dill, plus sprigs, for garnish
4	slices light whole-grain bread
1	package sliced smoked salmon (4 ounces)

1. From lemon, grate 1 teaspoon peel and squeeze 1 tablespoon juice. In medium bowl, combine lemon peel and juice, cream cheese, celery, carrot, green onions, and chopped dill. Stir to blend.

2. Spread cream-cheese mixture on one side of each bread slice; top with smoked salmon. Cut each sandwich into quarters; garnish with dill sprigs to serve.

EACH SANDWICH: About 150 calories, 10g protein, 15g carbohydrate, 7g total fat (4g saturated), 4g fiber, 23mg cholesterol, 462mg sodium

HOMEMADE SUSHI

Seafood, veggies, and rice encased in roasted seaweed and sprinkled with sesame seeds—sushi is the perfect heart-healthy wrap. The fillings can be as varied as your tastes dictate, and the rolls can be made up to six hours ahead and refrigerated until you're ready to serve them. Don't forget to provide plenty of pickled ginger, tamari, and wasabi on the side.

ACTIVE TIME: 1 hour 30 minutes **TOTAL TIME:** 2 hours plus chilling

MAKES: 100 pieces

SUSHI RICE

2½ cups water

2   cups Japanese short-grain rice

2   tablespoons sugar

1   teaspoon salt

½   cup seasoned rice vinegar

FILLINGS AND WRAPPING

6   ounces cooked, shelled, and deveined shrimp, thinly sliced lengthwise

6   ounces thinly sliced smoked salmon

1   ripe avocado, seeded, peeled, and cut into slices

1   carrot, peeled and cut crosswise in half, then lengthwise into pencil-thin sticks

1   small cucumber, cut lengthwise into 2" by ¼" matchstick strips

1   package (ten 8" by 7" sheets) roasted seaweed for sushi (nori)

ACCOMPANIMENTS

Pickled ginger

Soy sauce or tamari sauce

Wasabi (Japanese horseradish)

GARNISHES

Black sesame seeds

White sesame seeds, toasted

Minced chives

1. Prepare sushi rice: In 3-quart saucepan, bring water, rice, sugar, and salt to a boil over high heat. Reduce heat to low; cover and simmer, without stirring or lifting lid, until rice is tender and liquid has been absorbed (rice will be sticky), about 25 minutes. Remove saucepan from heat; stir in vinegar. Cover and keep warm.

2. Meanwhile, assemble fillings: Place shrimp, salmon, avocado, carrot, and cucumber in separate small bowls. Cover bowls with plastic wrap and place in 15 1/2″ by 10 1/2″ jelly-roll pan for easy handling. Refrigerate until ready to use.

3. Make sushi rolls: Place sushi mat or 12-inch-long piece of plastic wrap on work surface. Place small bowl of *water* within reach of work area; it's easiest to handle sticky sushi rice with damp hands.

4. Place 1 nori sheet, shiny (smooth) side down, with a short side facing you, on plastic wrap; top with generous 1/2 cup rice. With small metal spatula and damp hands, spread and pat rice into even layer over nori, leaving 1/4-inch border on all sides.

5. On top of rice, starting about 2 inches away from side facing you, arrange desired filling crosswise in 1 1/2-inch-wide strip.

6. Using end of plastic wrap closest to you, lift edge of nori, then firmly roll, jelly-roll fashion, away from you. Seal end of nori by pressing it to roll with water-dampened finger. Place sushi roll on tray or platter.

7. Repeat steps 3 through 6 to make 10 sushi rolls in total, using all fillings and changing plastic wrap when necessary. If desired, cover and refrigerate sushi rolls up to 6 hours.

8. Just before serving, place accompaniments in separate small serving bowls.

9. With serrated knife, slice each roll crosswise into ten 1/2-inch-thick slices. Arrange sliced rolls on platter. Garnish as desired with black and white sesame seeds and chives. Serve with accompaniments.

EACH PIECE: About 25 calories, 1g protein, 4g carbohydrate, 0g total fat, 0g fiber, 3mg cholesterol, 70mg sodium

PEANUT BUTTER, PEAR, AND CREAM CHEESE SANDWICHES

This may sound like an unlikely combination, but it creates a satisfying dessert sandwich or sweet snack for any time of the day. For photo, see page 66.

ACTIVE TIME: 10 minutes **TOTAL TIME:** 15 minutes

MAKES: 4 open-face sandwiches

4   slices cinnamon-raisin bread
¼   cup cream cheese, softened
1   tablespoon maple syrup
¼   teaspoon ground cinnamon

Pinch salt
1   small red Anjou pear
½   cup crunchy peanut butter

1. Toast bread.

2. Meanwhile, in medium bowl, stir together cream cheese, syrup, cinnamon, and salt until well blended. Thinly slice pear.

3. On each slice of bread, spread 2 tablespoons peanut butter and 1 tablespoon cream-cheese mixture. Arrange one-fourth of pear slices on top. Serve immediately.

EACH SANDWICH: About 355 calories, 12g protein, 32g carbohydrate, 23g total fat (5g saturated), 5g fiber, 16mg cholesterol, 345mg sodium

COOK'S TIP: THE ELUSIVE RIPE PEAR

Pears don't ripen well on the tree. Picked in a hard yet mature state, they soften from the inside out and can spoil very quickly if left at room temperature for too long.

• To get your money's worth, let the fruit stand in a cool place for a few days or up to a week. This allows for the changes in sugar and juice content that signal ripening. (To speed things up, keep pears out of direct sunlight in a loosely closed paper bag; they will absorb the natural ethylene gas that ripening fruit produces. Putting a ripe banana in the bag with them steps things up even more.)

• To tell if a pear is ripe, gently press the stem end. If the flesh yields slightly, the fruit is ready to eat.

NUTELLA AND BANANA ON CHALLAH

This chocolate and banana sandwich is definitely a treat, but you'll get potassium from the banana slices and healthy fats from the roasted almonds.

ACTIVE TIME: 10 minutes
TOTAL TIME: 15 minutes

MAKES: 2 open-face sandwiches

¼   cup Nutella or other chocolate-hazelnut spread
4   slices (each 1-inch thick) challah bread
2   tablespoons salted roasted almonds, chopped
1   large ripe banana, sliced

1. Prepare outdoor grill for direct grilling over medium heat, or heat grill pan to medium heat (see Tip).

2. Spread 1 tablespoon chocolate spread on one side of each slice of bread. Sprinkle with almonds, pressing gently to make nuts adhere. Arrange banana slices on 2 bread slices. Top with remaining 2 bread slices, spread side down.

3. Place sandwiches on hot grill grate. Place heavy 12-inch skillet on top of sandwiches, pressing down gently. Grill 5 to 6 minutes or until grill marks appear, turning over once. Cut into halves; serve immediately.

EACH SERVING: About 295 calories, 8g protein, 45g carbohydrate, 10g total fat (2g saturated), 3g fiber, 29mg cholesterol, 265mg sodium

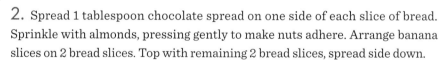

TIP
This sandwich can also be made in a panini press. Check for doneness after 3 minutes.

CROSTINI THREE WAYS

These crostini—topped with your choice of white bean, tuna and tomato, or caramelized onion and goat cheese—are great for snacks and parties. You can keep the white bean and caramelized onion toppings in an airtight container for up to two days; make the tuna and tomato topping the day you plan to eat it. If you're serving a crowd, you can toast large amounts of bread up to one week ahead. Just let it cool and store it in a tightly sealed container at room temperature until you're ready to add the toppings. To make smaller amounts for snacking, toast the bread in your toaster oven.

ACTIVE TIME: 5 minutes
TOTAL TIME: 15 minutes plus time to make toppings
MAKES: 40 crostini

1   baguette (10 ounces)
Topping of your choice (recipes follow)

1. Preheat oven to 400°F. Cut bread into 1/2-inch-thick slices; reserve ends for another use. Arrange slices on two cookie sheets. Toast in oven 8 to 10 minutes or until golden brown, rotating pans between upper and lower oven racks halfway through. Cool on wire rack.

2. Spread toast slices with topping as indicated in recipes.

WHITE BEAN TOPPING

From **1 lemon,** grate 1/2 teaspoon peel and squeeze 2 tablespoons juice. In food processor with knife blade attached, pulse lemon peel and juice with **2 cans (15 to 19 ounces each) white kidney beans,** rinsed and drained;

1 tablespoon olive oil; ¼ teaspoon ground cumin; 1 small crushed garlic clove; ¼ teaspoon salt; and ½ teaspoon ground black pepper until well blended but still slightly chunky. Spread about 1 tablespoon bean mixture on each piece of toasted bread. Sprinkle with **smoked paprika.**

EACH CROSTINO: About 45 calories, 2g protein, 8g carbohydrate, 1g total fat (0g saturated), 1g fiber, 0mg cholesterol, 95mg sodium

TUNA AND TOMATO TOPPING

In medium bowl, with fork, gently toss **2 cans (6 ounces each) white tuna packed in olive oil,** drained, with ⅓ **cup pitted Kalamata olives,** chopped; ¼ **cup loosely packed fresh parsley leaves,** chopped; **1 tablespoon drained capers,** chopped; **1 tablespoon olive oil**; and **16 grape tomatoes,** thinly sliced crosswise, until ingredients are evenly distributed. Place about 1 tablespoon on each piece of toasted bread, gently pressing mixture together without mashing tuna. (Don't top crostini until right before serving; they'll get soggy.)

EACH CROSTINO: About 40 calories, 3g protein, 4g carbohydrate, 1g total fat (0g saturated), 0g fiber, 2mg cholesterol, 80mg sodium

CARAMELIZED ONION AND GOAT CHEESE TOPPING

In deep 12-inch nonstick skillet, heat **2 tablespoons olive oil** over medium heat. Add **2 jumbo onions (1 pound each),** halved and thinly sliced; cover and cook 20 minutes, stirring occasionally. Uncover and cook 20 minutes longer or until onions are very tender and deep golden in color, stirring occasionally. Stir in **2 teaspoons fresh thyme leaves,** ¼ **teaspoon salt, and** ½ **teaspoon ground black pepper.** Top toasted bread slice with onion mixture. (If onion mixture was made ahead, reheat before assembling crostini.) Dollop each crostino with **1 level teaspoon soft goat cheese** (you'll need 6 ounces of cheese total).

EACH CROSTINO: About 45 calories, 2g protein, 6g carbohydrate, 2g total fat (1g saturated), 1g fiber, 2mg cholesterol, 75mg sodium

LEMON-CILANTRO EGGPLANT DIP

The light, nutty flavor of tahini, an essential ingredient in hummus, goes perfectly with rich roasted eggplant in this delicious dip. Serve it with toasted pita wedges and sticks of carrot, cucumber, and fresh peppers. To create a Mediterranean platter, pair it with Roasted Red Pepper Dip (page 100), some olives, and feta cheese.

ACTIVE TIME: 10 minutes
TOTAL TIME: 55 minutes plus chilling

MAKES: about 2 cups

2	eggplants (1 pound each), cut lengthwise in half
4	garlic cloves, not peeled
3	tablespoons tahini (sesame seed paste)
3	tablespoons fresh lemon juice
¾	teaspoon salt
¼	cup loosely packed fresh cilantro or mint leaves, chopped

1. Preheat oven to 450°F. Line 15 ½″ by 10 ½″ jelly-roll pan with foil and spray with nonstick cooking spray. Place eggplant halves, skin sides up, in foil-lined pan. Wrap garlic in foil and place in pan with eggplants. Roast 45 to 50 minutes or until eggplants are very tender and skin is shriveled and browned. Unwrap garlic. Cool eggplants and garlic until easy to handle.

2. When cool, scoop eggplant flesh into food processor with knife blade attached. Squeeze out garlic pulp from each clove and add to food processor with tahini, lemon juice, and salt; pulse to coarsely chop. Spoon dip into serving bowl; stir in cilantro. Cover and refrigerate at least 2 hours before serving. Refrigerate leftovers in an airtight container up to 3 days.

EACH 2-TABLESPOON SERVING: About 20 calories, 0g protein, 4g carbohydrate, 0g total fat, 4g fiber, 0mg cholesterol, 220mg sodium

LEMONY HUMMUS

This Middle Eastern dip has become a standby and is easy to make from scratch. Serve with toasted whole-wheat pita triangles or vegetable sticks for dipping.

TOTAL TIME: 15 minutes plus chilling

MAKES: about 2 cups

4	garlic cloves, peeled
1	large lemon
1	can (15 to 19 ounces) reduced-sodium garbanzo beans (chickpeas), rinsed and drained
2	tablespoons tahini (sesame seed paste)
2	tablespoons olive oil
3	tablespoons water
¼	teaspoon salt
⅛	teaspoon cayenne (ground red) pepper
½	teaspoon paprika
2	tablespoons chopped fresh cilantro (optional)

1. In 1-quart saucepan, bring *2 cups water* to a boil over high heat. Add garlic and cook 3 minutes to blanch; drain.

2. From lemon, grate 1 teaspoon peel and squeeze 3 tablespoons juice. In food processor with knife blade attached, combine beans, tahini, blanched garlic, lemon peel and juice, oil, water, salt, and cayenne. Puree until smooth. Transfer to platter; cover and refrigerate up to 3 days.

3. To serve, sprinkle with paprika and cilantro, if using.

EACH 2-TABLESPOON SERVING: About 60 calories, 2g protein, 4g carbohydrate, 4g total fat (0g saturated), 4g fiber, 0mg cholesterol, 118mg sodium

COOK'S TIP: MEZE

Meze, little savory dishes nibbled before a meal or with drinks, are a tradition in Greece, Turkey, and the Middle East. Try Lemony Hummus, Roasted Red Pepper Dip (page 100), or Lemon-Cilantro Eggplant Dip (opposite) with pita or French bread, along with feta cheese chunks, olives, radishes, sliced cucumbers, or tomato wedges.

ROASTED RED PEPPER DIP

A rich-tasting dip with a Middle Eastern accent. Serve it with vegetables and pita chips, or spread it on a sandwich or burger.

TOTAL TIME: 45 minutes

MAKES: about 2 cups

4	red peppers, roasted (see box)
½	teaspoon ground cumin
2	ounces walnuts (½ cup), toasted
2	slices firm white bread, torn into pieces
2	tablespoons balsamic or raspberry vinegar
1	tablespoon olive oil
½	teaspoon salt
⅛	teaspoon cayenne (ground red) pepper

1. Cut roasted peppers into large pieces. In small skillet, toast cumin over low heat, stirring constantly, until very fragrant, 1 to 2 minutes.

2. In food processor with knife blade attached, process walnuts until ground. Add roasted peppers, cumin, bread, vinegar, oil, salt, and cayenne; puree until smooth. Transfer to bowl. If not serving right away, cover and refrigerate up to 4 hours.

EACH 2-TABLESPOON SERVING: About 50 calories, 0g protein, 4g carbohydrate, 4g total fat (0g saturated), 0.5g fiber, 0mg cholesterol, 92mg sodium

COOK'S TIP: ROASTING RED PEPPERS

This technique brings out the sweetness in red peppers and adds smoky goodness to whatever dish you use them in.

1. Position oven rack 5 to 6 inches from heat source and preheat broiler. Line broiling pan with foil. Arrange peppers, cut lengthwise in half with stems and seeds removed, cut side down, in prepared broiling pan. Broil, without turning peppers, until skin is charred and blistered, 8 to 10 minutes.

2. Wrap peppers in foil and allow to steam at room temperature 15 minutes or until cool enough to handle.

3. Peel off and discard skin. Cover and refrigerate up to 3 days.

SPRING PEA DIP

This delicious dip has a luscious green color, fresh flavors, and a delicate texture. Serve it with assorted vegetables for dipping, such as cucumber strips, yellow and red pepper strips, and baby carrots, or with toasted pita wedges.

ACTIVE TIME: 20 minutes **TOTAL TIME:** 25 minutes

MAKES: about 1 cup

1	pound fresh peas in the pod (see Tip)
¼	cup loosely packed fresh mint leaves, chopped
¼	teaspoon salt
¼	teaspoon ground black pepper
⅓	cup part-skim ricotta cheese
2	tablespoons freshly grated Parmesan cheese

1. Run thumb along length of seam to open pod and release peas.

2. In 1-quart saucepan, bring *1 inch water* to a boil over high heat; add peas and return to a boil. Reduce heat to medium; cover and cook 3 minutes or just until peas are tender. Drain peas and rinse under cold running water; drain well.

3. In food processor with knife blade attached, puree peas with mint, salt, and pepper. Transfer to small bowl; stir in ricotta and Parmesan. Serve dip right away, or cover and refrigerate to serve later.

EACH ¼-CUP SERVING: About 80 calories, 4g protein, 8g carbohydrate, 4g total fat (1g saturated), 4g fiber, 8mg cholesterol, 220mg sodium

TIP

To save a bit of time, or if it just isn't the right season, use 1 cup thawed frozen peas instead of the fresh, and skip straight to step 3.

PERFECT GUACAMOLE

Our favorite avocados for guacamole are the varieties with thick, pebbly green skin, such as Hass, Pinkerton, and Reed. While guacamole is usually served as a dip, it's also great as a condiment for tacos or burritos or on top of a veggie burger; however you serve it, it's full of vitamins and healthy fats. If you're dipping, opt for baked tortilla chips or veggie sticks to keep unhealthy fats in check.

TOTAL TIME: 15 minutes

MAKES: about 1¾ cups

1   jalapeño chile, seeded and finely chopped
⅓   cup loosely packed fresh cilantro leaves, chopped
¼   cup finely chopped sweet onion, such as Vidalia or Maui
½   teaspoon salt
2   ripe avocados
1   ripe plum tomato

1. In mortar, combine jalapeño, cilantro, onion, and salt; with pestle, grind until mixture becomes juicy and thick (onion can still be slightly chunky).

2. Cut each avocado lengthwise in half around seed. Twist halves in opposite directions to separate. Slip spoon between pit and fruit and work pit out. With spoon, scoop fruit from peel onto cutting board.

3. Cut tomato crosswise in half. Squeeze halves to remove seeds and juice. Coarsely chop tomato.

4. If mortar is large enough, add avocado and chopped tomato to onion mixture in mortar. If mortar is too small, combine avocado, tomato, and onion mixture in bowl. Mash slightly with pestle or spoon until blended but still somewhat chunky.

5. Guacamole is best when served as soon as it's made. If not serving right away, press plastic wrap directly onto surface of guacamole to prevent discoloration and refrigerate up to 1 hour.

EACH 2-TABLESPOON SERVING: About 50 calories, 0g protein, 2g carbohydrate, 4g total fat (0g saturated), 6g fiber, 0mg cholesterol, 90mg sodium

HEART-SMART INGREDIENT:
AVOCADOS

Avocados contain heart-healthy antioxidants that have been shown to reduce levels of bad (LDL) cholesterol, while elevating good (HDL) cholesterol. Enjoy them not only in guacamole, but as a topper for salads, sandwiches, or chilled soups.

HEALTHY MAKEOVER NACHOS SUPREME

This Tex-Mex treat has fewer than half the calories (and 80% less fat!) than your typical restaurant nachos. Our low-cal creamy sauce—a blend of low-fat milk and reduced-fat cheese—smothers homemade "baked" tortilla chips, slimmed-down refried beans, and fresh, vitamin C–rich tomatoes.

ACTIVE TIME: 20 minutes **TOTAL TIME:** 25 minutes

MAKES: 6 appetizer servings

8	corn tortillas, cut into quarters
¼	teaspoon salt
¼	cup pickled sliced jalapeño chiles
1	can (15 ounces) no-salt-added black beans, rinsed and drained
1	cup low-fat (1%) milk
1	tablespoon cornstarch
1	tablespoon water
4	ounces reduced-fat (50%) extra-sharp Cheddar cheese, shredded
2	plum tomatoes, finely chopped
1	green onion, thinly sliced

1. Sprinkle one side of each tortilla with salt. In four batches, place tortillas between two paper towels on microwave-safe plate in single layer, spaced ½ inch apart. Microwave on High 2 minutes or until crisp.

2. Finely chop half of jalapeños; reserve remaining for serving. Reserve ¼ cup beans; place remaining in medium bowl.

3. In 1½- to 2-quart saucepan, heat milk over medium heat until just bubbling around edges. In small bowl, stir cornstarch and water until cornstarch dissolves. With wire whisk, stir cornstarch mixture into hot milk. Heat to simmering, whisking constantly; simmer 2 minutes or until thickened, whisking constantly. Remove from heat. Add cheese and whisk until melted and smooth. Stir in chopped jalapeños.

4. Pour ¼ cup cheese sauce over beans in bowl. With potato masher or fork, mash beans until almost smooth.

5. Place tortilla chips on serving plate. Spoon mashed beans over, then top with remaining sauce. Top with tomatoes, green onion, reserved beans, and reserved jalapeños.

EACH SERVING: About 200 calories, 13g protein, 29g carbohydrate, 4g total fat (3g saturated), 6g fiber, 12mg cholesterol, 315mg sodium

SLIMMED-DOWN POTATO SKINS

Our version of these tasty appetizers weighs in at just 120 calories per serving—versus the classic's 350—and has one-fifth the saturated fat. Our secret? Lighter ingredients (reduced-fat sour cream, Pecorino Romano cheese) that pack a lot of flavor.

ACTIVE TIME: 35 minutes **TOTAL TIME:** 1 hour 10 minutes

MAKES: 8 servings

4	large baking potatoes (12 ounces each), well scrubbed
4	slices center-cut bacon
1	tablespoon extra-virgin olive oil
⅛	teaspoon salt
⅛	teaspoon ground black pepper
⅓	cup reduced-fat sour cream
1	ounce Pecorino Romano cheese, finely grated
1	large ripe tomato (10 to 12 ounces), finely chopped
2	tablespoons snipped fresh chives

1. Preheat oven to 400°F.

2. With fork, pierce each potato three times. Place potatoes on parchment paper. Microwave on High, 8 minutes. Turn over; microwave on High 10 minutes longer or until tender. Cover with kitchen towel; let cool.

3. Meanwhile, in 18″ by 12″ jelly-roll pan, arrange bacon in single layer. Roast 10 to 12 minutes or until browned and crisp. Drain on paper towels. When cool, crumble. Discard fat from pan but do not wipe clean; set pan aside. Increase oven temperature to 475°F.

4. Cut each potato in quarters lengthwise. With spoon, scoop potato from skins, leaving about ¼-inch of potato with skin and being careful not to break through skin. Reserve cooked potato flesh for another use.

5. Arrange potato quarters, skin side up, in single layer on reserved pan. Brush with oil; sprinkle with salt and pepper.

6. Roast 13 to 15 minutes or until browned and crisp. Transfer, skin sides down, to serving plate.

7. To assemble, spread 1 teaspoon sour cream on each skin. Top with cheese, tomato, bacon, and chives.

EACH SERVING: About 120 calories, 4g protein, 16g carbohydrate, 5g total fat (2g saturated), 3g fiber, 13mg cholesterol, 160mg sodium

KALE CHIPS

Our crispy kale chips are essentially fat-free—perfect for guilt-free snacking.

ACTIVE TIME: 10 minutes
TOTAL TIME: 25 minutes

MAKES: 6 servings

TIP

Kale chips are best when eaten the same day you make them. For longer storage, place uncooked dry rice in the bottom of an airtight container, then add the kale chips. The rice will absorb excess moisture so your kale chips stay crisp.

1   bunch kale (10 ounces), rinsed and dried well
Nonstick cooking spray
½   teaspoon kosher salt

Preheat oven to 350°F. From kale, remove and discard thick stems; tear leaves into large pieces. Spread leaves in single layer on 2 large cookie sheets. Spray leaves with nonstick cooking spray to coat lightly; sprinkle with salt. Bake 12 to 15 minutes or just until crisp but not browned. Cool on cookie sheets on wire racks.

EACH 1-CUP SERVING: About 15 calories, 1g protein, 3g carbohydrate, 0g total fat, 1g fiber, 0mg cholesterol, 175mg sodium

SPICED CHICKPEA MUNCHIES

Instead of munching on potato chips or pretzels, which we all know are loaded with saturated fat and sodium, try these unassuming roasted snacks. The chickpeas boast a mild, nutty flavor that pairs well with cayenne and coriander—and they're a heart-healthy treat to reach for when you get the urge to nibble.

ACTIVE TIME: 5 minutes **TOTAL TIME:** 30 minutes

MAKES: about 1 cup

1	can (15 ounces) chickpeas, rinsed and drained
2	tablespoons vegetable oil
1	teaspoon ground coriander
¼	teaspoon cayenne (ground red) pepper
¼	teaspoon salt
1	tablespoon all-purpose flour

1. Preheat oven to 425°F. In jelly-roll pan, toss chickpeas with oil, coriander, cayenne, and salt. Sprinkle on flour and toss again to coat.

2. Roast 25 minutes or until golden and crisp, stirring once. Cool on paper towels. Store in an airtight container up to 1 day.

EACH 2-TABLESPOON SERVING: About 50 calories, 3g protein, 10g carbohydrate, 4g total fat (0g saturated), 2g fiber, 0mg cholesterol, 85mg sodium

HOT-PEPPER NUTS

If you like, use cashews, pecans, or almonds instead of walnuts. Although nuts contain heart-healthy fats, these crispy and spicy nibbles can become addictive, so we recommend portioning them into a small bowl or resealable plastic bag so that you don't eat them all in one sitting! Serve them with crisp slices of apple or pear to complete the snack.

ACTIVE TIME: 5 minutes **TOTAL TIME:** 30 minutes

MAKES: 2 cups

8	ounces walnuts (2 cups)
1	tablespoon margarine or butter, melted
2	teaspoons soy sauce
½	teaspoon hot pepper sauce, or to taste

1. Preheat oven to 350°F. Lightly grease jelly-roll pan.

2. In prepared pan, toss walnuts with melted margarine until coated. Bake, stirring occasionally, until well toasted, about 25 minutes. Drizzle soy sauce and hot pepper sauce over nuts, tossing until well mixed. Taste nuts and add more hot sauce if desired. Cool completely in pan on wire rack. Store nuts in airtight container up to 1 month.

EACH 2-TABLESPOON SERVING: About 105 calories, 2g protein, 3g carbohydrate, 10g total fat (2g saturated), 1g fiber, 2mg cholesterol, 58mg sodium

CHILI NUTS

Prepare nuts as directed above but substitute **1 tablespoon chili powder** and **½ teaspoon salt** for soy sauce and hot pepper sauce.

SWEET-AND-SPICY NUTS

Prepare nuts as directed above but substitute **2 tablespoons sugar, 1½ teaspoons Worcestershire sauce, ½ teaspoon cayenne (ground red) pepper,** and **¼ teaspoon salt** for soy sauce and hot pepper sauce.

POKER CHIPS

Save on cleanup by lining the cookie sheets with heavy-duty foil or parchment paper.

ACTIVE TIME: 10 minutes **TOTAL TIME:** 20 minutes plus cooling
MAKES: 8 dozen chips

½ cup olive oil
1 tablespoon freshly grated Parmesan or Pecorino Romano cheese
1 tablespoon chili powder
1 teaspoon ground cumin
1 package (12 ounces) white or whole-wheat pitas

1. Preheat oven to 425°F. In cup, with fork, mix oil, cheese, chili powder, and cumin.

2. With knife or kitchen shears, carefully split each pita. Brush insides of pita halves lightly with oil mixture. Cut each half into 8 wedges.

3. Transfer pita wedges to 2 ungreased cookie sheets (wedges can overlap slightly). Place cookie sheets on 2 oven racks and bake pita chips until edges are golden, 8 to 10 minutes. Watch carefully, as they can burn quickly.

4. Transfer cookie sheets to wire racks and cool completely. Store chips in airtight container up to 1 week.

EACH CHIP: About 20 calories, 0g protein, 2g carbohydrate, 1g total fat (0g saturated), 0g fiber, 0mg cholesterol, 20mg sodium

SHRIMP COCKTAIL

Everyone loves to dip shrimp into sauce; it's fun and it's tasty. Here's an alternative to the traditional red dipping sauce.

ACTIVE TIME: 17 minutes **TOTAL TIME:** 40 minutes plus chilling

MAKES: 8 first-course servings

1   lemon, thinly sliced
4   bay leaves
20   whole black peppercorns
10   whole allspice berries
2   teaspoons salt
24   extra-large shrimp (1 pound), shelled and deveined (see Tip, opposite)

MUSTARD DIPPING SAUCE
12   small romaine lettuce leaves
24   7-inch bamboo skewers

1. In 5-quart Dutch oven, combine *2 quarts water,* lemon, bay leaves, peppercorns, allspice berries, and salt; bring to a boil. Cover and boil 15 minutes.

2. Add shrimp and cook just until opaque throughout, 1 to 2 minutes. Drain and rinse with cold running water to stop cooking. Cover and refrigerate shrimp up to 24 hours.

3. Prepare Mustard Dipping Sauce.

4. Just before serving, place bowls of sauces in center of platter; arrange romaine leaves around bowls, leaf tips facing out. Thread each shrimp on a bamboo skewer and arrange skewers on romaine.

EACH SERVING (WITHOUT SAUCE): About 51 calories, 10g protein, 1g carbohydrate, 1g total fat (0g saturated), 0g fiber, 70mg cholesterol, 141mg sodium

MUSTARD DIPPING SAUCE

MAKES: about 1 cup

In small serving bowl, stir **1 cup reduced-fat sour cream, 3 tablespoons grainy Dijon mustard, 3 tablespoons chopped fresh parsley, 1/4 teaspoon freshly grated lemon peel, 1/4 teaspoon salt, and 1/8 teaspoon coarsely ground black pepper** until well combined. Cover and refrigerate up to 24 hours.

EACH TABLESPOON: About 28 calories, 1g protein, 1g carbohydrate, 2g total fat (1g saturated), 0g fiber, 5mg cholesterol, 111mg sodium

COOK'S TIP:
SHELLING AND DEVEINING RAW SHRIMP

With kitchen shears or a small knife, cut the shrimp shell along the outer curve, just deep enough into the flesh to expose the dark vein.

Peel back the shell from the cut and gently separate the shell from the shrimp. Discard the shell (or use to make fish stock).

Remove the vein with the tip of a small knife; discard. Rinse the shrimp with cold running water. Pat dry with paper towel.

Quinoa-Stuffed Portobellos (page 154)

3 | VEGGIE & WHOLE-GRAIN MAINS

Looking to incorporate more greens and grains into your family's diet? We have the perfect solution: Go meatless a couple of nights a week. The great-tasting vegetarian meals in this chapter are sure to keep your family satisfied, and you'll feel good knowing that they're getting lots of heart-protective antioxidants and cholesterol-lowering soluble fiber.

Start with familiar favorites: Cauliflower Mac 'n' Cheese is every bit as luscious as the original, and sneaks in fresh tomatoes and broccoli to boot. You already know they love chili, so why not make them a big pot of our Two-Bean Harvest Chili, which features no-salt-added canned beans and tomatoes. For a creative take on pizza, try our easy Grilled Mexican Pizza, which is topped with ready-made black bean dip, pepper Jack cheese, chopped tomato, and other taco fixings.

If preparing vegetables for dinners sounds uninspiring, try filling them for a fun new twist. Quinoa-Stuffed Portobellos and Stuffed Acorn Squash are pretty enough for company (each diner is served a stuffed veggie of their own), and are loaded with veggies, grains, and legumes. Or work some tofu or tempeh into your next dinner; both are lower in saturated fat than their meaty counterparts. Kids will enjoy eating Barbecue Tempeh and Veggie Kabobs right off a stick and Fried Rice with Tofu and Veggies, a healthier alternative to the Chinese takeout standby.

And, of course, we haven't forgotten the pasta. Choose from innovative dishes like Grilled Ratatouille Pasta and Broccoli Pesto Pasta that are bursting with veggies. To learn why you should swap in whole-wheat or multigrain pasta, see our box on page 137.

TWO-BEAN HARVEST CHILI

This hearty chili recipe is perfect for chilly autumn days.

ACTIVE TIME: 25 minutes **TOTAL TIME:** 35 minutes

MAKES: 4 main-dish servings

2	teaspoons vegetable oil
1	large onion (10 to 12 ounces), finely chopped
2	cups peeled and finely chopped carrots (12 ounces)
4	garlic cloves, chopped
½	teaspoon salt
1	bunch collard greens (6 ounces), ribs and tough stems removed, leaves chopped
1	tablespoon salt-free chili powder
1	teaspoon ground cumin
¼	teaspoon dried oregano
1	can (28 ounces) no-salt-added diced tomatoes
2	cans (15 ounces each) no-salt-added beans, preferably black beans and pink beans, rinsed and drained
¼	cup reduced-fat sour cream

1. In 6-quart saucepot, heat oil over medium heat. Add onion, carrots, garlic, and ¼ teaspoon salt. Cook 8 to 10 minutes or until golden and tender, stirring occasionally.

2. Add collard greens and remaining ¼ teaspoon salt and cook 1 to 2 minutes or until collards are bright green and just tender, stirring. Add chili powder, cumin, and oregano and cook 1 minute, stirring.

3. Stir in tomatoes and beans. Simmer 10 minutes, stirring occasionally. Ladle into bowls; top with sour cream.

EACH SERVING: About 335 calories, 16g protein, 58g carbohydrate, 5g total fat (2g saturated), 17g fiber, 8mg cholesterol, 410mg sodium

HEART-SMART INGREDIENT:
BEANS

Beans are packed with protein and both insoluble and soluble fiber. (Insoluble fiber can help with weight control and regularity; soluble fiber can reduce blood cholesterol and help control blood-sugar levels in people with diabetes.) Beans are also high in saponin, a cancer-fighting plant compound.

STUFFED ACORN SQUASH

Pine nuts and cannellini beans impart rich flavor and texture to this wild-rice-stuffed acorn squash. The squash halves create natural bowls, so just grab a spoon and dig in.

ACTIVE TIME: 35 minutes **TOTAL TIME:** 55 minutes
MAKES: 4 main-dish servings

2	acorn squash (1½ pounds each), cut lengthwise in half and seeded
1	teaspoon olive oil
2	ounces meatless bacon, such as Lightlife™ or Morningstar Farms® brands, finely chopped (optional)
1	small onion, finely chopped
2	large stalks celery, finely chopped
⅛	teaspoon crushed red pepper
¼	teaspoon salt, plus additional to taste
¼	teaspoon ground black pepper, plus additional to taste
1	can (15 ounces) no-salt-added white kidney (cannellini) beans, rinsed and drained
¼	cup water
1	package (7 to 7½ ounces) precooked wild rice
4	teaspoons pine nuts
½	cup packed fresh basil leaves, thinly sliced

1. Preheat oven to 375°F. Line 15½" by 10½" jelly-roll pan with foil.

2. On large microwave-safe plate, arrange squash halves in single layer, cut sides down. Microwave on High 9 to 11 minutes or until knife pierces flesh easily.

3. Meanwhile, in 12-inch skillet, heat oil over medium-high heat until hot. Add meatless bacon pieces, if using, and cook 3 to 4 minutes or until browned and crisp, stirring frequently. With spatula, transfer to paper towels to drain; do not remove skillet from heat. Add onion, celery, crushed red pepper, and ¼ teaspoon each salt and black pepper to skillet. Cook 4 to 5 minutes or until vegetables are tender and golden brown, stirring frequently. Remove from heat. In small bowl, mash ¼ cup beans with water. Into vegetables in skillet stir rice, mashed beans, whole beans, bacon, 2 teaspoons pine nuts, and half of basil. Season with salt and pepper, if desired.

4. On prepared jelly-roll pan, arrange squash pieces, cut side up. Divide bean mixture among squash halves, pressing firmly into cavities and mounding on top. Cover pan with foil. Bake 15 minutes. Uncover and bake 5 to 7 minutes longer or until squash and vegetables are golden on top. Garnish with remaining pine nuts and basil.

EACH SERVING: About 320 calories, 12g protein, 63g carbohydrate, 4g total fat (0g saturated), 11g fiber, 0mg cholesterol, 346mg sodium

TOMATO TART TATIN

Frozen puff pastry is the low-carb secret to this single-skillet dish.

ACTIVE TIME: 30 minutes **TOTAL TIME:** 1 hour

MAKES: 8 main-dish servings

1 sheet frozen puff pastry (half 17.3-ounce package), thawed
1 tablespoon olive oil
1 medium onion (8 to 10 ounces), chopped
1 large yellow pepper (8 to 10 ounces), chopped
½ teaspoon salt
¼ teaspoon freshly ground black pepper
1 teaspoon chopped fresh thyme leaves
2 tablespoons butter (no substitutions)
1½ pounds firm ripe plum tomatoes, seeded and cut in half lengthwise
3 ounces goat cheese, crumbled
8 small fresh basil leaves

1. Preheat oven to 400°F. On lightly floured surface, with floured rolling pin, roll pastry into 12-inch square; cut into 12-inch round. Place on waxed paper–lined cookie sheet; refrigerate.

2. In 12-inch heavy ovenproof skillet, heat oil over medium heat. Add onion, yellow pepper, and ⅛ teaspoon each salt and pepper. Cook 6 minutes or just until tender, stirring. Stir in thyme; cook 1 minute. Transfer to bowl.

3. In same pan, melt butter. Add tomatoes, cut sides down, in single layer; cover, cook 2 minutes, then uncover. Cook 3 to 4 minutes longer or until most of pan juices are reduced and thickened, swirling pan frequently. Turn tomatoes over; sprinkle with ¼ teaspoon salt and remaining ⅛ teaspoon pepper. Cook 2 minutes or until softened and most of liquid has evaporated, swirling pan. (Any remaining liquid should be thick and glossy.)

4. Remove pan from heat. Sprinkle onion mixture over and between tomatoes. Carefully invert dough (still on waxed paper) onto mixture in pan; discard paper. Cut 6 small slits in top of dough. Bake 30 to 35 minutes or until crust is dark golden brown. Cool in pan on wire rack 10 minutes.

5. To unmold, place platter over top of tart. Quickly and carefully turn platter with skillet upside down to invert tart; remove skillet. Sprinkle tart with remaining ⅛ teaspoon salt, goat cheese, and basil. Serve immediately.

EACH SERVING: About 210 calories, 5g protein, 11g carbohydrate, 14g total fat (5g saturated), 2g fiber, 13mg cholesterol, 330mg sodium

WHOLE-WHEAT PIZZA DOUGH

This basic pizza dough can be made ahead and frozen, so it's ready whenever you want homemade pizza. We used half whole-wheat flour for added fiber and flavor. If you're short on time, look to your local pizzeria. Many of them—and some supermarkets—sell dough, ready to roll out and top. Some even offer whole-wheat dough.

TOTAL TIME: 20 minutes

MAKES: enough dough for 1 (15-inch) pizza

- 1¼ cups whole-wheat flour
- 1½ cups all-purpose flour
- 1 package quick-rise yeast
- 1 teaspoon salt
- 1 cup very warm water (120°F to 130°F)
- 2 teaspoons cornmeal

1. In medium bowl, whisk together whole-wheat and all-purpose flours. In large bowl, combine 2 ¼ cups flour blend, yeast, and salt. Stir in water until dough is blended and comes away from side of bowl.

2. Turn dough onto floured surface and knead until smooth and elastic, about 8 minutes, working in more flour (about ½ cup) while kneading. Shape dough into ball; cover with plastic wrap and let rest 10 minutes.

3. Grease 15-inch pizza pan; sprinkle with cornmeal. Pat dough onto bottom of pan, shaping dough into ½-inch-high rim at edge of pan.

BISTRO PIZZA

This sophisticated pizza is topped with yellow pepper strips, asparagus, dollops of low-fat ricotta, and a sprinkling of Parmesan.

ACTIVE TIME: 20 minutes plus time to make dough   **TOTAL TIME:** 40 minutes
MAKES: 8 main-dish servings

Whole-Wheat Pizza Dough (opposite)
1   pound thin asparagus, trimmed and cut into 2-inch pieces
1   teaspoon olive oil
¼   teaspoon salt
1   medium yellow pepper, cut into thin strips
1   cup part-skim ricotta cheese
2   tablespoons grated Parmesan cheese
¼   teaspoon coarsely ground black pepper

1. Prepare pizza dough. Preheat oven to 450°F.

2. In small bowl, toss asparagus with oil and salt. Top pizza dough with pepper strips and asparagus. Dollop with teaspoons of ricotta; sprinkle with Parmesan and black pepper.

3. Bake pizza on bottom rack of oven until crust is browned, 20 to 25 minutes.

EACH SERVING: About 215 calories, 10g protein, 35g carbohydrate, 4g total fat (2g saturated), 4g fiber, 11mg cholesterol, 405mg sodium

GRILLED MEXICAN PIZZA

For an easy weeknight dinner or backyard barbecue, top a ready-made pizza crust with black bean dip, Mexican cheese blend, and fresh vegetables, including avocado, which is loaded with healthy fats. Serve it with our Watermelon Slushies (page 446) if it's a festive occasion.

TOTAL TIME: 15 minutes

MAKES: 4 main-dish servings

⅓ cup prepared black bean dip

1 large thin baked whole-wheat pizza crust (10 ounces)

2 slices reduced-sodium pepper Jack cheese, roughly chopped or torn

1 ripe avocado, pitted, peeled, and cut into chunks

2 tablespoons fresh lime juice

2 cups shredded romaine lettuce

¼ teaspoon grated lime peel

1 ripe medium tomato (6 to 8 ounces), chopped

1. Prepare outdoor grill for covered, direct grilling over medium heat.

2. Spread black bean dip evenly on crust, leaving ½-inch border; sprinkle with cheese. Place crust on hot grill rack; cover and cook until grill marks appear and cheese melts, 8 to 9 minutes.

3. Meanwhile, gently stir avocado with 1 tablespoon lime juice. Toss romaine with lime peel and remaining 1 tablespoon lime juice.

4. Top cooked pizza with romaine mixture and tomato, then with avocado. Cut into slices.

EACH SERVING: About 330 calories, 13g protein, 44g carbohydrate, 14g total fat (4g saturated), 11g fiber, 8mg cholesterol, 466mg sodium

GARDEN PIZZA

Everyone's favorite takeout gets a low-fat, high-fiber makeover with a heap of fresh vegetables, a whole-wheat crust, and a sprinkle of part-skim mozzarella.

ACTIVE TIME: 20 minutes plus time to make dough **TOTAL TIME:** 40 minutes

MAKES: 8 main-dish servings

Whole-Wheat Pizza Dough (page 122)

1	tablespoon vegetable oil
1	small zucchini (6 ounces), cut into ¼-inch pieces
1	small yellow straightneck squash (6 ounces), cut into ¼-inch pieces
1	large tomato, seeded and cut into ¼-inch pieces
½	teaspoon dried oregano
¼	teaspoon ground black pepper
¼	teaspoon salt
1	cup (4 ounces) shredded part-skim mozzarella cheese

1. Prepare pizza dough. Preheat oven to 450°F.

2. In 12-inch skillet, heat oil over medium-high heat. Add zucchini and yellow squash and cook until tender. Stir in tomato, oregano, pepper, and salt.

3. Top pizza dough with squash mixture; sprinkle evenly with shredded mozzarella cheese. Bake pizza on bottom rack of oven until crust is golden and crisp, 20 to 25 minutes.

EACH SERVING: About 215 calories, 9g protein, 34g carbohydrate, 5g total fat (2g saturated), 4g fiber, 10mg cholesterol, 455mg sodium

WHOLE-WHEAT PENNE GENOVESE

An onion-flecked white bean sauté adds heft to this fresh and healthy pesto pasta dish, making it light yet satisfying.

ACTIVE TIME: 20 minutes **TOTAL TIME:** 30 minutes

MAKES: 6 main-dish servings

12	ounces whole-wheat penne or rotini
1½	cups packed fresh basil leaves
1	garlic clove
3	tablespoons water
3	tablespoons extra-virgin olive oil
¼	teaspoon salt
¼	teaspoon ground black pepper
½	cup freshly grated Parmesan cheese
1	small onion, chopped
1	can (15 to 19 ounces) white kidney beans (cannellini), rinsed and drained
1	pint grape tomatoes (red, yellow, and orange mix if available), cut into quarters

1. Cook pasta in *boiling salted water* as package label directs.

2. Meanwhile, make pesto: In food processor with knife blade attached, blend basil, garlic, water, 2 tablespoons oil, salt, and pepper until pureed, stopping processor occasionally and scraping bowl with rubber spatula. Add Parmesan; pulse to combine. Set aside.

3. In 12-inch skillet, heat remaining 1 tablespoon oil over medium heat until very hot; add onion and cook 5 to 7 minutes or until beginning to soften. Mix in white beans and cook 5 minutes longer, stirring occasionally.

4. Reserve *¼ cup pasta cooking water*. Drain pasta and return to saucepot; stir in white bean mixture, pesto, cut-up tomatoes, and reserved cooking water. Toss to coat.

EACH SERVING: About 375 calories, 15g protein, 59g carbohydrate, 10g total fat (2g saturated), 9g fiber, 5mg cholesterol, 435mg sodium

SPAGHETTI WITH RED CABBAGE & GOLDEN RAISINS

This savory, subtly spiced red cabbage pasta dish is rich in B vitamins and fiber—be sure to cook the cabbage only until just tender to preserve its nutritional content.

ACTIVE TIME: 10 minutes **TOTAL TIME:** 25 minutes

MAKES: 6 side-dish servings

2½ teaspoons salt
1 small head red cabbage (about 1½ pounds)
1 tablespoon olive oil
1 small onion, chopped
1 garlic clove, crushed with garlic press
1 cup apple juice
½ cup golden raisins
Pinch ground cloves
8 ounces thin spaghetti

1. Bring large covered saucepot of *water* and 2 teaspoons salt to a boil over high heat.

2. Meanwhile, discard any tough outer leaves from cabbage. Cut cabbage into quarters; cut core from each quarter. Thinly slice cabbage.

3. In nonstick 12-inch skillet, heat oil over medium heat. Add onion and cook 8 minutes or until tender, stirring occasionally. Add garlic and cook 1 minute, stirring. Stir in cabbage, apple juice, raisins, cloves, and remaining ½ teaspoon salt. Cover and cook 15 minutes or until cabbage is tender, stirring occasionally.

4. About 5 minutes before cabbage is done, add pasta to boiling water and cook as label directs.

5. Reserve *¼ cup pasta cooking water*; drain pasta. Stir pasta into cabbage mixture in skillet; add cooking water if mixture seems dry.

EACH SERVING: About 255 calories, 7g protein, 52g carbohydrate, 3g total fat (0g saturated), 4g fiber, 0mg cholesterol, 275mg sodium

GNOCCHI

Usually served as a first course, these Italian potato dumplings are perfect with Marinara Sauce (page 144).

ACTIVE TIME: 1 hour 15 minutes **TOTAL TIME:** 1 hour 45 minutes
MAKES: 8 first-course servings

5   all-purpose potatoes (1½ pounds)
1   teaspoon salt
1½ cups all-purpose flour

1. In 4-quart saucepan, bring potatoes and *enough water to cover* to a boil over high heat. Reduce heat; cover and simmer until potatoes are tender, 20 to 25 minutes. Drain. Cool slightly; peel potatoes.

2. Press warm potatoes through food mill or ricer. With wooden spoon, stir in salt and flour until dough begins to come together. Gently press dough into a ball; divide in half.

3. On floured surface, with floured hands, knead each dough half until smooth. Divide each half into 6 equal pieces. On lightly floured surface, roll one piece of dough at a time into about ¾-inch-thick rope. Cut rope into ¾-inch pieces.

4. Place one piece of dough on inside curve of fork tines, gently pressing on dough with thumb as you roll dough along tines. Allow dough to drop off fork, slightly curling in on itself, forming an oval. One side of gnocchi will have ridges and opposite side will have an indentation. Repeat rolling, cutting, and shaping with remaining dough. (Gnocchi can be made up to 4 hours ahead to this point. Arrange in single layer in floured jelly-roll pan; cover and refrigerate.)

5. In 5-quart saucepot, bring *4 quarts water* to a boil over high heat. Add one third of gnocchi to boiling water. When gnocchi float to surface, cook 30 seconds. With slotted spoon, transfer gnocchi to warm shallow serving bowl. Repeat with remaining gnocchi.

EACH SERVING (WITHOUT SAUCE): About 160 calories, 4g protein, 35g carbohydrate, 0g total fat, 2g fiber, 0mg cholesterol, 295mg sodium

GRILLED RATATOUILLE PASTA

This unique take on ratatouille invites you to pair that delicious summertime grilled flavor with pasta.

ACTIVE TIME: 35 minutes **TOTAL TIME:** 50 minutes

MAKES: 6 main-dish servings

3	tablespoons red wine vinegar
3	tablespoons extra-virgin olive oil
2	garlic cloves, crushed with garlic press
1	red onion
2	medium zucchini (8 ounces each)
1	large eggplant (2¼ to 2½ pounds)
2	large orange or yellow peppers (10 ounces each), cut into quarters
1	pound ripe plum tomatoes (about 4), cut lengthwise in half
1	pound gemelli or elbow pasta
1	tablespoon Dijon mustard
2	tablespoons chopped fresh flat-leaf parsley leaves
¾	teaspoon salt
¼	teaspoon ground black pepper

1. Prepare outdoor grill for direct grilling over medium-high heat. Bring large covered pot of *salted water* to a boil over high heat.

2. In small bowl, whisk vinegar, oil, and garlic.

3. Cut onion crosswise into ½-inch-thick slices. Trim zucchini and eggplant; cut diagonally into ½-inch-thick slices. Brush half of vinegar mixture onto one side of onion, zucchini, eggplant, peppers, and tomatoes.

4. Grill, turning over once, until all vegetables are tender and charred; tomatoes take about 6 minutes, zucchini and eggplant 10 minutes, and peppers and onion 12 minutes. Transfer vegetables to cutting board. Cool slightly, then cut into ½-inch chunks.

5. Meanwhile, cook pasta in *boiling salted water* as label directs. Drain; return to pot.

6. Stir mustard into remaining vinegar mixture. Toss with pasta along with parsley, vegetables, salt, and pepper.

EACH SERVING: About 425 calories, 14g protein, 75g carbohydrate, 9g total fat (1g saturated), 9g fiber, 0mg cholesterol, 465mg sodium

PASTA PRIMAVERA

This dish is traditionally made when the first tender young vegetables appear in gardens and markets—thus the name *primavera*, which means "spring" in Italian. With an abundance of first-of-the-season veggies and fiber-rich whole-grain spaghetti, you'll never miss the cream sauce—or the calories.

TOTAL TIME: 30 minutes

MAKES: 4 main-dish servings

12	ounces whole-grain spaghetti
1	tablespoon extra-virgin olive oil
2	leeks (1¼ pounds), cut lengthwise in half, then crosswise into ¼-inch-wide slices and cleaned (see Tip)
½	teaspoon salt
½	teaspoon ground black pepper
1	pound thin asparagus, trimmed and cut into 1½-inch pieces
1	cup frozen peas
1	pint grape tomatoes, cut in half
¼	cup packed fresh flat-leaf parsley leaves, finely chopped
¼	cup freshly grated Parmesan cheese

TIP

To savor leeks' flavor minus the grit, trim and discard the roots and dark green tops. Discard tough outer leaves. After cutting leeks into ¼-inch-wide slices, place them in a large bowl of cold water; with one hand, swish to remove any sand. Transfer leeks to a colander. Repeat the process with fresh water, changing the water several times, until all the sand is removed. Drain well.

1. Cook pasta in *boiling salted water* as package label directs.

2. Meanwhile, in 12-inch skillet, heat oil over medium heat until hot. Add leeks and ⅛ teaspoon each salt and pepper; cook 9 to 10 minutes or until tender and golden, stirring occasionally.

3. Increase heat under skillet to medium-high. Add asparagus and ⅛ teaspoon each salt and pepper; cook 1 minute or until bright green, stirring. Add peas, tomatoes, and remaining ¼ teaspoon each salt and pepper. Cook 2 minutes or until peas are bright green. From saucepot with pasta, scoop *1 cup water;* pour into skillet with vegetables. Cook 5 minutes or until liquid has reduced and tomatoes have softened.

4. Drain pasta; transfer to large serving bowl. Add vegetable mixture. With tongs, toss until well combined. Divide among serving plates, and top with parsley and Parmesan.

EACH SERVING: About 485 calories, 22g protein, 90g carbohydrate, 8g total fat (2g saturated), 12g fiber, 5mg cholesterol, 480mg sodium

WHOLE-GRAIN SHELLS WITH GOAT CHEESE AND WALNUTS

A substantial vegetarian dish, this pasta showcases the winning combination of goat cheese and walnuts, which provides protein and healthy omega-3s.

ACTIVE TIME: 10 minutes **TOTAL TIME:** 25 minutes

MAKES: 6 main-dish servings

2   ounces walnuts (½ cup), chopped

2   garlic cloves, chopped

1   tablespoon extra-virgin olive oil

⅜   teaspoon salt

⅜   teaspoon ground black pepper

1   box (13¼ ounces) medium whole-grain shells

1   pound frozen peas

6   ounces goat cheese, softened

1. Bring a large covered pot of *salted water* to a boil over high heat.

2. In 8- to 10-inch skillet, combine walnuts, garlic, and oil. Cook over medium heat until golden and fragrant, stirring occasionally. Stir in ⅛ teaspoon each salt and pepper.

3. Add pasta to boiling water in pot. Cook 1 minute less than minimum time indicated on label, stirring occasionally. Add peas; cook 1 minute longer. Reserve *1 cup cooking water.* Drain pasta and peas; return to pot. Add goat cheese, half of reserved cooking water, and remaining ¼ teaspoon each salt and pepper. If mixture is dry, toss with additional cooking water. To serve, top with garlic-and-walnut mixture.

EACH SERVING: About 430 calories, 20g protein, 59g carbohydrate, 15g total fat (5g saturated), 9g fiber, 13mg cholesterol, 350mg sodium

SUMMER PESTO PENNE

Fresh asparagus and frozen peas are the unexpected vegetables in this appealing twist on the ever-popular, warm-weather classic.

ACTIVE TIME: 20 minutes **TOTAL TIME:** 25 minutes

MAKES: 6 servings

1	cup packed parsley leaves
1/2	cup packed mint leaves
1/3	cup walnut halves
2	tablespoons lemon juice
2	cloves garlic, smashed
3/4	teaspoon salt
1/4	teaspoon pepper
1/3	cup olive oil
1/4	cup water
1	pound penne
1	bunch asparagus, cut into 1-inch pieces
2	cups frozen peas
1/3	cup ricotta cheese

1. Heat large covered saucepot of *salted water* to boiling on high.

2. Meanwhile, make pesto: In food processor, pulse parsley, mint, walnut halves, lemon juice, garlic, 1/2 teaspoon salt, and pepper until almost smooth. With motor running, slowly add olive oil, then water, until smooth.

3. Cook penne as label directs, but 4 minutes before penne is done cooking, add asparagus. Then, 2 minutes before penne is done, add peas. Drain.

4. Toss pasta mixture with pesto and salt. Top with 1/4 teaspoon salt and ricotta cheese.

EACH SERVING: About 490 calories, 16g protein, 67g carbohydrate, 19g total fat (4g saturated), 7g fiber, 7mg cholesterol, 445mg sodium

FUSILLI WITH HERBED RICOTTA AND GRAPE TOMATOES

Add a little bit of the pasta cooking water to ricotta and you've got an almost instant sauce for fusilli.

ACTIVE TIME: 10 minutes
TOTAL TIME: 20 minutes

MAKES: 4 main-dish servings

1	cup part-skim ricotta cheese
1	tablespoon fresh oregano leaves, chopped
¼	cup freshly grated Pecorino Romano cheese, plus more for serving (optional)
¼	cup packed fresh basil leaves, chopped
12	ounces fusilli or corkscrew pasta
1	pint grape tomatoes

1. Bring large saucepot of *salted water* to a boil over high heat.

2. Meanwhile, in small bowl, combine ricotta, oregano, Pecorino, and half of basil.

3. Add pasta to boiling water and cook as label directs, adding tomatoes when 3 minutes of cooking time remain.

4. Drain pasta and tomatoes, reserving *¼ cup cooking water*. Return pasta and tomatoes to pot. Add reserved pasta cooking water to ricotta mixture; stir into pasta and tomatoes. Toss with remaining basil. Serve with additional cheese, if you like.

EACH SERVING: About 440 calories, 20g protein, 71g carbohydrate, 8g total fat (4g saturated), 3g fiber, 24mg cholesterol, 295mg sodium

COOK'S TIP: PASTA POINTERS

Everyone can cook pasta, right? But not everyone knows how to keep noodles from clumping or the secret to using the leftover cooking water in sauces. Follow these tips to ensure pasta perfection:

• **Make room.** Fill a large (6- to 8-quart) saucepot with cold water (use at least 4 quarts per pound). This prevents sticking and helps dilute the starch released during cooking so you don't end up with a gluey mess.

• **Put a lid on it.** Cover the pot, and use high heat so water will reach the boiling point sooner (it still takes about 10 minutes).

• **Add salt to the pasta water.** This only slightly affects the sodium content of the finished dish but noticeably boosts the flavor.

• **Go slow.** Add the pasta gradually, stirring with a wooden spoon or fork to keep it from sticking together or to the bottom of the pot. If cooking long strands like spaghetti or linguine, use the spoon to bend them as they soften until completely submerged; stir well.

• **Boil again.** Partially cover the pot until the water bubbles once more, then uncover and adjust the heat so water is boiling, but not so fast that it will overflow.

• **Don't add oil.** Your mother may have told you it keeps noodles from sticking, but so does frequent stirring. Besides, an oily coating makes it harder for sauce to stick.

• **Test it.** Italians have been cooking their pasta al dente, literally "to the tooth," for years, and with good reason: Pasta becomes gummy and absorbs too much sauce when overcooked. A noodle should offer some resistance— but never crunch—when you bite it. Just remember that whole-grain and whole-wheat pastas require longer cooking times.

• **Save the water.** It helps to reserve 1/2 to 1 cup of the water before draining in case you need more sauce for your finished dish (often the case with angel-hair pasta, which seems to soak sauces right up). Gradually stir the water into tomato, veggie, or cream sauces.

• **Serve pronto.** Drain pasta quickly and use immediately. Rinsing in cold water is unnecessary unless the noodles will be served cold—the cool splash removes surface starch, which helps sauces stick.

CAULIFLOWER MAC 'N' CHEESE

This baked macaroni and cheese hides cauliflower and carrots in the cheese sauce, making it a "stealth health" meal for picky kids and adults alike.

ACTIVE TIME: 30 minutes **TOTAL TIME:** 1 hour 15 minutes

MAKES: 6 main-dish servings

1	head cauliflower (1½ pounds), core discarded, flowerets cut into 2-inch pieces
4	carrots, peeled and thinly sliced
1	cup unsalted vegetable broth
¼	cup reduced-fat cream cheese (Neufchâtel)
1	teaspoon Dijon mustard

Pinch cayenne (ground red) pepper

¾	cup Gruyère cheese, shredded (3 ounces)
½	teaspoon salt
½	teaspoon ground black pepper
12	ounces elbow macaroni
8	ounces (3 cups) small broccoli flowerets
2	medium plum tomatoes, cored, seeded, and chopped
¼	cup Parmesan cheese, freshly grated

1. Preheat oven to 400°F. Bring 8-quart stockpot of *salted water* to a boil over high heat.

2. Add cauliflower and carrots to boiling water. Cook 15 minutes or until very tender.

3. Meanwhile, in blender, combine broth, cream cheese, mustard, cayenne, Gruyère, salt, and black pepper. With slotted spoon, transfer cauliflower and carrots to blender (leave pot over heat). Puree until very smooth.

4. Add pasta to same pot of boiling water. Cook half as long as label directs, adding broccoli flowerets during last minute of cooking. Drain; return pasta to pot. Stir in cauliflower sauce and half of chopped tomatoes. Spread in 2½-quart shallow baking dish. Top with Parmesan and remaining tomatoes.

5. Bake 35 minutes or until golden brown on top and heated through.

EACH SERVING: About 345 calories, 16g protein, 53g carbohydrate, 9g total fat (5g saturated), 5g fiber, 25mg cholesterol, 480mg sodium

VEGETABLE LASAGNA

This satisfying pasta dish is overflowing with mushrooms, zucchini, spinach, herbs, and cheese. We chose part-skim ricotta and mozzarella to keep it skinny. To get a head start, prepare the lasagna through step 5, cover it, and refrigerate overnight. Just pop it in the oven, and you can have a delicious dinner on the table in less than 45 minutes.

ACTIVE TIME: 45 minutes **TOTAL TIME:** 1 hour 10 minutes

MAKES: 16 main-dish servings

9	lasagna noodles
1	tablespoon olive oil
1	onion, finely chopped
8	ounces mushrooms, thinly sliced
2	medium zucchini (8 to 10 ounces each), sliced ¼-inch thick
1	bunch (8 ounces) spinach, tough stems trimmed
2	ripe plum tomatoes, finely chopped
2	garlic cloves, minced
2	tablespoons chopped fresh parsley
2	tablespoons chopped fresh basil
½	teaspoon salt
½	teaspoon coarsely ground black pepper
1	container (15 ounces) part-skim ricotta cheese
8	ounces part-skim mozzarella cheese, shredded (2 cups)
¼	cup freshly grated Parmesan cheese
¼	cup low-fat (1%) milk
⅛	teaspoon ground nutmeg
¾	cup Marinara Sauce (page 144)

1. In saucepot, cook lasagna noodles in *boiling salted water* as label directs. Drain noodles and rinse with cold running water to stop cooking; drain again. Layer noodles between sheets of waxed paper.

2. Meanwhile, in nonstick 12-inch skillet, heat oil over medium-high heat until hot. Add onion and mushrooms and cook 5 minutes, stirring often. Add zucchini and cook 4 minutes, stirring often. Add spinach and tomatoes and cook until spinach wilts, vegetables are tender, and most liquid in skillet has evaporated, 2 to 3 minutes, stirring often. Stir in garlic, parsley, basil, and ¼ teaspoon each salt and pepper; cook 30 seconds, stirring. Set vegetable mixture aside.

3. In medium bowl, stir ricotta, mozzarella, Parmesan, milk, nutmeg, and remaining ¼ teaspoon each salt and pepper until blended.

4. Preheat oven to 425°F. Spoon 1 cup vegetable mixture evenly into 13″ by 9″ glass baking dish. Arrange 3 noodles over vegetables; evenly spread 1½ cups cheese mixture over noodles and top with 3 noodles. Spoon remaining vegetable mixture over noodles and top with remaining 3 noodles. Evenly spread remaining cheese mixture over noodles; top with marinara sauce.

5. Bake lasagna until hot and bubbly, 25 to 30 minutes (35 to 40 minutes if cold). Let stand 10 minutes for easier serving.

EACH SERVING: About 165 calories, 10g protein, 17g carbohydrate, 7g total fat (3g saturated), 2g fiber, 18mg cholesterol, 300mg sodium

MARINARA SAUCE

This simple, basic sauce can be topped with chicken sausage or low-fat ricotta—and it's delicious on its own.

ACTIVE TIME: 15 minutes **TOTAL TIME:** 35 minutes

MAKES: 3 1/3 cups (enough to coat 1 pound pasta for 6 main-dish servings)

2	tablespoons olive oil
1	small onion, chopped
1	garlic clove, finely chopped
1	can (28 ounces) whole plum tomatoes
2	tablespoons tomato paste
2	tablespoons chopped fresh basil or parsley (optional)
1/2	teaspoon salt

1. In nonreactive 3-quart saucepan, heat oil over medium heat; add onion and garlic and cook, stirring, until onion is tender, about 5 minutes.

2. Stir in tomatoes with their juice, tomato paste, basil if using, and salt. Bring to a boil, breaking up tomatoes with side of spoon. Reduce heat; partially cover and simmer, stirring occasionally, until sauce has thickened slightly, about 20 minutes.

EACH 1-CUP SERVING: About 67 calories, 1g protein, 7g carbohydrate, 4g total fat (1g saturated), 1g fiber, 0mg cholesterol, 388mg sodium

PESTO

Pesto is the perfect use for all that fresh summer basil. To serve the pesto with pasta, add ¼ cup pasta cooking water. To store pesto, spoon into half-pint containers and top with a few tablespoons of olive oil. Cover and refrigerate up to one week.

TOTAL TIME: 10 minutes

MAKES: about ¾ cup sauce (enough to coat 1 pound pasta for 6 main-dish servings)

2   cups firmly packed fresh basil leaves
1   garlic clove, crushed with garlic press
2   tablespoons pine nuts (pignoli) or walnuts
¼   cup olive oil
1   teaspoon salt
¼   teaspoon coarsely ground black pepper
½   cup freshly grated Parmesan cheese

In blender or in food processor with knife blade attached, puree basil, garlic, pine nuts, oil, salt, and pepper until smooth. Add Parmesan and blend until combined.

EACH 1-TABLESPOON SERVING: About 66 calories, 20g protein, 67g carbohydrate, 9g total fat (1g saturated), 0g fiber, 3mg cholesterol, 256mg sodium

FETTUCCINI WITH MUSHROOM SAUCE

The combination of dried porcini and fresh shiitake mushrooms gives this sauce a rich, earthy flavor.

ACTIVE TIME: 45 minutes **TOTAL TIME:** 1 hour

MAKES: 6 main-dish servings

½	cup boiling water
1	package (.35 ounce) dried porcini mushrooms
2	tablespoons olive oil
1	medium onion, chopped
2	garlic cloves, finely chopped
8	ounces shiitake mushrooms, stems removed and caps thinly sliced
12	ounces white mushrooms, trimmed and thinly sliced
½	teaspoon salt
¼	teaspoon freshly ground black pepper
1¼	cups chicken broth
1	pound fresh fettuccine
2	tablespoons butter, cut into pieces (optional)
¼	cup chopped fresh parsley

1. In small bowl, pour boiling water over porcini mushrooms; let stand about 15 minutes. With slotted spoon, remove porcini, reserving liquid. Rinse fresh mushrooms to remove any grit, then chop. Strain mushroom liquid through sieve lined with paper towels; set aside.

2. In 12-inch skillet, heat 1 tablespoon oil over low heat. Add onion and garlic and cook, stirring frequently, until onion is tender. Add shiitake mushrooms; increase heat to medium and cook, stirring, 5 minutes. Add remaining 1 tablespoon oil, white and porcini mushrooms, salt, and pepper; cook until mushrooms are tender, about 7 minutes. Add reserved mushroom liquid and cook, stirring frequently, until liquid has evaporated, about 2 minutes. Add broth and bring to a boil; cook until broth has reduced by one-third.

3. Meanwhile, in large saucepot, cook pasta as label directs. Drain. In warm serving bowl, toss pasta with mushroom sauce, butter if using, and parsley.

EACH SERVING (WITHOUT BUTTER): About 366 calories, 13g protein, 64g carbohydrate, 6g total fat (1g saturated), 5g fiber, 0mg cholesterol, 475mg sodium

SPAGHETTI WITH GARLIC AND OIL

The classic combination of garlic and oil gives this simple pasta its heady flavor. Serve with lots of freshly grated Parmesan or Pecorino Romano cheese.

ACTIVE TIME: 5 minutes **TOTAL TIME:** 30 minutes

MAKES: 6 main-dish servings

1	package (16 ounces) spaghetti or linguine
¼	cup olive oil
1	large garlic clove, finely chopped
⅛	teaspoon crushed red pepper (optional)
¾	teaspoon salt
¼	teaspoon coarsely ground black pepper
2	tablespoons chopped fresh parsley

1. In large saucepot, cook pasta as label directs. Drain, reserving *½ cup cooking water.*

2. Meanwhile, in 1-quart saucepan, heat oil over medium heat. Add garlic and cook just until golden, about 1 minute; add crushed red pepper if using, and cook 30 seconds longer. Remove saucepan from heat; stir in salt and black pepper. In warm serving bowl, toss pasta with sauce and parsley, using cooking water to moisten pasta as necessary.

EACH SERVING: About 362 calories, 10g protein, 57g carbohydrate, 10g total fat (1g saturated), 3g fiber, 0mg cholesterol, 361mg sodium

GARLICKY BROCCOLI PASTA

Pasta with garlic and broccoli is a time-honored tradition and for good reason: it is absolutely delicious.

TOTAL TIME: 25 minutes

MAKES: 6 main-dish servings

1   package (16 ounces) orecchiette or fusilli pasta
1   bunch broccoli (about 1 pound)
2   tablespoons extra-virgin olive oil
3   garlic cloves, thinly sliced
¼   cup water
½   teaspoon salt
½   cup freshly grated Pecorino Romano cheese

1. In large saucepot, cook pasta as label directs.

2. Meanwhile, trim broccoli. Coarsely chop stems and florets. You should have about 5 cups broccoli.

3. In nonstick 12-inch skillet, heat oil over medium heat until hot. Add garlic and cook, stirring, until golden, 2 to 3 minutes. Stir in broccoli, water, and salt. Cover and cook, stirring occasionally, until broccoli is tender, 8 to 10 minutes.

4. Drain pasta, reserving *½ cup pasta cooking water.* Return pasta to saucepot. Add Pecorino, broccoli mixture, and reserved cooking water to pasta; toss until well combined.

EACH SERVING: About 370 calories, 14g protein, 61g carbohydrate, 8g total fat (2g saturated), 5g fiber, 7mg cholesterol, 395mg sodium

WHOLE-WHEAT PASTA WITH GARLICKY GREENS

This delicious, heart-healthy dish makes a great first course, or a light lunch or supper on its own.

ACTIVE TIME: 17 minutes **TOTAL TIME:** 29 minutes

MAKES: about 10 cups or 6 main-dish servings

1	large bunch broccoli rabe (1 pound)
1	bunch Swiss chard (½ pound)
1	pound whole-wheat penne or ziti
2	tablespoons extra-virgin olive oil
3	garlic cloves, finely chopped
¼	teaspoon crushed red pepper
½	cup water
¼	teaspoon salt
½	cup freshly grated Parmesan cheese

1. Bring a large covered saucepot of *salted water* to a boil over high heat.

2. Meanwhile, trim and discard tough stem ends from broccoli rabe and Swiss chard. Coarsely chop tender stems and leaves. You should have about 20 cups chopped greens.

3. Add pasta to boiling water and cook as label directs. While pasta cooks, in nonstick 12-inch skillet, heat oil over medium heat until hot. Add garlic and crushed red pepper; cook 2 minutes or until garlic is golden, stirring. Stir half of greens, the ½ cup water, and salt into skillet. Increase to medium-high heat heat; cover and cook 2 to 3 minutes or until greens in skillet wilt. Stir in remaining greens; cover and cook 10 to 12 minutes or until greens are tender, stirring occasionally.

4. Drain pasta, reserving *¼ cup of cooking water.* Return pasta to saucepot. Add Parmesan, greens mixture, and reserved cooking water to pasta in saucepot; toss until well combined.

EACH SERVING: About 360 calories, 16g protein, 60g carbohydrate, 8g total fat (2g saturated), 8g fiber, 6mg cholesterol, 412mg sodium

THAI MIXED VEGETABLE STIR-FRY

Stir-fries are all about rapid cooking, and this recipe is no exception. Brown your tofu (toss it gently so it doesn't get mashed), then stir-fry your veggies until they're tender-crisp. Add the tofu to the veggies—and dinner is served.

ACTIVE TIME: 30 minutes **TOTAL TIME:** 40 minutes

MAKES: 4 main-dish servings

¾ cup light coconut milk

2 tablespoons reduced-sodium soy sauce

1 tablespoon packed brown sugar

2 limes

4 teaspoons vegetable oil

1 package (14 to 16 ounces) firm tofu, drained and cut into ¾" by ½" pieces

12 ounces green beans, ends trimmed and halved

2 carrots, peeled and thinly sliced

½ cup water

8 ounces cremini mushrooms, trimmed and quartered

1 tablespoon peeled, minced fresh ginger

3 garlic cloves, minced

¼ teaspoon crushed red pepper flakes

1 ripe tomato, chopped

2 cups lightly packed fresh basil leaves, torn

1. In small bowl, stir coconut milk, soy sauce, and brown sugar. From 1 lime, grate ½ teaspoon peel and squeeze 1 tablespoon juice. Cut remaining lime into 8 wedges.

2. In large skillet, heat 2 teaspoons oil over medium heat until hot. Add tofu and cook, turning occasionally, until browned, about 5 minutes. Transfer tofu to paper towel-lined plate.

3. In same skillet, heat remaining 2 teaspoons oil over medium-high heat until hot. Add green beans and carrots; stir-fry 2 minutes. Reduce heat to medium and add water to skillet. Cover and cook 1 minute. Increase heat to high and add mushrooms; stir-fry 2 minutes. Add ginger, garlic, and red pepper flakes; stir-fry 1 minute. Add coconut-milk mixture; cook for 1 minute.

4. Remove skillet from heat and stir in tomato, basil, lime juice, and lime peel. Toss in tofu to rewarm. Serve with lime wedges on the side.

EACH SERVING: About 240 calories, 12g protein, 20g carbohydrate, 14g total fat (3g saturated), 5g fiber, 0mg cholesterol, 480mg sodium

NUTRITIONAL NOTE:
TASTE THE RAINBOW

The vibrant colors of fruits and vegetables do more than add visual appeal to a drab dinner. Natural pigments in produce, called phytochemicals, keep your body healthy, too. Scientists are still learning about the wide range of phytochemicals in nature, so don't expect to get these helpers from a pill. Instead, eat a colorful diet filled with reds, yellows, oranges, and greens.

FRIED RICE WITH TOFU AND VEGGIES

Tasty and thrifty, this is the perfect dish for cleaning out the bits and pieces in your fridge—part of a head of broccoli, a lone carrot, a couple of eggs, a container of leftover rice. We've included some tofu for a low-fat source of protein; as for the vegetables, swap in whatever you have in your crisper.

ACTIVE TIME: 35 minutes **TOTAL TIME:** 50 minutes

MAKES: 4 main-dish servings

2	tablespoons vegetable oil
1	package (14 to 16 ounces) extra-firm tofu, drained, patted dry, and cut into ½-inch cubes
2	large eggs, beaten
1	tablespoon peeled, minced fresh ginger
2	garlic cloves, minced
8	ounces asparagus, trimmed and cut diagonally into ¾-inch pieces
2	cups small broccoli flowerets
1	large carrot, peeled and shredded
4	ounces shiitake mushrooms, stems discarded and caps thinly sliced
¼	cup water
1	cup brown jasmine rice, cooked as label directs and chilled, or 2 cups cold leftover rice
¾	cup frozen peas, thawed
2	tablespoons reduced-sodium soy sauce
2	green onions, finely chopped
1½	teaspoons toasted sesame oil
¼	cup chopped fresh cilantro

1. In large skillet, heat 2 teaspoons vegetable oil over medium heat. Add tofu and cook, turning occasionally, until lightly browned on all sides, about 3 minutes. Transfer to medium bowl.

2. Heat 1 teaspoon vegetable oil in skillet and pour in eggs. Cook, stirring, until softly scrambled, about 1 minute. Add to bowl with tofu.

3. In 12-inch nonstick skillet, heat remaining 1 tablespoon vegetable oil over medium heat. Add ginger and garlic and stir-fry 1 minute. Add asparagus, broccoli, carrot, and mushrooms; stir-fry 3 minutes. Add water and increase heat to medium-high. Stir-fry until water evaporates and vegetables are tender-crisp, about 1 minute. Add rice, peas, and soy sauce; stir-fry until rice is hot, about 3 minutes. Stir in green onions and sesame oil.

4. Remove from heat, add tofu, and toss to warm. Sprinkle with cilantro and serve.

EACH SERVING: About 450 calories, 19g protein, 51g carbohydrate, 20g total fat (2g saturated), 8g fiber, 0mg cholesterol, 480mg sodium

NUTRITIONAL NOTE: GLUTEN-FREE GRAINS

If you're on a gluten-free diet or cooking for family or friends with celiac disease, explore these gluten-free grains:

- buckwheat
- corn
- millet
- quinoa
- rice
- sorghum
- teff
- wild rice
- oats (look for an organic brand that specifies "gluten-free" on its label)

QUINOA-STUFFED PORTOBELLOS

This healthy meal is low in calories, yet hearty enough to serve as a main course. Meaty portobello mushrooms combine with protein-rich quinoa, creamy feta, and vitamin-dense Brussels sprouts on the side to create a flavorful dish packed with nutrients. Quinoa, which has a mild, slightly nutty flavor, packs more protein than any other grain. For photo, see page 114.

TOTAL TIME: 30 minutes

MAKES: 4 main-dish servings

½   cup quinoa, rinsed
¾   cup water
1¼   pounds Brussels sprouts
4   teaspoons extra-virgin olive oil
⅜   teaspoon salt
¼   teaspoon ground black pepper
4   large portobello mushroom caps (about 1 pound)
1   teaspoon fresh thyme leaves, finely chopped
⅔   cup frozen corn
3   ounces feta cheese, crumbled (¾ cup)
½   teaspoon ground cumin

1. Preheat oven to 450°F. In 2-quart saucepan, combine quinoa and water. Bring to a boil over high heat; reduce heat to medium-low. Cover and cook 15 minutes or until liquid is absorbed.

2. Meanwhile, trim and halve Brussels sprouts. In 18" by 12" jelly-roll pan, toss sprouts, 2 teaspoons oil, ¼ teaspoon salt, and pepper to evenly coat. Roast 10 minutes.

3. While sprouts cook, brush mushrooms with remaining 2 teaspoons oil and sprinkle with remaining ⅛ teaspoon salt. Combine thyme, corn, feta, cumin, and cooked quinoa in bowl.

4. When sprouts have roasted 10 minutes, push to one side of pan and arrange mushrooms, gill sides up, on other side. Divide quinoa mixture among mushrooms; roast 10 minutes or until mushrooms are tender.

EACH SERVING: About 290 calories, 14g protein, 38g carbohydrate, 11g total fat (4g saturated), 9g fiber, 19mg cholesterol, 430mg sodium

CHUNKY VEGETABLE BULGUR SALAD

Made from bulgur with lots of chopped mint and parsley, this squash-studded salad is reminiscent of tabbouleh. Serve it with toasted pita wedges and a drizzle of yogurt, if you like.

TOTAL TIME: 20 minutes plus standing

MAKES: 4 main-dish servings

2	cups bulgur
2½	cups boiling water
2	lemons
1	tablespoon olive oil
1	small red onion, finely chopped
1	cup cherry tomatoes, halved
1	medium zucchini (8 ounces), chopped
1	medium yellow summer squash (8 ounces), chopped
½	cup loosely packed fresh mint leaves, chopped
½	cup loosely packed fresh parsley leaves, chopped
½	teaspoon salt
¼	teaspoon coarsely ground black pepper

1. In large bowl, stir together bulgur and boiling water. Cover and let stand until liquid is absorbed, about 30 minutes.

2. Meanwhile, from lemons, grate 1 teaspoon peel and squeeze ¼ cup juice; set aside.

3. In nonstick 12-inch skillet, heat oil over medium-high heat until hot. Add onion and cook until it begins to soften, 3 to 4 minutes. Add tomatoes, zucchini, and squash, and cook until vegetables are tender, 6 to 8 minutes, stirring occasionally.

4. Stir vegetables into bulgur with lemon peel and juice, mint, parsley, salt, and pepper. Serve immediately, or spoon into container with tight-fitting lid and refrigerate up to 1 day.

EACH SERVING: About 320 calories, 12g protein, 64g carbohydrate, 4g total fat (0g saturated), 16g fiber, 0mg cholesterol, 320mg sodium

BARBECUE TEMPEH AND VEGGIE KABOBS

Meaty tempeh and colorful mixed vegetables are skewered for a satisfying and delicious dinner that's a cinch to make on the grill. Not familiar with tempeh? See the box opposite for details.

ACTIVE TIME: 30 minutes **TOTAL TIME:** 40 minutes
MAKES: 12 kabobs or 6 main-dish servings

1   package (8 ounces) tempeh
2/3   cup barbecue sauce
1   red pepper, seeded and cut into 1-inch pieces
1   small red onion, cut into 6 wedges, each wedge halved crosswise
1   zucchini, cut into ¼-inch-thick half-moons
1   tablespoon canola oil plus additional for grill
Salt to taste
Ground black pepper to taste
1   teaspoon chili powder

1. Prepare outdoor grill for direct grilling over medium heat. Presoak 12 wooden skewers in cold water at least 30 minutes to prevent burning.

2. Cut tempeh into 24 equal-size chunks.

3. Heat 10-inch nonstick skillet over medium heat. Add tempeh and barbecue sauce and simmer until sauce thickens and sticks to tempeh, about 15 minutes, stirring occasionally. Remove skillet from heat.

4. Meanwhile, in medium bowl, gently toss red pepper, onion, and zucchini with 1 tablespoon oil, salt, pepper, and chili powder.

5. Assemble kabobs using 1 piece onion and 2 pieces of other items on each skewer.

6. Grill, turning kabobs occasionally, until browned and tender, 12 to 15 minutes. Remove to large platter.

EACH SERVING (2 KABOBS): About 160 calories, 9g protein, 20g carbohydrate, 6g total fat (1g saturated), 4g fiber, 0mg cholesterol, 354mg sodium

HEART-SMART INGREDIENT: TEMPEH

Made by fermenting whole soybeans (or other beans plus grains) into dense, chewy blocks, tempeh has a much meatier texture than the more familiar tofu, and lends itself to baking, braising, grilling, or frying. In Indonesia, where it originated, it remains an affordable everyday protein to many who only eat meat on special occasions.

Tempeh contains 22 grams of protein per 4-ounce serving (comparable to the protein found in chicken legs or pork chops); because this is a fermented food, the protein is easy to assimilate. It also contains omega-6 fatty acids, which can help stabilize blood pressure, and omega-3 fatty acids, which can boost heart health and lower triglycerides.

BULGUR AND CASHEW-STUFFED EGGPLANT

Grains, nuts, and vegetables come together to make a satisfying Middle Eastern–inspired entrée.

ACTIVE TIME: 15 minutes
TOTAL TIME: 20 minutes

MAKES: 4 main-dish servings

3	tablespoons olive oil
3	cloves garlic, crushed with garlic press
1	cup golden raisins
1	teaspoon curry powder
2	teaspoons salt
1	cup quick-cooking bulgur wheat
2	cups water
2	medium eggplants
1	cup cashews, chopped

Chopped fresh mint (for garnish)

1. In small saucepot, heat 1 tablespoon olive oil over medium heat. Add crushed garlic, raisins, curry powder, and 1 teaspoon salt. Cook 2 minutes, stirring.

2. Add bulgur and water and heat to simmering. Cover and simmer 15 minutes, or until bulgur is tender.

3. Meanwhile, cut eggplants in half lengthwise. Scoop out seeds. Arrange eggplant on foil-lined baking sheet, cut sides up. Brush with 2 tablespoons olive oil and sprinkle with 1 teaspoon salt. Broil over high heat (6 inches from heat source), 7 minutes or until tender.

4. Remove eggplant from oven; cover with foil. With fork, fluff bulgur; stir in cashews. Stuff eggplant with bulgur mixture and garnish with chopped mint.

EACH SERVING: About 460 calories, 11g protein, 69g carbohydrate, 19g total fat (3g saturated), 16g fiber, 0mg cholesterol, 450mg sodium

SOUTHWESTERN RICE AND CORN FRITTATA

A hearty, one-skillet dish that's perfect for a weeknight supper or a Sunday brunch.

ACTIVE TIME: 25 minutes **TOTAL TIME:** 50 minutes

MAKES: 6 main-dish servings (cut frittata into wedges)

1	package (8 to 9 ounces) precooked brown rice (scant 2 cups)
4	teaspoons olive oil
1	small onion, chopped
1	jalapeño chile, seeded and finely chopped
1	garlic clove, finely chopped
1	cup frozen corn kernels
8	large eggs
¼	cup milk
¼	cup loosely packed fresh cilantro leaves, chopped
½	teaspoon salt
½	cup shredded Mexican cheese blend
	Prepared salsa (optional)

1. Heat brown rice as label directs.

2. Meanwhile, preheat oven to 400°F. In oven-safe nonstick 10-inch skillet, heat 2 teaspoons oil over medium heat until hot. Add onion and cook 4 to 5 minutes or until lightly browned, stirring occasionally. Stir in jalapeño and garlic; cook 30 seconds, stirring. Add corn and cook 1 minute or until corn is thawed, stirring occasionally. Transfer corn mixture to bowl.

3. In large bowl, with wire whisk, beat eggs, milk, cilantro, and ½ teaspoon salt until well blended. Stir in rice, corn mixture, and cheese.

4. In same skillet, heat remaining 2 teaspoons oil over medium heat until hot. Pour in egg mixture; cover and cook 3 minutes or until it starts to set around the edge.

5. Remove cover, place skillet in oven. Bake 20 minutes or until knife inserted 2 inches from edge comes out clean. Remove frittata from oven; let stand 5 minutes.

6. To serve, loosen frittata from skillet; slide onto warm platter.

EACH SERVING: About 245 calories, 13g protein, 19g carbohydrate, 14g total fat (5g saturated), 2g fiber, 293mg cholesterol, 355mg sodium

8 QUICK & EASY WAYS
TO GET YOUR GRAINS

• Use a combination of wild and brown rice in place of white rice in your favorite pilaf or rice-salad recipes, making sure to adjust the rice's cooking time (soak brown rice in cold water overnight in the fridge to cut the cooking time in half).

• Slice whole-wheat or multigrain bread into ½-inch cubes; toss with olive oil and bake until golden for tasty and healthy croutons.

• For a new twist, stir some plain vanilla yogurt and fruit jam into hot oatmeal before serving.

• Slice precooked polenta logs into rounds. Place on a cookie sheet and top with spaghetti sauce and cheese; bake until hot and bubbly for an easy entrée.

natural and wild rice

brown rice

whole oats

wheat berries

• Sprinkle a spoonful of toasted wheat germ or ground flaxseed on your breakfast cereal (choose a cereal that lists whole grains in the ingredients or states that it is 100 percent whole wheat).

• Toss cooked bulgur, chopped parsley, and finely chopped celery, carrots, and red onion with your favorite vinaigrette for a tasty side dish.

• Your secret weapon—a few teaspoons of wheat germ added with the flour when making cookie dough or cake batter—will make each mouthful more nutritious.

• Mix cooked quinoa with canned corn, butter, and chopped basil for a new side dish.

millet

buckwheat

flaxseeds

sesame seeds

EASY SUMMER TOMATO RISOTTO

Heat-beating and hands-off, this convenient risotto, featuring the summer bounty of corn and tomatoes, is simmered in the microwave from beginning to end, so there's no toiling over a steamy stove. A little grated Parmesan gives it the classic creaminess.

ACTIVE TIME: 30 minutes
TOTAL TIME: 40 minutes

MAKES: 6 main-dish servings

1	bag (12 ounces) microwave-in-bag green beans
1	can (14½ ounces) reduced-sodium vegetable broth
2	cups water
2	tablespoons margarine or butter
1	small onion, chopped
2	cups Arborio rice
2	pounds ripe tomatoes
2	cups fresh corn kernels
¼	cup finely grated Parmesan cheese
⅜	teaspoon salt
¼	teaspoon ground black pepper
2	tablespoons chopped fresh basil

1. Cook beans as label directs. Cool slightly; cut into 1-inch pieces.

2. In 2-quart saucepan, bring broth and water to a boil.

3. Meanwhile, in 4-quart microwave-safe bowl, microwave margarine and onion, uncovered, on High 3 minutes or until softened. Stir in rice. Cook on High, 1 minute.

4. Stir broth mixture into rice mixture. Cover with vented plastic wrap; microwave on Medium (50% power), 10 minutes.

5. Meanwhile, in food processor, puree half of tomatoes; strain juice through sieve into measuring cup, pressing on solids. Discard solids. Chop remaining tomatoes.

6. Stir 1½ cups tomato juice into rice mixture. Re-cover bowl with vented plastic wrap; microwave over medium heat 5 minutes or until most of liquid is absorbed.

7. Stir corn into rice mixture and cover again with vented plastic wrap; microwave over medium heat 3 minutes or until corn is heated through.

8. Stir Parmesan, green beans, chopped tomatoes, salt, pepper, and half of basil into risotto. Sprinkle with remaining basil before serving.

EACH SERVING: About 390 calories, 12g protein, 70g carbohydrate, 8g total fat (5g saturated), 6g fiber, 8mg cholesterol, 430mg sodium

CAULIFLOWER PLANKS WITH MEDITERRANEAN RELISH

These "steaks" are quick-grilled then baked and topped with a relish of sweet oranges and dates, briny olives, toasted almonds, and fresh herbs. They're the creation of Janice Elder, a finalist in the second Cook Your Heart Out Contest. Add a side of greens and dinner is served.

ACTIVE TIME: 20 minutes **TOTAL TIME:** 35 minutes

MAKES: 4 servings

1	head cauliflower, trimmed
1	tablespoon canola oil
½	teaspoon salt
½	teaspoon freshly ground black pepper, plus more to taste
2	teaspoons extra-virgin olive oil
1	shallot, peeled and finely chopped
½	cup chopped pitted dates
2	tablespoons sherry vinegar
¼	cup coarsely chopped whole almonds, lightly toasted
¼	cup Kalamata olives, drained well and chopped
2	tablespoons finely chopped fresh flat-leaf parsley, plus more for garnish
1	teaspoon fresh thyme leaves, plus more (for garnish)
1	orange, peel grated and set aside

1. Preheat oven to 350°F. Spray a rimmed baking sheet with nonstick cooking spray.

2. Using large, heavy knife, cut cauliflower into four 1-inch-thick slices, starting at top and center of head and cutting all the way through to stem end. Brush cut sides of cauliflower with some of canola oil and sprinkle with salt and pepper. Any leftover cauliflower pieces may be set aside for another use.

3. Brush large skillet or grill pan with any remaining canola oil and heat over medium-high heat. When hot, add cauliflower slices, working in batches if necessary, and cook until lightly browned, about 4 minutes per side. Transfer cauliflower to prepared baking sheet and bake in preheated oven 12 to 15 minutes until tender.

4. Meanwhile, heat olive oil in saucepan over medium heat. When hot, add shallot, stirring until translucent, 2 to 3 minutes. Add dates and vinegar, stirring until dates are softened, about 5 minutes. Reduce heat to low; add almonds, olives, parsley, thyme, and orange peel. Season with pepper and stir gently to combine. Remove and discard white pith from orange; cut into segments. Add orange segments to saucepan and toss and heat until relish is warmed throughout.

5. Arrange cauliflower planks on serving platter and spoon warm relish on top. Garnish with additional fresh parsley and thyme and serve immediately.

EACH SERVING: About 230 calories, 5g protein, 30g carbohydrate, 12g total fat (1g saturated), 6g fiber, 0mg cholesterol, 445mg sodium

SIX-BEAN SALAD WITH TOMATO VINAIGRETTE

Trying to eat less meat? Check out this powerhouse of protein, iron, and bone-building vitamin K. The tomato dressing adds a zesty finish.

ACTIVE TIME: 20 minutes **TOTAL TIME:** 25 minutes plus chilling
MAKES: 8 main-dish servings

BEAN SALAD
¾   teaspoon salt
8   ounces green beans, trimmed and cut into 1-inch pieces
8   ounces wax beans, trimmed and cut into 1-inch pieces
1   can (15 to 19 ounces) no-salt-added garbanzo beans
1   can (15 to 19 ounces) no-salt-added black beans or black soybeans
1   can (15 to 19 ounces) no-salt-added red kidney beans
1½ cups (half 16-ounce bag) frozen shelled green soybeans (edamame), thawed
1   head Boston lettuce, separated into leaves, for serving

TOMATO VINAIGRETTE
1   small ripe tomato, coarsely chopped
1   small shallot, coarsely chopped
¼   cup olive oil
2   tablespoons red wine vinegar
1   tablespoon Dijon mustard
½   teaspoon salt
¼   teaspoon ground black pepper

1. Prepare salad: In 12-inch skillet, place *1 inch water;* add salt and bring to a boil over high heat. Add green and wax beans; return water to boil. Reduce heat to low; simmer until beans are tender-crisp, 6 to 8 minutes. Drain beans. Rinse with cold running water to stop cooking; drain again. Transfer beans to large serving bowl.

2. Rinse and drain garbanzo, black, and kidney beans. Add canned beans and green soybeans to bowl with green and wax beans.

3. Prepare dressing: In blender, combine tomato, shallot, oil, vinegar, mustard, salt, and pepper. Blend until smooth.

4. Add vinaigrette to beans in bowl. Toss until beans are evenly coated. Cover and refrigerate to blend flavors, at least 1 hour or up to 8 hours.

EACH SERVING: About 270 calories, 14g protein, 36g carbohydrate, 8g total fat (1g saturated), 13g fiber, 0mg cholesterol, 263mg sodium

Seared Salmon with Sweet Potatoes (page 182)

4 | **FISH &** SHELLFISH

If your goal is a heart-healthy family (and we know that's the case because you're reading this book!), then serve fish for dinner twice a week—the oilier, the better. All oily fish contain omega-3 fatty acids, polyunsaturated fats that protect against heart disease (see "Get Your Omega-3s" on page 179 to learn more). Because salmon boasts the highest levels of these good-for-you fats, we open this chapter with recipes starring this winner. Whether you choose to oven roast it in dishes like Salmon with Mustard Glaze or grill it in recipes like Smoky Spanish Salmon, make this fish a part of your regular dinnertime rotation.

If you're cooking for picky kids (or a partner who insists he or she doesn't like fish), try serving them mild Almond-Crusted Tilapia or fun Flounder Pesto Roll-Ups. Or take the stealth-health approach and sneak some fish into a big bowl of noodles, as in Rustic Pasta Toss with Tuna and Tomatoes. You'll likely be surprised by your family members' positive reactions—and they'll benefit from the lean protein, vitamins, and minerals that these dishes deliver.

And don't forget the shellfish: Scallops, Scampi-Style and Italian-Spiced Shrimp Casserole are always popular. Do your family a favor and try replacing the white rice in the casserole with brown; the soluble fiber in brown rice can help lower cholesterol levels in all who dig in regularly.

SALMON STEAKS WITH TRICOLOR PEPPER RELISH

Consider roasted salmon one of your go-to heart-healthy dinner options: It's high in omega-3 fatty acids, which can help lower blood cholesterol levels.

ACTIVE TIME: 12 minutes **TOTAL TIME:** 45 minutes

MAKES: 4 main-dish servings

¼ cup sliced almonds

3 medium peppers (4 to 6 ounces each), preferably red, yellow, and orange, thinly sliced

1 small onion (4 to 6 ounces), thinly sliced

1 tablespoon olive oil

⅜ teaspoon salt

⅜ teaspoon freshly ground black pepper

2 salmon steaks (12 to 14 ounces each)

½ cup packed fresh basil leaves, finely chopped, plus additional for garnish

¼ cup oil-packed sun-dried tomatoes, patted dry and chopped

1 tablespoon capers, coarsely chopped

Cooked brown or white rice, for serving

1. Preheat oven to 450°F. In 18″ by 12″ jelly-roll pan, spread almonds in single layer. Roast 4 to 6 minutes or until toasted. Transfer to plate; set aside. In same pan, combine peppers, onion, oil, and ⅛ teaspoon each salt and black pepper. Spread in single layer; roast 15 minutes or until tender. Stir vegetables; push to one side of pan to make space for salmon.

2. Sprinkle salmon with remaining ¼ teaspoon each salt and black pepper to season both sides. Place in pan with peppers. Roast 8 to 10 minutes or until salmon is just opaque and knife pierces easily through flesh. (Instant-read thermometer inserted horizontally in center of fillet should reach 145°F.)

3. Meanwhile, in large bowl, combine basil, tomatoes, and capers. Add roasted peppers and onion and stir well. Cut each salmon steak lengthwise in half; remove and discard bones. Divide salmon among serving plates and top with pepper relish and almonds. Serve with rice, garnished with chopped basil.

EACH SERVING: About 395 calories, 40g protein, 14g carbohydrate, 20g total fat (3g saturated), 4g fiber, 101mg cholesterol, 385mg sodium

GINGER-CRUSTED SALMON WITH MELON SALSA

Spicy and fresh, this healthy, flavorful dinner combines rich salmon and a salsa made with a duet of melons and herbs.

ACTIVE TIME: 20 minutes **TOTAL TIME:** 30 minutes

MAKES: 4 main-dish servings

2	cups cubed cantaloupe (cut into ⅓-inch pieces)
1	cup cubed honeydew (cut into ⅓-inch pieces)
¼	cup packed fresh cilantro leaves, finely chopped
2	tablespoons fresh mint leaves, finely chopped
1	jalapeño chile, stemmed, seeded, and finely chopped
2	tablespoons fresh lime juice
⅜	teaspoon salt
2	tablespoons peeled, grated fresh ginger
2	teaspoons curry powder
½	teaspoon ground black pepper
4	pieces skinless salmon fillet (6 ounces each)
2	teaspoons vegetable oil

1. In medium bowl, combine both melons, cilantro, mint, jalapeño, lime juice, and ¼ teaspoon salt; stir until well mixed and set aside.

2. In small bowl, stir together ginger, curry powder, remaining ⅛ teaspoon salt, and black pepper. Spread mixture evenly over non-skin side of each fillet.

3. In 12-inch nonstick skillet, heat oil over medium heat 1 minute. Add salmon, ginger side down, and cook 10 minutes or until salmon just turns opaque in center, turning over once. (Instant-read thermometer inserted horizontally in center of fillet should reach 145°F.) Serve salmon with melon salsa.

EACH SERVING: About 350 calories, 40g protein, 13g carbohydrate, 15g total fat (2g saturated), 2g fiber, 108mg cholesterol, 325mg sodium

SMOKY SPANISH SALMON

Simply grilled salmon and ripe summer vegetables get an extra layer of smokiness from this famous paprika.

ACTIVE TIME: 25 minutes **TOTAL TIME:** 40 minutes

MAKES: 4 main-dish servings

1	teaspoon smoked paprika
3/8	teaspoon salt
1/8	teaspoon ground black pepper
4	pieces (6 ounces each) salmon fillet with skin
5	teaspoons extra-virgin olive oil
4	large tomatoes (2 pounds), cored, cut in half, and seeded
2	large yellow peppers (10 ounces each), cut into quarters and seeded
1	large red onion (10 to 12 ounces), cut into 1/2-inch-thick rounds
1/3	cup sliced green olives
1/4	cup torn fresh flat-leaf parsley leaves

1. Prepare grill for covered direct grilling over medium-high heat. Mix paprika, 1/4 teaspoon salt, and black pepper. Rub salmon with 1 teaspoon oil, then two-thirds of paprika mixture. Add 2 teaspoons oil to remaining paprika mixture; brush on cut sides of tomatoes.

2. Brush yellow peppers and onion with remaining 2 teaspoons oil; place on grill along with tomatoes. Cover; cook until onions and peppers are tender-crisp, 10 to 15 minutes, turning over once; let cool slightly.

3. Meanwhile, place salmon, skin side down, on grill. Cover; cook 6 minutes or until just opaque throughout. (Instant-read thermometer inserted horizontally in center of fillet should reach 145°F.)

4. Slice yellow peppers; place in bowl. Chop onion and tomatoes; add to bowl. Stir in olives, parsley, and remaining 1/8 teaspoon salt; serve with salmon.

EACH SERVING: About 435 calories, 42g protein, 21g carbohydrate, 21g total fat (3g saturated), 5g fiber, 110mg cholesterol, 475mg sodium

COLD POACHED SALMON STEAKS WITH WATERCRESS SAUCE

Fast and easy, this is one of the best warm-weather entrées around.

ACTIVE TIME: 15 minutes **TOTAL TIME:** 20 minutes plus cooling

MAKES: 4 main-dish servings

1	medium lemon
4	salmon steaks, 1-inch thick (6 ounces each)
¾	teaspoon salt
½	teaspoon coarsely ground black pepper
1	medium onion, thinly sliced

Watercress Sauce

1. From lemon, squeeze juice; reserve for Watercress Sauce. Set lemon shells aside. Rub salmon steaks evenly with salt and pepper.

2. In 12-inch skillet, bring *½-inch water* to a boil over high heat. Add salmon, onion, and lemon shells; bring to a boil. Reduce heat; cover and simmer until fish is just opaque throughout, 5 to 8 minutes. With slotted spatula, transfer fish to platter. Let cool 30 minutes, or cover and refrigerate to serve later.

3. Meanwhile, prepare Watercress Sauce.

4. Remove skin and bones from salmon, if you like. Serve with sauce.

EACH SERVING (WITHOUT SAUCE): About 274 calories, 30g protein, 0g carbohydrate, 16g total fat (3g saturated), 0g fiber, 88mg cholesterol, 231mg sodium

WATERCRESS SAUCE

In blender or in food processor with knife blade attached, puree ½ **bunch watercress**, tough stems trimmed (1 cup), ½ **cup sour cream, 1 tablespoon fresh lemon juice, 1 teaspoon chopped fresh tarragon (or ⅛ teaspoon dried tarragon), 1 ½ teaspoons sugar**, and ½ **teaspoon salt** until smooth. Cover and refrigerate. Makes about ½ cup sauce.

EACH 1-TABLESPOON SERVING: About 35 calories, 1g protein, 2g carbohydrate, 3g total fat (2g saturated), 0g fiber, 6mg cholesterol, 165mg sodium

BROILED SALMON STEAKS

Broiling is a quick—and easy—way to get healthful, flavorful salmon steaks onto the dinner table in less than 15 minutes.

ACTIVE TIME: 5 minutes **TOTAL TIME:** 15 minutes

MAKES: 4 main-dish servings

4   salmon steaks, 1-inch thick (6 ounces each)
1   teaspoon vegetable oil
Pinch salt
Pinch ground black pepper

1. Preheat broiler. Rub both sides of salmon steaks with oil and sprinkle with salt and pepper.

2. Place salmon on rack in broiling pan. Place pan in broiler, 4 inches from heat source. Broil salmon 5 minutes, then turn and broil until fish is just opaque throughout, about 5 minutes longer.

EACH SERVING: About 284 calories, 30g protein, 0g carbohydrate, 17g total fat (3g saturated), 0g fiber, 88mg cholesterol, 123mg sodium

SALMON WITH MUSTARD GLAZE

Here's a fix-it-and-forget-it dish to prepare when you're entertaining a crowd. A zippy mustard glaze and dilled sour cream sauce make the meal seem fancier than it is. Carrot and Zucchini Ribbons (page 391) would make a pretty side dish.

ACTIVE TIME: 10 minutes **TOTAL TIME:** 30 minutes
MAKES: 12 main-dish servings

2	lemons, thinly sliced, plus additional lemon wedges, for garnish
½	cup spicy brown mustard
¼	cup light mayonnaise
2	tablespoons sugar
2	tablespoons cider vinegar
½	cup loosely packed chopped fresh dill, plus additional for garnish
1	whole boneless side of salmon (3¼ pounds)
¼	teaspoon salt
¼	teaspoon freshly ground black pepper
¾	cup reduced-fat sour cream

1. Preheat oven to 450°F. In 18″ by 12″ jelly-roll pan, arrange lemon slices in single layer to form diagonal line stretching from one corner of pan to opposite corner.

2. In medium bowl, stir mustard, mayonnaise, sugar, vinegar, and half of chopped dill until sugar dissolves.

3. Place salmon, skin side down, on lemons in prepared pan. In medium bowl, set aside half of mustard mixture; spread remaining mixture on top of salmon. Sprinkle salt and pepper on top. Roast 13 to 15 minutes or until just opaque throughout. (Instant-read thermometer inserted horizontally into thickest part of salmon should register 145°F.)

4. Meanwhile, stir sour cream and remaining dill into remaining mustard mixture. Place salmon on large serving platter; garnish with lemon wedges and dill. Serve salmon with sauce.

EACH SERVING: About 255 calories, 28g protein, 3g carbohydrate, 12g total fat (3g saturated), 0g fiber, 85mg cholesterol, 255mg sodium

BAKED SALMON FILLETS

Thick center-cut pieces of salmon take about 20 minutes to bake. If using thinner pieces, cut nearer the tail, check after 15 minutes. Try with Salmoriglio Sauce.

ACTIVE TIME: 5 minutes **TOTAL TIME:** 25 minutes
MAKES: 4 main-dish servings

4	pieces salmon fillet with skin (6 ounces each)
1	teaspoon olive oil
⅛	teaspoon salt
⅛	teaspoon ground black pepper

1. Preheat oven to 400°F and grease 13" by 9" baking dish.

2. With tweezers, remove any bones from salmon fillets. Arrange fillets in prepared baking dish; rub with oil and sprinkle with salt and pepper. Bake until salmon is just opaque throughout, 15 to 20 minutes.

EACH SERVING: About 331 calories, 34g protein, 0g carbohydrate, 21g total fat (4g saturated), 0g fiber, 100mg cholesterol, 174mg sodium

SALMORIGLIO SAUCE

For an optional substitution, use 1 tablespoon fresh oregano instead of dried.

ACTIVE TIME: 10 minutes **TOTAL TIME:** 40 minutes
MAKES: a scant ⅔ cup

¼	cup fresh lemon juice (1 to 2 lemons)
1	garlic clove, crushed with side of chef's knife
1	teaspoon dried oregano, crumbled
¼	teaspoon salt
¼	teaspoon coarsely ground black pepper
⅓	cup extra-virgin olive oil

1. In medium bowl, combine everything except oil. Let stand 30 minutes.

2. With wire whisk, in thin, steady stream, whisk in oil until blended. Serve, or let stand up to 4 hours at room temperature. Whisk again just before serving.

EACH 1-TABLESPOON SERVING: About 66 calories, 0g protein, 1g carbohydrate, 7g total fat (1g saturated), 1g fiber, 0mg cholesterol, 57mg sodium

FIVE-SPICE SALMON FILLETS

Chinese five-spice powder adds an intriguing hint of licorice to rich salmon. This blend is also luscious on tuna steaks.

ACTIVE TIME: 5 minutes **TOTAL TIME:** 15 minutes

MAKES: 4 main-dish servings

4	pieces salmon fillet or tuna steaks (4 ounces each), skin removed
2	teaspoons Chinese five-spice powder
1	teaspoon all-purpose flour
½	teaspoon salt
¼	teaspoon cracked black pepper
2	teaspoons vegetable oil

1. With tweezers, remove any bones from salmon fillets. On waxed paper, combine five-spice powder, flour, salt, and pepper. Use to rub on both sides of fillets.

2. In nonstick 10-inch skillet, heat oil over medium heat until hot. Add salmon; cook until just opaque throughout, 4 to 5 minutes per side.

EACH SERVING: About 222 calories, 21g protein, 2g carbohydrate, 14g total fat (3g saturated), 1g fiber, 63mg cholesterol, 353mg sodium

NUTRITIONAL NOTE: GET YOUR OMEGA-3S

Despite their reputation for clogging arteries and packing on unwanted pounds, not all fats are villainous. Indeed, one type of polyunsaturated fat, omega-3, is thought to combat heart disease. Omega-3s help inhibit the formation of blood clots and reduce the incidence of heartbeat abnormalities. You'll find omega-3s in fish—and the oilier the fish, the more omega-3 it contains. So be sure to include oily fish like salmon, bluefin tuna, mackerel, and sardines in your diet.

ROAST SALMON WITH TARRAGON AND CAPERS

A whole salmon fillet with a crumb-and-herb topping looks festive, tastes fabulous, and is surprisingly quick and easy to prepare.

ACTIVE TIME: 10 minutes **TOTAL TIME:** 40 minutes

MAKES: 6 main-dish servings

3	tablespoons butter or margarine
⅓	cup plain dried breadcrumbs
¼	cup loosely packed fresh parsley leaves, minced
3	tablespoons drained capers, minced
1	teaspoon dried tarragon, minced
¼	teaspoon salt
¼	teaspoon coarsely ground black pepper
2	pounds salmon fillet, in one piece

Lemon wedges, for garnish

1. Preheat oven to 450°F. Line jelly-roll pan with foil; grease foil.

2. In 1-quart saucepan, melt butter over low heat. Remove saucepan from heat; stir in breadcrumbs, parsley, capers, tarragon, salt, and pepper.

3. Place salmon, skin side down, in prepared pan. Pat crumb mixture on top. Roast until salmon turns opaque throughout and topping is lightly browned, about 30 minutes. (Instant-read thermometer inserted horizontally into thickest part of filet should register 145°F.)

4. With two large spatulas, carefully transfer salmon to platter (it's okay if salmon skin sticks to foil). Serve with lemon wedges.

EACH SERVING: About 325 calories, 28g protein, 5g carbohydrate, 21g total fat (4g saturated), 0g fiber, 76mg cholesterol, 425mg sodium

SEARED SALMON WITH SWEET POTATOES

Simple salmon and sweet potatoes become a gourmet meal in minutes when topped with an easy, tangy lemon-caper sauce. For photo, see page 168.

ACTIVE TIME: 15 minutes **TOTAL TIME:** 30 minutes
MAKES: 4 main-dish servings

1	pound sweet potatoes, peeled and cut into ½-inch cubes
¼	cup water
⅜	teaspoon salt
¼	teaspoon freshly ground black pepper
1	bag (6 ounces) baby spinach
⅛	teaspoon cayenne (ground red) pepper
4	pieces skinless center-cut salmon fillet (5 ounces each)
1	lemon
1	cup dry white wine
2	teaspoons capers, rinsed
¼	cup chopped fresh flat-leaf parsley

1. In large microwave-safe bowl, combine potatoes, water, and ¼ teaspoon each salt and pepper. Cover with vented plastic wrap; microwave on High 9 minutes or until tender, stirring halfway through. Add spinach; replace cover and microwave 2 minutes longer.

2. Meanwhile, sprinkle cayenne and remaining ⅛ teaspoon salt on salmon to season both sides. In nonstick 12-inch skillet over medium heat, cook salmon 10 minutes or until knife pierces center easily, turning over once halfway through. (Instant-read thermometer inserted horizontally in center of fillet should reach 145°F.) Transfer to plate. From lemon, finely grate ½ teaspoon peel onto fish; into cup, squeeze 1 tablespoon juice.

3. To skillet, add wine and capers. Boil over high heat 2 minutes or until liquid is reduced by half, scraping browned bits from pan. Remove from heat; stir in lemon juice and parsley.

4. Divide potato mixture among plates; top with fish. Spoon sauce over fish.

EACH SERVING: About 300 calories, 31g protein, 22g carbohydrate, 9g total fat (1g saturated), 4g fiber, 78mg cholesterol, 430mg sodium

PAN-SEARED TUNA

This is a great way to cook tuna steaks: Get the oil in the pan very hot and sear the fish very quickly. The oil in the marinade moistens the fish but adds hardly any fat.

ACTIVE TIME: 20 minutes **TOTAL TIME:** 1 hour

MAKES: 4 main-dish servings

4	large lemons
6	tablespoons olive oil
6	tablespoons chopped fresh parsley
½	teaspoon salt
¼	teaspoon ground black pepper
4	tuna steaks, ¾-inch thick (5 ounces each)

1. From lemons, grate 1 teaspoon peel and squeeze ⅔ cup juice, reserving it in a cup. In 9-inch square baking dish, with wire whisk, whisk lemon peel and juice, 3 tablespoons oil, 5 tablespoons parsley, salt, and pepper until mixed. Add tuna, turning to coat. Cover and refrigerate 45 minutes to marinate, turning occasionally.

2. In 10-inch cast-iron or other heavy skillet, heat remaining 3 tablespoons oil over medium-high heat until hot. Add tuna and cook until pale pink in center (medium), about 3 minutes per side, or until desired doneness. Transfer to plates and sprinkle with remaining 1 tablespoon parsley.

EACH SERVING: About 246 calories, 30g protein, 1g carbohydrate, 13g total fat (2g saturated), 0g fiber, 48mg cholesterol, 341mg sodium

RUSTIC PASTA TOSS WITH TUNA AND TOMATOES

This heart-smart pasta salad is loaded with farm-stand zucchini, squash, and tomatoes. Just combine the raw veggies with canned tuna and campanelle pasta for a beat-the-heat—and beat-the-clock—meal.

ACTIVE TIME: 15 minutes **TOTAL TIME:** 30 minutes

MAKES: 6 main-dish servings

1	pound campanelle or fusilli pasta
2	medium zucchini
1	medium yellow squash
1	pint cherry or grape tomatoes (see Tip)
¼	cup pitted Kalamata olives
¼	cup fresh flat-leaf parsley leaves
3	tablespoons red wine vinegar
¼	cup extra-virgin olive oil
1	garlic clove, crushed with garlic press
¼	teaspoon salt
⅛	teaspoon freshly ground black pepper
2	cans (5 ounces each) tuna in water, drained

1. Cook pasta in *boiling salted water* as package label directs.

2. Meanwhile, trim zucchini and squash, cut lengthwise into quarters, then cut crosswise into thin slices. Slice tomatoes in half. Slice olives and finely chop parsley.

3. In large bowl, whisk vinegar, oil, garlic, salt, and pepper; stir in tomatoes.

4. Drain pasta well. Add to tomato mixture along with tuna, zucchini, squash, olives, and parsley. Toss until well mixed.

EACH SERVING: About 470 calories, 21g protein, 66g carbohydrate, 14g total fat (2g saturated), 5g fiber, 16mg cholesterol, 435mg sodium

TIP

If you're lucky enough to find some nice, ripe regular tomatoes, substitute 2 medium tomatoes for the cherry tomatoes called for here. Chop them in step 2 and add them along with the other vegetables at the end. Their extra juices will add more moisture to the sauce.

SWORDFISH STEAKS BROILED WITH MAÎTRE D'HÔTEL BUTTER

Swordfish is terrific with this classic lemon-and-herb butter. If you like, top each steak with an additional tablespoon of it before serving.

ACTIVE TIME: 10 minutes **TOTAL TIME:** 20 minutes

MAKES: 4 main-dish servings

4   teaspoons Maître d'Hôtel Butter
4   swordfish steaks, 1-inch thick (6 ounces each)

1. Prepare Maître d'Hôtel Butter.

2. Preheat broiler. Place swordfish on rack in broiling pan. Spread ½ teaspoon maître d'hôtel butter on each side of each fish steak. Place pan in broiler, 4 inches from heat source. Broil swordfish, without turning, until just opaque throughout, 8 to 10 minutes. Spoon pan juices over fish to serve.

EACH SERVING: About 217 calories, 30g protein, 0g carbohydrate, 10g total fat (4g saturated), 0g fiber, 69mg cholesterol, 175mg sodium

MAÎTRE D'HÔTEL BUTTER

This butter takes just 10 minutes and can be prepared ahead. Freeze to eliminate last-minute fussing.

In medium bowl, beat ½ **cup butter or margarine** (1 stick), softened, with wooden spoon until creamy. Beat in **2 tablespoons chopped fresh parsley**, ¼ **teaspoon freshly grated lemon peel**, and **1 tablespoon fresh lemon juice**. Blend well. Transfer flavored butter to waxed paper and shape into log about 6 inches long; wrap, twisting ends of waxed paper to seal. Overwrap in plastic or foil before chilling or freezing. Flavored butters can be refrigerated up to 2 days or frozen up to 1 month. To serve, cut into ½-inch-thick slices. Makes 12 servings.

ROASTED COD AND MUSHROOM RAGOUT

The rich earthiness of sweet potatoes and mushrooms blends with meaty cod to deliver an entrée that's low in calories—and loaded with antioxidants.

ACTIVE TIME: 20 minutes **TOTAL TIME:** 30 minutes

MAKES: 4 main-dish servings

1	large sweet potato (1 pound), peeled and cut into 1/2-inch chunks
2	tablespoons extra-virgin olive oil
2	large shallots, thinly sliced
1/2	teaspoon salt
1/2	teaspoon ground black pepper
2	packages (10 ounces each) sliced mushrooms
2	tablespoons water
4	skinless cod fillets (6 ounces each)
1/4	cup packed fresh flat-leaf parsley leaves, finely chopped
1/2	cup dry white wine

1. Preheat oven to 450°F.

2. On 18" by 12" jelly-roll pan, combine sweet potatoes, 1 tablespoon oil, half of shallots, and 1/8 teaspoon each salt and pepper. Arrange in single layer on one side of pan. Roast 15 minutes.

3. Meanwhile, in 12-inch skillet, heat remaining 1 tablespoon oil over medium-high heat. Add remaining shallots and cook 2 to 3 minutes or until tender and golden brown, stirring occasionally. Add mushrooms and water; cook 8 minutes or until liquid evaporates, stirring occasionally.

4. Arrange cod on other side of roasting pan. Sprinkle with 1/8 teaspoon each salt and pepper. Roast alongside potato mixture 8 to 10 minutes or until fish is just opaque throughout. (Instant-read thermometer inserted horizontally into thickest part of fish should register 145°F.)

5. Stir parsley, wine, and remaining ¼ teaspoon each salt and pepper into mushroom-shallot mixture. Cook 1 to 2 minutes or until wine is reduced by half.

6. Divide potato and cod among serving plates. Spoon mushroom ragout over cod.

EACH SERVING: About 295 calories, 33g protein, 22g carbohydrate, 9g total fat (1g saturated), 4g fiber, 65mg cholesterol, 420mg sodium

BROILED COD STEAKS MONTAUK

A flavored mayonnaise topping is a quick way to add punch to broiled fish.

ACTIVE TIME: 5 minutes **TOTAL TIME:** 15 minutes

MAKES: 4 main-dish servings

¼   cup reduced-fat mayonnaise

½   teaspoon Dijon mustard

⅛   teaspoon salt

⅛   teaspoon ground black pepper

4   cod steaks, ½-inch thick (6 ounces each)

1. Preheat broiler.

2. In small bowl, mix mayonnaise, mustard, salt, and pepper until blended.

3. Lightly oil rack in broiling pan. Place cod on rack in broiling pan. Place pan in broiler, 4 inches from heat source. Broil cod until just opaque throughout, 5 to 7 minutes. Remove broiling pan from broiler. Brush mayonnaise mixture on fish. Return pan to broiler; broil until mayonnaise mixture is lightly browned and bubbling, 1 to 2 minutes longer.

EACH SERVING: About 222 calories, 27g protein, 0g carbohydrate, 3g total fat (1g saturated), 0g fiber, 72mg cholesterol, 247mg sodium

LEMON TOPPING

Prepare as directed but substitute **½ teaspoon freshly grated lemon peel** for Dijon mustard.

HORSERADISH TOPPING

Prepare as directed but substitute **1 teaspoon bottled white horseradish** for Dijon mustard.

DILL-PEPPER TOPPING

Prepare as directed but substitute **2 tablespoons chopped fresh dill** for Dijon mustard and **¼ teaspoon coarsely ground black pepper** for ground black pepper.

DRIED TOMATO TOPPING

Prepare as directed but substitute **1 dried tomato,** finely chopped, for Dijon mustard.

LIME-JALAPEÑO TOPPING

Prepare as directed but substitute **½ teaspoon freshly grated lime peel** for Dijon mustard and add **1 small jalapeño**, seeded and minced, to mayonnaise mixture.

PARMESAN TOPPING

Prepare as directed but substitute **2 tablespoons freshly grated Parmesan cheese** for Dijon mustard.

COD VERACRUZ

This is fish, Mexican-style. Chile aficionados may want to add a little more cayenne pepper or hot chili powder.

TOTAL TIME: 40 minutes

MAKES: 4 main-dish servings

4	tablespoons vegetable oil
1	yellow pepper, cut into thin strips
1	medium onion, thinly sliced
1	jalapeño chile, seeded and finely chopped
1	garlic clove, thinly sliced
¾	teaspoon chili powder
½	teaspoon salt
1	can (14½ to 16 ounces) tomatoes in puree
½	teaspoon ground coriander
¼	teaspoon ground cumin
⅛	teaspoon cayenne (ground red) pepper
4	cod steaks, ¾-inch thick (4 ounces each)

1. In nonstick 12-inch skillet, heat 2 tablespoons oil over medium heat. Add yellow pepper and onion and cook, stirring, until tender and golden, 15 minutes. Add jalapeño, garlic, ½ teaspoon chili powder, and ¼ teaspoon salt and cook, stirring, 3 minutes.

2. Add tomatoes with their puree and cook, breaking up tomatoes with side of spoon, until mixture has slightly reduced, about 10 minutes.

3. Meanwhile, in cup, combine coriander, cumin, remaining ¼ teaspoon each chili powder and salt, and ground red pepper. Sprinkle both sides of cod steaks with spice mixture.

4. In 10-inch skillet, heat remaining 2 tablespoons oil over medium-high heat until hot. Add cod and cook until steaks are just opaque throughout and nicely browned, 3 to 4 minutes per side. To serve, arrange fish on platter and top with warm tomato sauce.

EACH SERVING: About 225 calories, 19g protein, 10g carbohydrate, 11g total fat (1g saturated), 2g fiber, 43mg cholesterol, 369mg sodium

THAI SNAPPER IN FOIL PACKETS

Tender fillets seasoned with lime and ginger are cooked in a foil packet for ease. This helps to seal in the juices, too. Pair with ½ cup steamed edamame beans per person.

ACTIVE TIME: 20 minutes
TOTAL TIME: 30 minutes

MAKES: 4 main-dish servings

3 tablespoons fresh lime juice

1 tablespoon sugar-free Asian fish sauce

1 tablespoon olive oil

1 teaspoon grated, peeled fresh ginger

½ teaspoon minced garlic

4 red snapper fillets (6 ounces each)

1 large carrot, peeled and cut into 2-inch-long matchstick-thin strips

1 green onion, thinly sliced

¼ cup packed fresh cilantro leaves

TIP

The "secret ingredient" in southeast Asian cooking, Asian fish sauce, is a thin, translucent, salty brown liquid extracted from salted, fermented fish. Red Boat™ fish sauce is sugar-free and available online.

1. Prepare outdoor grill for direct grilling over medium heat.

2. In small bowl, mix together lime juice, fish sauce, olive oil, ginger, and garlic.

3. From roll of foil, cut four 16" by 12" sheets. Fold each sheet crosswise in half and open up again.

4. Place 1 red snapper fillet, skin side down, on half of each piece of foil. Top with carrot strips, green onion slices, then cilantro leaves. Spoon lime juice mixture over snapper and vegetables. Fold other half of foil over fish. Fold and crimp foil edges all around to create sealed packets.

5. Place packets on hot grill rack; grill 8 minutes, until fish flakes easily when tested with fork.

6. To serve, with kitchen shears, cut an X in the top of each packet so steam can escape, then transfer each fillet to plate.

EACH SERVING: About 220 calories, 36g protein, 5g carbohydrate, 6g total fat (1g saturated), 1g fiber, 62mg cholesterol, 445mg sodium

BAKED SNAPPER WITH PEPPERS AND MUSHROOMS

This fast fish recipe is ultra low-fat and low-cal, but it doesn't scrimp on flavor. Serve with a side of bulgur or brown rice.

ACTIVE TIME: 20 minutes **TOTAL TIME:** 35 minutes

MAKES: 6 main-dish servings

1	tablespoon olive oil
2	orange and/or yellow peppers, thinly sliced
1	onion, chopped
1	package (10 ounces) sliced mushrooms
½	cup dry white wine
1	teaspoon fresh thyme leaves, chopped, plus additional leaves for garnish
6	skinless, boneless snapper, sole, or flounder fillets (4 ounces each)
2	tablespoons fresh lemon juice
¼	teaspoon salt
¼	teaspoon ground black pepper

1. Preheat oven to 450°F. In 12-inch skillet, heat oil over medium heat until hot. Add peppers and onion and cook 10 minutes or until tender, stirring often. Add mushrooms, wine, and thyme; cook over medium-high heat 3 minutes, stirring often.

2. Meanwhile, spray bottom and sides of 13" by 9" glass or ceramic baking dish with nonstick cooking spray. Arrange fillets in baking dish, folding narrow ends under. Sprinkle with lemon juice, salt, and pepper.

3. Spoon hot vegetable mixture from skillet on top of fish in baking dish. Bake fish 15 to 18 minutes or until opaque throughout. Garnish with additional thyme leaves.

EACH SERVING: About 175 calories, 26g protein, 9g carbohydrate, 4g total fat (1g saturated), 2g fiber, 42mg cholesterol, 175mg sodium

RED SNAPPER IN PARCHMENT WITH TOMATOES AND BASIL

Here, the snapper juices mingle with the tomatoes and basil in a parchment packet to create a fabulous sauce.

ACTIVE TIME: 25 minutes **TOTAL TIME:** 40 minutes

MAKES: 4 main-dish servings

1	tablespoon margarine or butter
1	large garlic clove, finely chopped
1	pound ripe plum tomatoes, seeded and chopped (2 cups)
3/8	teaspoon salt
1/4	teaspoon ground black pepper
1/3	cup chopped fresh basil
4	red snapper fillets (6 ounces each), skin removed
4	squares (12 inches each) parchment paper or foil

1. Preheat oven to 400°F.

2. In 12-inch skillet, melt margarine over medium-high heat. Add garlic and cook, 30 seconds. Add tomatoes, 1/4 teaspoon salt, and 1/8 teaspoon pepper. Cook, stirring frequently, until liquid has almost evaporated, about 5 minutes. Remove from heat and stir in basil.

3. With tweezers, remove any bones from snapper fillets. Place 1 fillet, skin side down, on one half of each parchment square. Sprinkle with remaining 1/8 teaspoon each salt and pepper; top with tomato mixture.

4. Fold unfilled half of parchment over fish. To seal packets, beginning at a corner where parchment is folded, make 1/2-inch-wide folds, with each new fold overlapping previous one, until packet is completely sealed. Packet will resemble half-circle. Place packets in jelly-roll pan. Bake 15 minutes (packets will puff up and brown). Cut packets open to serve.

EACH SERVING: About 205 calories, 33g protein, 65g carbohydrate, 5g total fat (2g saturated), 0g fiber, 65mg cholesterol, 359mg sodium

FLOUNDER PESTO ROLL-UPS

This simple, satisfying meal comes together in minutes. If you have extra time, make our pesto on page 145.

ACTIVE TIME: 15 minutes **TOTAL TIME:** 35 minutes

MAKES: 4 main-dish servings

4	flounder fillets (about 6 ounces each)
8	teaspoons ready-made basil pesto (see Tip)
¼	teaspoon salt
¼	cup dry white wine
4	plum tomatoes, chopped
¼	cup loosely packed fresh parsley leaves, chopped

1. Preheat oven to 400°F. Place fillets, skin side down, on work surface. Spread 2 teaspoons pesto on each fillet; sprinkle with salt. Starting at narrow end of each fillet, roll up jelly-roll fashion. Place roll-ups, seam side down, in 8-inch square glass baking dish.

2. Pour wine over fillets and top with tomatoes. Cover dish and bake 20 minutes or until fish flakes easily when tested with a fork. (Instant-read thermometer inserted from top into center of roll should reach 145°F.) Sprinkle with parsley to serve.

EACH SERVING: About 205 calories, 31g protein, 5g carbohydrate, 6g total fat (1g saturated), 1g fiber, 76mg cholesterol, 335mg sodium

TIP
The ready-made pesto sold in the store's refrigerator case will taste fresher than the type found in the bottled condiments aisle.

BAKED FLOUNDER WITH SAVORY CRUMB TOPPING

Need a fast and flavorful midweek supper recipe? Our tasty flounder is the answer. If you don't have an open bottle of dry white wine, substitute dry vermouth or reduced-sodium chicken broth.

ACTIVE TIME: 15 minutes **TOTAL TIME:** 25 minutes

MAKES: 4 main-dish servings

1½ cups fresh breadcrumbs (about 3 slices bread)
2   tablespoons chopped fresh parsley
¼   cup dry white wine
4   flounder fillets (5 ounces each)
¼   teaspoon salt
¼   cup mayonnaise

1. Preheat oven to 400°F. In 10-inch skillet, toast breadcrumbs over medium heat, stirring frequently, until golden, about 10 minutes. Remove from heat and stir in parsley.

2. Pour wine into 13" by 9" baking dish; add flounder fillets, turning to coat. Arrange fillets, skinned side up, in dish, tucking thin ends under. Sprinkle with salt and spread mayonnaise on top. Gently pat breadcrumb mixture over mayonnaise. Bake until fish is just opaque throughout and topping has crisped, about 10 minutes.

EACH SERVING: About 295 calories, 29g protein, 11g carbohydrate, 13g total fat (2g saturated), 0.5g fiber, 76mg cholesterol, 452mg sodium

PARMESAN CHEESE FILLETS

Prepare as directed above but use only ⅔ **cup plain dried breadcrumbs** and add ⅓ **cup freshly grated Parmesan cheese** to breadcrumb mixture.

SESAME SEED FILLETS

Prepare as directed above but use only ¾ **cup plain dried breadcrumbs** and add ¼ **cup sesame seeds** to breadcrumb mixture.

ALMOND-CRUSTED TILAPIA

Skip the breadcrumbs: Here, mild-mannered tilapia is topped with a crunchy coating of heart-healthy almonds instead. A medley of green beans and mushrooms completes the meal.

TOTAL TIME: 25 minutes

MAKES: 4 main-dish servings

2 to 3 lemons

2   tablespoons olive oil

½   teaspoon salt

¼   teaspoon coarsely ground black pepper

4   tilapia fillets (6 ounces each)

¼   cup sliced natural almonds

1   small onion (4 to 6 ounces), chopped

1   bag (12 ounces) trimmed fresh green beans

1   package (10 ounces) sliced white mushrooms

2   tablespoons water

1. Preheat oven to 425°F. From 1 or 2 lemons, grate 1 teaspoon peel and squeeze 3 tablespoons juice, reserving in a cup; cut remaining lemon into wedges. Mix lemon peel and 1 tablespoon juice, 1 tablespoon oil, ¼ teaspoon salt, and ⅛ teaspoon pepper.

2. Spray 13" by 9" baking dish with nonstick cooking spray; place tilapia, dark side down, in dish. Drizzle with lemon mixture; press almonds on top. Bake 15 minutes or until just opaque throughout.

3. Meanwhile, in 12-inch skillet, heat remaining 1 tablespoon oil over medium-high heat 1 minute. Add onion and cook 5 to 6 minutes or until golden, stirring occasionally. Stir in green beans, mushrooms, water, and remaining ¼ teaspoon salt and ⅛ teaspoon pepper. Cook about 6 minutes or until most of liquid evaporates and beans are tender-crisp. Toss with remaining 2 tablespoons lemon juice. Serve bean mixture alongside tilapia and garnish with lemon wedges.

EACH SERVING: About 315 calories, 33g protein, 15g carbohydrate, 15g total fat (1g saturated), 5g fiber, 0mg cholesterol, 380mg sodium

GREEK-STYLE TILAPIA

This healthy Mediterranean dish requires just five ingredients—and thirty minutes of your time. Instead of rice, the fish is served with orzo.

ACTIVE TIME: 20 minutes **TOTAL TIME:** 30 minutes
MAKES: 4 main-dish servings

2	lemons
1½	pounds tilapia fillets
1	tablespoon fresh oregano leaves, chopped, plus additional sprigs for garnish
¼	teaspoon salt
¼	teaspoon freshly ground black pepper
1	pint grape tomatoes, cut in half lengthwise
8	ounces orzo

1. Preheat oven to 400°F. From lemons, grate ½ teaspoon peel and squeeze ¼ cup juice, reserving in a cup.

2. In 13" by 9" glass or ceramic baking dish, arrange fillets. Evenly sprinkle fillets with lemon juice and peel, chopped oregano, salt, and pepper. Add tomatoes to baking dish around tilapia; cover with foil and roast 16 to 18 minutes or until tilapia is opaque throughout and tomatoes are tender. (Instant-read thermometer inserted horizontally into center of fillet should reach 145°F.)

3. Meanwhile, cook orzo in *boiling salted water* as package label directs. Drain well.

4. Serve tilapia, tomatoes, and orzo with juices from baking dish.

EACH SERVING: About 395 calories, 36g protein, 50g carbohydrate, 6g total fat (0g saturated), 2g fiber, 0mg cholesterol, 310mg sodium

FRIED CATFISH

Before frying, let the coated fish fillets stand for a few minutes to set the crust; it will adhere better and fry to crispy perfection.

ACTIVE TIME: 25 minutes **TOTAL TIME:** 45 minutes
MAKES: 6 main-dish servings

¾ cup cornmeal
2 tablespoons all-purpose flour
½ teaspoon salt
¼ teaspoon ground black pepper
¼ cup milk
6 catfish fillets (6 ounces each)
4 tablespoons vegetable oil
Lemon wedges

1. In zip-tight plastic bag, combine cornmeal, flour, salt, and pepper. Pour milk into pie plate. Dip catfish fillets, one at a time, into milk to coat well, then into cornmeal mixture, shaking bag to coat fish. Place coated catfish on wire rack set over waxed paper; let dry 20 minutes.

2. In 10-inch skillet, heat 2 tablespoons oil over medium-high heat until hot. Add 3 catfish fillets and fry until just opaque throughout and golden, 4 to 5 minutes per side. Transfer to paper towels to drain. Repeat with remaining 2 tablespoons oil and remaining catfish. Serve with lemon wedges.

EACH SERVING: About 377 calories, 28g protein, 16g carbohydrate, 22g total fat (4g saturated), 1g fiber, 58mg cholesterol, 255mg sodium

PANFRIED SCALLOPS

Try these during the fall and winter months, when small bay scallops are in season. Otherwise, substitute sea scallops and increase the cooking time accordingly.

TOTAL TIME: 10 minutes

MAKES: 4 main-dish servings

1   pound bay scallops
1   tablespoon olive oil
½   teaspoon salt
2   tablespoons chopped fresh parsley
4   lemon wedges

Pat scallops dry with paper towels. In 12-inch skillet, heat oil over medium-high heat until hot. Add scallops to skillet and sprinkle with salt. Cook, stirring, until just opaque throughout, about 4 minutes. Add parsley and toss. Serve with lemon wedges.

EACH SERVING: About 160 calories, 19g protein, 3g carbohydrate, 8g total fat (1g saturated), 1g fiber, 37mg cholesterol, 473mg sodium

SCALLOP AND ASPARAGUS STIR-FRY

Tossing this dish with chopped basil just before serving adds a pleasing touch of fresh flavor. With steamed rice, you have a complete meal.

TOTAL TIME: 35 minutes

MAKES: 4 main-dish servings

1 pound sea scallops
2 tablespoons reduced-sodium soy sauce
1 tablespoon minced, peeled fresh ginger
2 tablespoons vegetable oil
2 garlic cloves, thinly sliced
1½ pounds asparagus, trimmed and cut into 2-inch pieces
¼ teaspoon crushed red pepper
½ cup loosely packed fresh basil leaves, chopped, plus additional for garnish

1. Pull off and discard tough crescent-shaped muscle from each scallop. In bowl, toss scallops with 1 tablespoon soy sauce and ginger.

2. In 12-inch skillet, heat 1 tablespoon oil over medium-high heat. Add garlic and cook, stirring often, until golden. With slotted spoon, transfer garlic to medium bowl.

3. Add asparagus and crushed red pepper to skillet and cook, stirring frequently (stir-frying), until asparagus is tender-crisp, about 7 minutes. Transfer asparagus to bowl with garlic.

4. Add remaining 1 tablespoon oil to skillet; add scallop mixture and stir-fry until scallops are just opaque throughout, 3 to 5 minutes.

5. Return asparagus and garlic to skillet, along with remaining 1 tablespoon soy sauce; heat through. Add chopped basil, tossing to combine. Spoon mixture onto warm platter and top with basil leaves.

EACH SERVING: About 204 calories, 24g protein, 10g carbohydrate, 8g total fat (1g saturated), 2g fiber, 37mg cholesterol, 487mg sodium

SCALLOPS, SCAMPI-STYLE

Try this wholesome twist on shrimp scampi featuring scallops, which are low in fat, calories, and cholesterol, and high in vitamin B12.

ACTIVE TIME: 15 minutes **TOTAL TIME:** 25 minutes
MAKES: 4 main-dish servings

1	cup whole-wheat couscous
1¼	pounds sea scallops
1	lemon
1	garlic clove, crushed with garlic press
¼	teaspoon salt
¼	teaspoon coarsely grated black pepper
4	zucchini and/or yellow summer squash (8 ounces each)
1	tablespoon trans-fat free margarine or butter
2	tablespoons chopped fresh chives

1. Prepare couscous as label directs.

2. Meanwhile, pull off and discard tough crescent-shaped muscle, if any, from each scallop; rinse to remove sand from crevices. Pat scallops dry with paper towels.

3. From lemon, grate 1 teaspoon peel and squeeze 2 tablespoons juice, reserving in a small cup. In bowl, toss scallops with garlic, ½ teaspoon lemon peel, salt, and pepper.

4. With vegetable peeler, slice each squash lengthwise into thin, long ribbons until you reach core with seeds; discard core. Set aside squash ribbons.

5. In nonstick 12-inch skillet, heat margarine over medium-high heat until melted. Add scallops and cook, turning once, 5 to 6 minutes or until browned and just opaque throughout; transfer scallops to plate.

6. Add squash to same skillet and reduce heat to medium; cover and cook 2 minutes, stirring once. Uncover and cook 1 minute or until tender-crisp. Remove squash from heat; stir in lemon juice and remaining peel.

7. Spoon vegetable mixture onto plates; top with scallops and sprinkle with chives. Serve with couscous.

EACH SERVING: About 355 calories, 33g protein, 48g carbohydrate, 4g total fat (1g saturated), 9g fiber, 47mg cholesterol, 416mg sodium

THAI SHRIMP

Spoon this chunky shrimp-and-vegetable mixture over fragrant jasmine rice.

ACTIVE TIME: 40 minutes **TOTAL TIME:** 45 minutes

MAKES: 4 main-dish servings

2	medium limes
3	teaspoons vegetable oil
1	small onion, finely chopped
1	small red pepper, thinly sliced
2	teaspoons grated, peeled fresh ginger
1/8 to 1/4	teaspoon cayenne (ground red) pepper
4	ounces medium mushrooms, cut into quarters
1/2	teaspoon salt
1	can (13¾ to 15 ounces) light coconut milk (not cream of coconut)
1	pound large shrimp, shelled and deveined (see Tip, page 113)
2	ounces snow peas, strings removed and cut into 2" by 1/4" matchstick strips
1/3	cup loosely packed fresh cilantro leaves

1. From limes, with vegetable peeler, peel six 1" by ¾" strips of peel; squeeze 2 tablespoons juice. Set aside.

2. In nonstick 12-inch skillet, heat 2 teaspoons oil over medium heat. Add onion and cook until tender, about 5 minutes. Add sliced red pepper and cook 1 minute. Stir in ginger and cayenne pepper; cook 1 minute. Transfer onion mixture to small bowl.

3. In same skillet, heat remaining 1 teaspoon oil over medium heat. Add mushrooms and salt and cook until tender and lightly browned, about 5 minutes. Stir in coconut milk, lime peel and juice, and onion mixture and bring to a boil. Add shrimp and cook until shrimp are opaque throughout, about 2 minutes. Stir in snow peas and cilantro.

EACH SERVING: About 222 calories, 20g protein, 11g carbohydrate, 11g total fat (4g saturated), 2g fiber, 140mg cholesterol, 456mg sodium

ITALIAN-SPICED SHRIMP CASSEROLE

Both quick and flavorful, this healthful shrimp dish over rice gets its flavor from a variety of Italian herbs and spices.

ACTIVE TIME: 20 minutes **TOTAL TIME:** 40 minutes
MAKES: 6 main-dish servings

1	cup long-grain white rice
1¾	cups hot water
1	tablespoon olive oil
1	small onion, finely chopped
1	tablespoon fresh oregano leaves, minced
½	teaspoon crushed red pepper, or to taste
2	garlic cloves, crushed with garlic press
1	cup dry white wine
1	can (14½ ounces) no-salt-added diced tomatoes, drained well
½	teaspoon salt
½	teaspoon ground black pepper
1	pound (16- to 20-count) shrimp, shelled and deveined, tail part of shell left on if you like
8	leaves fresh basil, very thinly sliced, for garnish

1. Preheat oven to 400°F.

2. In 3-quart shallow baking dish, combine rice and water. Cover tightly with aluminum foil and bake 20 minutes.

3. Meanwhile, in 5- to 6-quart saucepot, heat oil over medium heat. Add onion, oregano, and crushed red pepper; cook 3 minutes, stirring occasionally. Add garlic and cook 30 seconds or until golden, stirring. Add wine and bring to a boil; reduce heat to medium-low and simmer 6 minutes or until wine is reduced by half, stirring occasionally. Stir in tomatoes, salt, and black pepper. Remove from heat.

4. Arrange shrimp in single layer on top of rice in baking dish. Pour tomato mixture evenly over shrimp; cover tightly with foil and bake casserole 15 minutes or until shrimp turn opaque. Garnish with basil.

EACH SERVING: About 245 calories, 16g protein, 35g carbohydrate, 4g total fat (1g saturated), 2g fiber, 93mg cholesterol, 300mg sodium

WARM LENTIL SALAD WITH SEARED SHRIMP

A Dijon mustard and sherry vinegar dressing tops this warm salad, which is an excellent source of low-fat protein and tummy-filling fiber.

ACTIVE TIME: 30 minutes **TOTAL TIME:** 1 hour 10 minutes
MAKES: 4 main-dish servings

8	ounces (1¼ cups) French green (de Puy) lentils, picked over and rinsed
2	large stalks celery, finely chopped
1	onion, finely chopped
1	large carrot, peeled and finely chopped
2	garlic cloves, crushed with garlic press
1	bay leaf
3	cups water
4	sprigs fresh thyme, plus additional for garnish
8	large shrimp, shelled and deveined, tail part of shell left on if you like
3	tablespoons extra-virgin olive oil
½	cup packed fresh flat-leaf parsley leaves, finely chopped
2	tablespoons sherry vinegar
2	teaspoons Dijon mustard
¼	teaspoon salt
¼	teaspoon freshly ground black pepper

1. In 4-quart saucepan, combine lentils, celery, onion, carrot, garlic, bay leaf, water, and 3 thyme sprigs. Bring to a boil over medium-high heat. Reduce heat to medium-low; cover and simmer 25 to 35 minutes or until lentils are tender.

2. Meanwhile, from remaining thyme sprig, remove leaves and finely chop; discard stem. In medium bowl, combine shrimp, 1 tablespoon olive oil, and chopped thyme. Let stand 15 minutes while lentils simmer. Heat 12-inch skillet over medium-high heat until very hot. Add shrimp in single layer and cook 1 to 2 minutes or until browned. Turn over and cook 2 minutes longer or until shrimp just turn opaque throughout.

3. Drain lentil mixture well and transfer to large bowl. Remove and discard bay leaf and thyme sprigs. Toss lentil mixture with parsley, vinegar, mustard, remaining 2 tablespoons oil, salt, and pepper. Divide salad among serving plates. Top each serving with 2 shrimp; garnish with fresh thyme sprigs.

EACH SERVING: About 345 calories, 20g protein, 42g carbohydrate, 11g total fat (2g saturated), 20g fiber, 22mg cholesterol, 225mg sodium

HEART-SMART INGREDIENT: LENTILS

These legumes may be small, but they're big on fill-you-up soluble fiber. Translation: they may help keep weight down and also help lower total and LDL (undesirable) cholesterol levels. Lentils are also high in protein, iron, and potassium, which helps keep blood pressure in check.

SHRIMP AND PINEAPPLE SALAD WITH BASIL

No grill basket? Thread shrimp onto skewers instead. If you use wooden skewers, presoak them in hot water for at least 30 minutes to prevent them from burning.

ACTIVE TIME: 10 minutes **TOTAL TIME:** 25 minutes

MAKES: 6 main-dish servings

3 to 4 limes
3 tablespoons olive oil
1½ cups loosely packed fresh basil leaves
½ teaspoon salt
¼ teaspoon coarsely ground pepper
1½ pounds large shrimp, shelled and deveined
1 pineapple (3 pounds)
12 corn tortillas
Olive oil cooking spray
1 bag (5 to 6 ounces) baby greens
2 medium heads Belgian endive, sliced

1. Prepare outdoor grill for direct grilling over medium heat.

2. Prepare dressing: From limes, grate ½ teaspoon peel and squeeze ¼ cup juice. In blender, place lime peel and juice, oil, ½ cup basil leaves, salt, and pepper. Blend until pureed.

3. Spoon 2 tablespoons dressing from blender into medium bowl. Add shrimp to bowl and toss to coat with dressing.

4. Cut off crown and stem ends from pineapple. Stand pineapple upright and slice off rind and eyes. Cut pineapple lengthwise into 8 wedges, then cut off core from each wedge.

5. Place pineapple wedges on hot grill rack over medium heat and cook until lightly charred and tender, about 10 minutes, turning over once. Place shrimp in grill basket on same grill rack with pineapple wedges and cook until opaque throughout, 5 to 8 minutes, turning over once. Transfer shrimp to large bowl. Transfer pineapple to cutting board and cut into ½-inch chunks.

6. Lightly spray both sides of tortillas with cooking spray and place on hot grill rack. Cook until toasted, 4 to 5 minutes, turning over once.

7. To bowl with shrimp, add greens, endive, pineapple, and remaining 1 cup basil and dressing; toss to coat. Place 2 tortillas on each of 6 plates; top with salad.

EACH SERVING: About 350 calories, 23g protein, 43g carbohydrate, 11g total fat (2g saturated), 6g fiber, 140mg cholesterol, 420mg sodium

TROPICAL CITRUS SHRIMP

This zippy ceviche was the grand-prize winner of *Good Housekeeping*'s first-ever Cook Your Heart Out contest. With just 1 gram of saturated fat and 155 calories per serving, it's heart-smart dining at its flavorful best. To keep the shrimp tender, plunge the cooked shrimp into an ice-water bath, advises Jan Valdez of Chicago, the recipe's creator.

TOTAL TIME: 35 minutes plus chilling

MAKES: 8 main-dish servings

1½ pounds medium shrimp, shelled and deveined
⅔ cup fresh orange juice
¼ cup fresh lemon juice
¼ cup fresh lime juice
¼ cup unsweetened pineapple juice
1 mango, peeled and diced
1 cup diced jicama
½ small red onion, minced
½ cup chopped fresh cilantro
1 jalapeño chile, seeded and minced
1 avocado, pitted, peeled, and diced
1 tablespoon extra-virgin olive oil
½ teaspoon salt
½ teaspoon freshly ground black pepper
Baked unsalted tortilla chips

1. Bring large covered saucepot of *water* to a boil over high heat. Fill large bowl with *ice and water*. Add shrimp to boiling water; cook 1 to 2 minutes or until just opaque throughout. Drain; transfer to bowl of ice water. Let stand until cold. Drain well. Cut shrimp into ½-inch pieces. Transfer to large bowl; stir in fruit juices. Cover and refrigerate 30 minutes.

2. Stir in mango, jicama, onion, cilantro, jalapeño, avocado, oil, salt, and black pepper. Cover and refrigerate 30 minutes longer. Serve with tortilla chips.

EACH SERVING: About 155 calories, 15g protein, 13g carbohydrate, 5g total fat (1g saturated), 3g fiber, 131mg cholesterol, 300mg sodium

MUSSELS WITH TOMATOES AND WHITE WINE

If you've never prepared mussels at home, see the Tip below. To enjoy every last drop, serve this saucy dish with some crusty bread—or a spoon.

ACTIVE TIME: 20 minutes **TOTAL TIME:** 45 minutes

MAKES: 4 main-dish servings

1	tablespoon olive oil
1	small onion, chopped
2	garlic cloves, finely chopped
¼	teaspoon crushed red pepper
1	can (14 to 16 ounces) no-salt-added whole tomatoes
¾	cup dry white wine
4	pounds large mussels, scrubbed and debearded if necessary
2	tablespoons chopped fresh parsley

1. In nonreactive 5-quart Dutch oven, heat oil over medium heat. Add onion and cook until tender and golden, 6 to 8 minutes. Add garlic and crushed red pepper and cook 30 seconds longer. Stir in tomatoes with their juice and wine, breaking up tomatoes with side of spoon. Bring to a boil; boil 3 minutes.

2. Add mussels; bring to a boil. Reduce heat; cover and simmer until mussels open, about 5 minutes, transferring mussels to large bowl as they open. Discard any mussels that have not opened after 5 minutes. Pour tomato sauce over mussels and sprinkle with parsley.

EACH SERVING: About 210 calories, 18g protein, 12g carbohydrate, 6g total fat (2g saturated), 2g fiber, 36mg cholesterol, 325mg sodium

MOULES À LA MARINIÈRE

Prepare as directed, but substitute **1 tbsp butter** for olive oil and **⅓ cup chopped shallots** for onion. Omit crushed red pepper and tomatoes; use **1½ cups dry white wine**.

> **TIP**
> Scrub mussels well under cold running water. Cultivated mussels usually do not have beards, but if yours do, grasp the hairlike beard firmly with your thumb and forefinger and pull it away, or scrape it off with a knife.

STEAMED SOFT-SHELL CLAMS

A great appetizer or main dish to have with an ice-cold beer on a hot summer day!

ACTIVE TIME: 5 minutes **TOTAL TIME:** 10 minutes

MAKES: 6 first-course servings

6   dozen steamer (soft-shell) clams
Melted butter or margarine (optional)

1. In very large bowl or in kitchen sink, place clams and enough *cold water* to cover; drain. Repeat rinsing and draining until sand no longer falls to bottom of bowl.

2. In steamer or 8-quart saucepot fitted with rack, bring enough *water* to cover pan bottom to a boil over high heat. Place clams on rack in steamer. Reduce heat; cover and steam until clams open, 5 to 10 minutes, transferring clams to bowl as they open. Discard any clams that have not opened.

3. Strain clam broth through sieve lined with paper towels and pour into 6 soup cups or mugs.

4. To eat, with fingers, pull clams from shells by neck; peel off and discard black sheath that covers neck. Dip clams first in broth to remove any sand, then into melted butter, if you like. When sand has settled to bottom, broth can be sipped, if desired.

EACH SERVING (WITHOUT BUTTER): About 76 calories, 13g protein, 3g carbohydrate, 1g total fat (0g saturated), 0g fiber, 35mg cholesterol, 57mg sodium

COOK'S TIP:
SCRUBBING AND SHUCKING CLAMS

1. Scrub the clams well under cold running water to remove all the grit.

2. Protecting your hand with a folded towel, hold the clam with the "hinge" facing you; wedge the thin edge of a clam knife between the shells.

3. Slide the knife around to separate the shells.

4. Open the shell. Cut the clam meat away from the top shell; discard the top shell.

5. Slide the knife underneath the meat in the bottom shell to release it.

Chicken and Raspberry Salad (page 222)

5 | CHICKEN & TURKEY

On busy weeknights, poultry is a convenient solution many of us turn to again and again—and it's a good-for-your-heart option, especially if you prepare white meat or remove the skin from dark meat before serving. The choice of cooking method is important, too. Here, we've gathered recipes with techniques that require just a spritz of cooking spray or a drizzle of olive oil, like baking, grilling, and stir-frying.

Another secret to heart-smart poultry dinners: include a rainbow of vegetables and fiber-rich whole grains. Toward this end, we share recipes such as Maple-Walnut Chicken, which comes with a side of whole-grain pilaf and steamed spinach, and Chicken and Apple Stew in Squash Bowls, a hearty chicken stew served in edible acorn-squash bowls.

We've made sure to round up lots of kid-friendly options, too, like Chicken-Stuffed Spuds, baked potatoes with a zesty chicken filling that you can make in the microwave and toaster oven. Other yummy dishes sure to recruit regular members of the clean-plate club include zippy Southwestern Turkey Fajitas, sweet Apricot Mustard Glazed Chicken, or a big bowl of Linguine with Carrot-Turkey Ragu.

If you prefer to spend a little time up front and then let the oven do its magic, check out Turkey Thighs Osso Buco Style and Sweet Potato Shepherd's Pie, which substitute turkey thighs for veal shanks and ground turkey for ground lamb. Both require little attention once they're in the oven and can be easily doubled to feed a crowd.

CHICKEN AND RASPBERRY SALAD

This satisfying, healthful salad features grilled avocado, a buttery counterpart to fresh antioxidant-rich berries and lean grilled chicken breast.

TOTAL TIME: 35 minutes

MAKES: 4 main-dish servings

2	tablespoons fresh lemon juice
2	tablespoons reduced-fat sour cream
1	tablespoon honey
1	teaspoon Dijon mustard
3/8	teaspoon salt
3/8	teaspoon ground black pepper
1	teaspoon poppy seeds
1	pound skinless, boneless chicken breast halves
1½	teaspoons olive oil
1	avocado, cut in half, pitted but not peeled
1	pint (12 ounces) raspberries
6	ounces mixed salad greens
¼	cup sliced almonds, toasted

1. Prepare outdoor grill for direct grilling over medium heat.

2. In bowl, whisk lemon juice, sour cream, honey, mustard, and ⅛ teaspoon each salt and pepper. Stir in poppy seeds. Cover; refrigerate dressing up to 1 day.

3. With meat mallet, pound chicken to even ½-inch thickness. Rub 1 teaspoon oil over chicken; sprinkle with remaining ¼ teaspoon each salt and pepper. Rub cut sides of avocado with remaining ½ teaspoon oil. Place chicken and avocado on grill. Cook chicken 8 to 10 minutes, turning over once, until instant-read thermometer inserted into center of breast registers 165°F. Grill avocado 3 to 5 minutes or until grill marks appear, turning over once. Let both rest 5 minutes. Discard avocado peel; slice. Slice chicken.

4. In bowl, toss raspberries with 1 tablespoon dressing. In large bowl, toss greens with remaining dressing; divide among plates. Top with raspberries, chicken, avocado, and almonds.

EACH SERVING: About 300 calories, 27g protein, 19g carbohydrate, 14g total fat (3g saturated), 8g fiber, 67mg cholesterol, 320mg sodium

SWEET CHIPOTLE CHICKEN

For a summery dish that may just become a family favorite, toss and grill chicken cutlets in a flavorful salsa marinade, then top them with fresh tomatoes and avocado.

ACTIVE TIME: 20 minutes **TOTAL TIME:** 30 minutes
MAKES: 4 main-dish servings

2½ pounds assorted heirloom tomatoes, cored and sliced
⅜ teaspoon salt
¼ cup packed fresh cilantro
1 tablespoon chopped chipotle chiles in adobo
1 tablespoon fresh lime juice
2 teaspoons honey
1 garlic clove
⅛ teaspoon ground cumin
4 thin chicken cutlets (1¼ pounds)
1 large avocado, pitted, peeled, and very thinly sliced
Taco-size corn tortillas (optional)

1. Prepare outdoor grill for covered direct grilling over medium-high heat. Sprinkle tomato slices with ⅛ teaspoon salt.

2. In food processor or blender, combine cilantro, chipotle, lime juice, honey, garlic, cumin, half of tomatoes, and remaining ¼ teaspoon salt; puree until smooth. Transfer ¼ cup of tomato salsa to large bowl. Set aside remaining salsa.

3. To large bowl, add chicken; toss to coat. Grill chicken (discarding marinade), covered, 3 minutes on each side or until cooked through. (Instant-read thermometer inserted into center of cutlet should reach 165°F.) Transfer to platter.

4. Divide remaining tomatoes among cutlets. Top with avocado. Serve with remaining salsa and corn tortillas, if desired.

EACH SERVING: About 280 calories, 32g protein, 16g carbohydrate, 11g total fat (2g saturated), 6g fiber, 78mg cholesterol, 335mg sodium

SPICED CHICKEN SKEWERS

Quick and healthy grilled kabobs seasoned with chili and lemon are served on a bed of bulgur.

TOTAL TIME: 30 minutes

MAKES: 4 main-dish servings

1	cup bulgur
1¾	cups water
1	pound skinless, boneless chicken breasts, cut into 1-inch chunks
2	teaspoons chili powder
2	teaspoons extra-virgin olive oil
½	teaspoon salt
½	teaspoon freshly ground black pepper
2	pints cherry tomatoes
2	lemons
1	garlic clove, crushed with garlic press
1	cup chopped fresh flat-leaf parsley leaves

1. Prepare outdoor grill for direct grilling or preheat large grill pan over medium-high heat.

2. In large microwave-safe bowl, combine bulgur and water. Microwave on High, stirring once, 10 minutes, or until bulgur is tender and water is absorbed.

3. In medium bowl, toss chicken with chili powder, 1 teaspoon oil, and ¼ teaspoon each salt and pepper until well coated. Thread chicken and tomatoes alternately onto skewers, spacing ¼ inch apart.

4. Grill chicken skewers, turning occasionally, 7 to 8 minutes, until chicken is cooked through (instant-read thermometer inserted horizontally into center of chicken should reach 165°F).

5. Meanwhile, from 1 lemon, finely grate 1 teaspoon peel and squeeze 3 tablespoons juice; cut remaining lemon into wedges. Place peel and juice in bowl with bulgur. Add garlic, parsley, remaining ¼ teaspoon each salt and pepper, and remaining 1 teaspoon oil. Stir well.

6. Divide bulgur mixture and chicken skewers among serving plates. Serve with lemon wedges.

EACH SERVING: About 305 calories, 29g protein, 37g carbohydrate, 6g total fat (1g saturated), 10g fiber, 63mg cholesterol, 390mg sodium

CURRIED CHICKEN WITH MANGO-CANTALOUPE SLAW

Gingery fruit slaw pairs perfectly with curried chicken.

ACTIVE TIME: 25 minutes **TOTAL TIME:** 35 minutes plus marinating

MAKES: 4 main-dish servings

1 to 3 limes

1   container (6 ounces) plain low-fat yogurt

¾   teaspoon curry powder

4   tablespoons chopped crystallized ginger

1   teaspoon salt

¼   teaspoon crushed red pepper

4   medium skinless, boneless chicken breast halves (1¼ pounds)

½   small cantaloupe, rind removed, cut into 2" by ¼" matchstick strips (2 cups)

1   large mango, peeled and cut into 2" by ¼" matchstick strips (2 cups)

½   cup loosely packed fresh cilantro leaves, chopped

1   head Boston lettuce

1. If desired for garnish, cut 1 lime into wedges and set aside. From remaining limes, grate ½ teaspoon peel and squeeze 2 tablespoons juice.

2. In large bowl, with wire whisk, whisk 1 tablespoon lime juice and ¼ teaspoon lime peel with yogurt, curry powder, 2 tablespoons ginger, ¾ teaspoon salt, and ⅛ teaspoon crushed red pepper. Add chicken, turning to coat with marinade. Cover and let stand 15 minutes at room temperature or 30 minutes in refrigerator, turning over occasionally.

3. Meanwhile, in medium bowl, with rubber spatula, gently stir cantaloupe and mango with cilantro and remaining 2 tablespoons ginger, 1 tablespoon lime juice, ¼ teaspoon lime peel, ¼ teaspoon salt, and ⅛ teaspoon crushed red pepper; set aside. Makes about 4 cups.

4. Prepare charcoal fire or preheat gas grill for covered direct grilling over medium heat.

5. Grease grill rack. Remove chicken breasts from marinade; discard marinade. Place chicken on hot rack. Cover grill and cook 10 to 12 minutes, turning over once, until instant-read thermometer inserted into center of breast reaches 165°F. Transfer chicken to cutting board; cool slightly until easy to handle, then cut into long, thin slices.

6. To serve, arrange lettuce leaves on dinner plates; top with chicken and slaw. Serve with lime wedges if you like.

EACH SERVING CHICKEN WITH LETTUCE: About 205 calories, 34g protein, 5g carbohydrate, 4g total fat (1g saturated), 1g fiber, 92mg cholesterol, 330mg sodium

EACH ½ CUP SLAW: About 50 calories, 1g protein, 13g carbohydrate, 0g total fat, 1g fiber, 0mg cholesterol, 150mg sodium

COFFEE-SPICE CHICKEN AND FRUIT-BASIL SALSA

A jerk-style seasoning of Jamaican allspice and java gives this Caribbean chicken its caffeinated kick. Balancing the heat: a cooling summer salsa.

ACTIVE TIME: 30 minutes **TOTAL TIME:** 40 minutes

MAKES: 8 main-dish servings

3	cups seedless watermelon cubes, cut into ½-inch chunks (from 4-pound piece of watermelon)
1	large ripe nectarine, pitted and cut into ½-inch chunks
3	tablespoons red onion, finely chopped
1	tablespoon fresh lemon juice
2	tablespoons instant coffee
1	tablespoon peeled, grated fresh ginger
1	tablespoon olive oil
1¼	teaspoons ground allspice
¾	teaspoon salt
8	skinless, boneless chicken breast halves (3 pounds)
½	cup packed fresh basil leaves, coarsely chopped

1. In medium bowl, combine watermelon, nectarine, red onion, and lemon juice. Cover and refrigerate salsa while preparing chicken. Makes 4 cups.

2. Prepare outdoor grill for covered direct grilling over medium heat.

3. In large bowl, with spoon or fingers, press coffee to pulverize. Add ginger, oil, allspice, and ½ teaspoon salt; stir to combine. Add chicken breasts and toss to coat evenly with spice mixture (you may need to pat spice mixture onto chicken with fingers).

4. Place chicken breasts on hot grill grate. Cover and cook 8 to 10 minutes, turning over once, until chicken is cooked through. (Instant-read thermometer inserted into center of breast should reach 165°F.)

5. Transfer chicken to cutting board and let rest 5 minutes. Meanwhile, stir basil and remaining ¼ teaspoon salt into salsa. Slice chicken crosswise and serve with salsa.

EACH SERVING: About 235 calories, 40g protein, 8g carbohydrate, 4g total fat (1g saturated), 1g fiber, 99mg cholesterol, 310mg sodium

BASIL-ORANGE CHICKEN WITH COUSCOUS

Marinating the chicken in orange and basil gives it a bright, fresh flavor. Served over whole-wheat couscous with steamed sugar snap peas, this light dish is perfect for warmer weather.

ACTIVE TIME: 20 minutes
TOTAL TIME: 30 minutes

MAKES: 4 main-dish servings

2	large navel oranges
3	lemons
½	cup packed fresh basil leaves, chopped
2	tablespoons olive oil
³/₈	teaspoon salt
³/₈	teaspoon ground black pepper
4	medium skinless, boneless chicken breast halves (1½ pounds)
½	teaspoon sugar
1	cup whole-wheat couscous
1	package (8 ounces) stringless sugar snap peas

1. From 1 orange, grate 1½ teaspoons peel and squeeze 4 tablespoons juice. From 2 lemons, grate 1½ teaspoons peel and squeeze ⅓ cup juice. Cut remaining orange and lemon into slices and set aside.

2. In medium bowl, combine 1 teaspoon of each peel and 1 tablespoon orange juice with half of basil, 1 tablespoon olive oil, ¼ teaspoon salt, and ¼ teaspoon pepper.

3. Place chicken breast between two sheets of plastic wrap and, with flat side of meat mallet, pound to an even ½-inch thickness. Add chicken to citrus mixture, turning to coat; set aside.

4. In small pitcher or bowl, combine sugar, remaining ⅛ teaspoon salt, remaining ⅛ teaspoon pepper, citrus peels, citrus juices, basil, and oil; set aside. (Dish can be made to this point up to 8 hours ahead. Cover chicken and citrus sauce and refrigerate.)

5. Preheat large ridged grill pan or prepare outdoor grill for direct grilling over medium-high heat. Meanwhile, prepare couscous as label directs. In 4-quart saucepan filled with *½-inch water,* place a vegetable steamer. Bring to a boil over high heat.

6. Add chicken to hot grill pan or grate; cook 4 minutes. Turn chicken over and cook 3 to 4 minutes longer or until no longer pink in center. Grill reserved citrus slices as well.

7. While chicken is cooking on second side, add snap peas to steamer; cook 2 to 3 minutes or until tender-crisp. Fluff couscous and spoon onto large platter; top with chicken and snap peas. Drizzle sauce over all. Garnish with grilled citrus slices.

EACH SERVING: About 400 calories, 46g protein, 33g carbohydrate, 9g total fat (1g saturated), 6g fiber, 99mg cholesterol, 365mg sodium

COOK'S TIP:
CHICKEN BREAST SAVVY

The demand for chicken breasts has increased with consumers' growing commitment to cut back on fat. Now companies market several variations. Skinless, boneless breast halves may be labeled exactly that, or they may be called skinless, boneless split breasts or portions. If the label doesn't indicate that the breast is cut into two pieces, it could be whole—the clues to look for are the words halves, split, or portions. Poultry companies also package tenderloins (the narrow pieces of chicken from the underside of breasts). These could be labeled tenders or fillets—either way, they are boneless, very tender, and perfect for chicken fingers, stir-fries, and salads. Thin-sliced chicken breast cutlets are breast halves cut horizontally for quicker cooking. They're great in place of pounded chicken breasts, or instead of veal for a lower-fat take on veal scaloppine.

LEMON-OREGANO CHICKEN

This fresh-flavored chicken dish is perfect for outdoor grilling on one of those surprisingly warm days in early spring. For even cooking, it's a good idea to pound chicken breasts to a uniform thickness with a meat mallet.

ACTIVE TIME: 15 minutes **TOTAL TIME:** 30 minutes

MAKES: 4 main-dish servings

3   medium zucchini (8 ounces each)
2   tablespoons olive oil
½   teaspoon salt
½   cup loosely packed fresh mint leaves, chopped
4   medium skinless, boneless chicken breast halves (1½ pounds)
3   lemons
1   tablespoon chopped fresh oregano
½   teaspoon coarsely ground black pepper

1. Prepare outdoor grill for covered direct grilling over medium heat.

2. With mandoline or sharp knife, slice zucchini very thinly lengthwise. In large bowl, toss zucchini with 1 tablespoon oil, ¼ teaspoon salt, and half of mint.

3. Place chicken breast between two sheets of plastic wrap and, with meat mallet, pound to uniform ¼-inch thickness. From 2 lemons, grate 1 tablespoon peel and squeeze 2 tablespoons juice. Cut remaining lemon into 4 wedges; set aside. In medium bowl, combine lemon peel and juice with oregano, pepper, and remaining 1 tablespoon oil and ¼ teaspoon salt. Add chicken to bowl and toss until evenly coated.

4. Place zucchini slices, in batches, on hot grill rack over medium heat and cook until grill marks appear and zucchini is tender, 2 to 4 minutes, turning over once. Remove zucchini from grill; place on large platter and sprinkle with remaining mint.

5. Place chicken on hot grill rack. Cover grill and cook chicken until juices run clear when chicken is pierced with tip of knife, 6 to 8 minutes, turning over once. Transfer chicken to platter with zucchini; serve with lemon wedges.

EACH SERVING: About 280 calories, 42g protein, 8g carbohydrate, 9g total fat (2g saturated), 3g fiber, 99mg cholesterol, 390mg sodium

ASPARAGUS CHICKEN ROULADES

When food is "butterflied," it is cut horizontally almost in half, then opened flat, resembling a butterfly.

TOTAL TIME: 30 minutes

MAKES: 4 main-dish servings

4	medium skinless, boneless chicken breast halves (¼ pound each)
1	lemon
3	ounces goat cheese, softened
½	cup loosely packed fresh mint leaves, chopped
¾	pound thin asparagus, trimmed
¼	teaspoon ground black pepper
¼	teaspoon salt
1	tablespoon olive oil
½	cup chicken broth

1. Butterfly the chicken: Holding knife parallel to work surface and against a long side of chicken breast half, cut chicken almost in half, making sure not to cut all the way through. Open breast half and spread flat like a book. Repeat with remaining chicken.

2. From lemon, grate ½ teaspoon peel and squeeze 1 tablespoon juice; set aside juice. In small bowl, stir goat cheese, mint, and lemon peel until mixed.

3. Spread goat-cheese mixture evenly on cut sides of breast halves. Place one-fourth of uncooked asparagus on a long side of each breast half. Roll up each breast half to enclose asparagus, allowing ends of stalks to stick out if necessary; secure with toothpicks. Sprinkle chicken roulades with pepper and salt.

4. In 12-inch skillet, heat oil over medium-high heat until hot. Add roulades; cook, covered, 9 to 11 minutes or until chicken loses its pink color throughout, turning roulades to brown all sides. Transfer to cutting board; keep warm.

5. To same skillet, add broth and lemon juice; bring to a boil, scraping up any browned bits. Remove skillet from heat.

6. To serve, discard toothpicks from roulades. Cut roulades crosswise into 1-inch-thick slices. Place each sliced roulade on a plate; drizzle with pan sauce.

EACH SERVING: About 265 calories, 39g protein, 2g carbohydrate, 10g total fat (4g saturated), 2g fiber, 92mg cholesterol, 450mg sodium

GRILLED CHICKEN BRUSCHETTA

Add grilled chicken breasts to this popular appetizer, and you have a lean dinner, rich in fiber and vitamin C, that's good for your heart—and your taste buds.

ACTIVE TIME: 20 minutes **TOTAL TIME:** 25 minutes
MAKES: 4 main-dish servings

- 3 garlic cloves, peeled
- 3 teaspoons extra-virgin olive oil
- 3/8 teaspoon salt
- 3/8 teaspoon ground black pepper
- 4 skinless, boneless chicken breast halves (6 ounces each)
- 1 3/4 pounds tomatoes, chopped
- 1 small shallot, finely chopped
- 1/4 cup packed fresh basil leaves, finely chopped
- 2 tablespoons red wine vinegar
- 1 round loaf crusty whole-wheat bread (8 ounces), sliced

1. Preheat outdoor grill over medium heat. Crush 2 garlic cloves with press.

2. In 9-inch pie plate, mix together crushed garlic, 1 teaspoon oil, and 1/4 teaspoon each salt and pepper, then rub all over chicken.

3. In large bowl, combine tomatoes, shallot, basil, vinegar, 1 teaspoon oil, and 1/8 teaspoon each salt and pepper. Let stand.

4. Grill chicken, covered, 10 to 13 minutes or until juices run clear when thickest part of chicken is pierced, turning once. Transfer to cutting board. Let rest 10 minutes; slice.

5. Brush bread with remaining 1 teaspoon oil. Grill 1 minute, turning once. Cut remaining garlic clove in half. Rub cut sides all over bread. Divide bread and chicken among serving plates; top with tomato mixture.

EACH SERVING: About 365 calories, 45g protein, 31g carbohydrate, 7g total fat (1g saturated), 5g fiber, 99mg cholesterol, 325mg sodium

PACIFIC RIM CHICKEN AND RICE BOWLS

This satisfying meal in a bowl was created by Teresa Ralston, finalist in the kid-friendly category of *Good Housekeeping*'s second Cook Your Heart Out contest.

TOTAL TIME: 25 minutes plus time to make rice

MAKES: 4 main-dish servings

1	tablespoon extra-virgin olive oil
1	tablespoon honey
1	tablespoon reduced-sodium soy sauce
2	teaspoons fresh lime juice
1½	teaspoons peeled and finely grated fresh ginger
½	teaspoon finely grated fresh garlic
¼	teaspoon Asian chili sauce (Sriracha)
2	cups sugar snap peas
1	cup julienned red bell pepper
½	cup matchstick-cut carrots
12	ounces boneless, skinless chicken breast halves
2	cups hot cooked brown rice
¾	cup diced fresh pineapple

1. In small bowl, whisk together oil, honey, soy sauce, lime juice, ginger, garlic, and chili sauce. Set aside.

2. Blanch sugar snap peas in pot of *boiling water* for 90 seconds or until tender-crisp. Transfer to ice bath to stop cooking. Blanch red bell pepper and carrots in boiling water for 60 seconds or until tender-crisp; remove to ice bath to stop cooking. Drain vegetables and pat dry.

3. Spray nonstick grill pan with cooking spray and heat over medium heat. Add chicken to pan and cook 7 to 10 minutes, turning over once, until cooked through. Let rest for 5 minutes, then slice thinly and uniformly across grain.

4. Divide hot cooked rice among serving bowls. Top each with chicken, sugar snap peas, red bell pepper, carrots, and pineapple. Drizzle each with sauce and serve immediately.

EACH SERVING: About 300 calories, 21g protein, 38g carbohydrate, 7g total fat (1g saturated), 1g fiber, 47mg cholesterol, 200mg sodium

GREEN-CHILE SKILLET CHICKEN

This Tex-Mex specialty relies on canned green chiles for its heat—choose mild, medium, or hot, depending on your preference.

ACTIVE TIME: 10 minutes **TOTAL TIME:** 20 minutes

MAKES: 4 main-dish servings

4	medium skinless, boneless chicken breast halves (1¼ pounds)
¼	teaspoon salt
⅛	teaspoon ground black pepper
1	tablespoon olive oil
1	can (4 to 4½ ounces) diced green chiles, drained
1	cup grape tomatoes, cut in half
¾	cup reduced-sodium chicken broth
½	teaspoon ground cumin
1	garlic clove, crushed with garlic press
2	tablespoons chopped fresh cilantro

1. With meat mallet, pound chicken breast halves to even ½-inch thickness (or place chicken between two sheets of plastic wrap or waxed paper and pound with rolling pin). Sprinkle with salt and pepper.

2. In nonstick 12-inch skillet, heat oil over medium heat until hot. Add chicken breasts and cook, turning once, until chicken is browned on both sides and loses its pink color throughout, 6 to 7 minutes. Transfer chicken breasts to platter; cover loosely with foil to keep warm.

3. To skillet, add chiles, tomatoes, broth, cumin, garlic, and juices from platter; cook, stirring occasionally, until sauce is slightly reduced, about 3 minutes. Stir in cilantro. To serve, spoon sauce over chicken.

EACH SERVING: About 205 calories, 33g protein, 4g carbohydrate, 5g total fat (1g saturated), 0g fiber, 82mg cholesterol, 445mg sodium

ALMOND-CRUSTED CHICKEN WITH RAINBOW SLAW

An easy source of healthy protein, these quick-cooking chicken cutlets get their oven-crisped coating from chopped almonds. The colorful, crunchy slaw combines carrots, red cabbage, oranges, and yellow peppers.

ACTIVE TIME: 20 minutes **TOTAL TIME:** 30 minutes

MAKES: 4 main-dish servings

2	oranges
4	cups thinly sliced red cabbage (12 ounces)
2	large carrots, peeled and cut into thin matchsticks
1	large yellow pepper, very thinly sliced
2	tablespoons snipped chives
3	tablespoons white wine vinegar
4	teaspoons canola oil
½	teaspoon salt
½	teaspoon freshly ground black pepper
1	tablespoon all-purpose flour
½	cup almonds, very finely chopped
1	large egg white
¼	teaspoon ground cumin
¼	teaspoon no-salt-added chili powder
4	skinless, boneless chicken breast cutlets (1 pound)

1. Arrange oven rack in lowest position and place 15″ by 10″ jelly-roll pan on rack. Preheat oven to 450°F.

2. Cut peel and white pith from oranges; discard trimmings. Cut oranges into segments; transfer, with their juices, to large bowl. Add cabbage, carrots, yellow pepper, chives, vinegar, 1 teaspoon oil, and ¼ teaspoon each salt and black pepper. Toss well; let slaw stand while you prepare chicken.

3. Spread flour over medium heat plate; spread almonds on separate plate. In pie plate, beat egg white until foamy.

4. Sprinkle cumin, chili, and remaining ¼ teaspoon each salt and black pepper over chicken. Press one side of 1 piece chicken in flour; shake off excess. Dip same side in egg white; press into almonds. Repeat with remaining chicken.

5. Remove hot pan from oven; brush with remaining 1 tablespoon oil. Add chicken pieces, nut sides down; roast 10 to 12 minutes or until chicken is cooked through. (Instant-read thermometer inserted horizontally into cutlet should register 165°F.) Serve with slaw.

EACH SERVING: About 350 calories, 30g protein, 28g carbohydrate, 15g total fat (2g saturated), 7g fiber, 63mg cholesterol, 425mg sodium

CHICKEN WITH ORANGE RELISH

Incredibly healthy and full of flavor, this quick main dish is so refreshingly tasty, you'll forget it's good for you!

TOTAL TIME: 25 minutes

MAKES: 4 servings

4	skinless, boneless chicken breast cutlets (1 pound)
¾	teaspoon peeled, grated fresh ginger
¼	teaspoon ground black pepper
¼	teaspoon salt
1	large orange
3	stalks celery, finely chopped
2	green onions, sliced
1	tablespoon red wine vinegar
¼	cup packed fresh cilantro leaves, finely chopped
1	cup whole-wheat couscous

1. Preheat oven to 425°F. Spray jelly-roll pan with nonstick cooking spray. Arrange chicken on pan. Rub chicken with ½ teaspoon ginger; sprinkle with pepper and ⅛ teaspoon salt. Roast 10 to 12 minutes or until cooked through. (Instant-read thermometer inserted horizontally into center of cutlet should reach 165°F.)

2. Meanwhile, with knife, cut peel and white pith from orange; discard. Cut on either side of membrane to remove each segment from orange; place half of segments in 2-quart saucepan. Squeeze juice from membranes into saucepan.

3. To same saucepan, add celery, onions, vinegar, remaining ¼ teaspoon ginger, and remaining ⅛ teaspoon salt. Bring to a boil over high heat. Reduce heat to simmer; cook 7 minutes or until celery is tender-crisp, stirring occasionally. Remove from heat; stir in cilantro and reserved orange segments.

4. Cook couscous as label directs. Serve chicken with relish and couscous.

EACH SERVING: About 320 calories, 30g protein, 45g carbohydrate, 3g total fat (1g saturated), 8g fiber, 63mg cholesterol, 245mg sodium

APRICOT MUSTARD GLAZED CHICKEN

Convenient ingredients like microwave-in-a-bag spinach, boneless chicken breasts, and apricot preserves make for a quick and healthy tasty dish.

TOTAL TIME: 30 minutes

MAKES: 4 main-dish servings

4	medium skinless, boneless chicken breast halves (1½ pounds)
³⁄₈	teaspoon salt
¼	teaspoon freshly ground black pepper
4	teaspoons olive oil
1	lemon
1	small onion (4 to 6 ounces), chopped
⅓	cup apricot preserves
⅓	cup chicken broth
1	tablespoon Dijon mustard
1	package (9 ounces) microwave-in-the-bag spinach

1. Place chicken between two sheets of plastic wrap. With meat mallet, pound to an even ½-inch thickness; season with ¼ teaspoon salt and ⅛ teaspoon pepper.

2. In 12-inch skillet, heat 2 teaspoons oil over medium heat. Add chicken and cook 6 to 8 minutes or until browned on both sides, turning over once. (Instant-read thermometer inserted horizontally into center of chicken should reach 165°F.) Transfer chicken to dish. Meanwhile, from lemon, grate ½ teaspoon peel and squeeze 1 tablespoon juice; set aside.

3. To same skillet, over medium heat, place remaining 2 teaspoons oil. When oil is hot, add onion and cook 6 minutes or until tender. Add preserves, broth, mustard, and lemon peel; bring to a boil over medium-high heat. Boil 1 minute. Return chicken to skillet; reduce heat to medium-low and simmer 4 to 6 minutes or until chicken is glazed and cooked through, spooning preserve mixture over breasts frequently. (Instant-read thermometer inserted into center of breast should reach 165°F.)

4. Meanwhile, cook spinach as label directs. Transfer to serving bowl and toss with lemon juice and remaining ⅛ teaspoon each salt and pepper. Serve spinach with glazed chicken; spoon any extra preserve mixture over chicken.

EACH SERVING: About 325 calories, 42g protein, 22g carbohydrate, 7g total fat (1g saturated), 7g fiber, 99mg cholesterol, 480mg sodium

WARM CHICKEN AND ORZO PILAF

Chunky vegetables and goat cheese pair with whole-wheat orzo and lemony chicken in this well-rounded meal.

TOTAL TIME: 30 minutes

MAKES: 4 main-dish servings

1	lemon
1	pint cherry tomatoes, halved
1	orange pepper (8 ounces), chopped
3	garlic cloves, crushed with garlic press
2	tablespoons extra-virgin olive oil
¼	teaspoon dried oregano
¼	teaspoon salt
¼	teaspoon freshly ground black pepper
1	pound skinless, boneless chicken breasts, cut into 1-inch chunks
1	cup whole-wheat orzo pasta
4	stalks celery, thinly sliced at an angle
2	ounces fresh goat cheese, crumbled (½ cup)

1. Preheat oven to 450°F. From lemon, finely grate 1 teaspoon peel and squeeze 2 tablespoons juice. Set aside.

2. On one side of 18″ by 12″ jelly-roll pan, toss tomatoes and orange pepper with garlic, 1 tablespoon oil, and ⅛ teaspoon each oregano, salt, and black pepper. Spread in even layer. On other side of pan, toss chicken with lemon peel, remaining 1 tablespoon oil, and remaining ⅛ teaspoon each oregano, salt, and black pepper. Spread in even layer. Roast 13 minutes or until chicken is cooked through (165°F).

3. While chicken and vegetables roast, cook orzo in *boiling salted water* as label directs. Drain well and transfer to large bowl. Add chicken and vegetables, with their juices, to orzo, along with celery and lemon juice. Toss until well mixed. Top with goat cheese.

EACH SERVING: About 420 calories, 34g protein, 41g carbohydrate, 14g total fat (4g saturated), 7g fiber, 79mg cholesterol, 325mg sodium

CHICKEN PARM STACKS

Chicken Parmesan goes healthy with grilled—rather than breaded—chicken and fresh veggies. Whole-wheat breadcrumbs add great crunch and some fiber.

ACTIVE TIME: 20 minutes **TOTAL TIME:** 30 minutes

MAKES: 4 main-dish servings

1	slice whole-wheat bread
1	tablespoon plus 1 teaspoon olive oil
¼	cup packed fresh flat-leaf parsley leaves
1	garlic clove
⅜	teaspoon salt
⅜	teaspoon freshly ground black pepper
1	pound chicken breast cutlets
1	pound yellow squash, cut into ½-inch-thick slices
1	pound ripe tomatoes, cut into ½-inch-thick slices
1	ounce Parmesan cheese

Basil leaves, for garnish

1. Place oven rack 6 inches from broiler heat source. Preheat broiler. Line 18" by 12" jelly-roll pan with foil. Preheat large ridged grill pan or prepare outdoor grill for direct grilling over medium-high heat.

2. Tear bread into large chunks. In food processor with knife blade attached, pulse bread into fine crumbs. In small bowl, combine breadcrumbs with 1 teaspoon oil.

3. To food processor, add parsley, garlic, ¼ teaspoon each salt and pepper, and remaining 1 tablespoon oil. Pulse until very finely chopped.

4. On large plate, rub half of parsley mixture all over chicken cutlets. Add chicken to hot grill pan or place on hot grill grate; cook 4 minutes. Turn chicken over and cook 3 to 4 minutes longer or until instant-read thermometer inserted horizontally into cutlet reaches 165°F.

5. Meanwhile, arrange squash in single layer in prepared pan. Coat with remaining parsley mixture. Broil 7 to 9 minutes or until squash is tender and browned. Transfer squash to serving platter in single layer. Place chicken on top.

6. In same pan, arrange tomato slices in single layer. Divide crumb mixture evenly over tomatoes. Sprinkle with remaining ⅛ teaspoon each salt and pepper. Broil 30 seconds or until crumbs are golden brown.

7. Arrange crumb-topped tomato slices on top of chicken. With vegetable peeler, shave paper-thin slices of Parmesan directly over tomatoes. Garnish with fresh basil leaves.

EACH SERVING: About 250 calories, 29g protein, 12g carbohydrate, 10g total fat (3g saturated), 3g fiber, 69mg cholesterol, 415mg sodium

MAPLE-WALNUT CHICKEN

Maple syrup adds a sweet glaze to lean chicken breasts, while spinach, walnuts, and whole-grain pilaf deliver heart-boosting antioxidants and fiber.

TOTAL TIME: 30 minutes

MAKES: 4 main-dish servings

4	skinless, boneless chicken breast halves (6 to 7 ounces each)
1	tablespoon olive oil
1	tablespoon packed fresh thyme leaves
¼	teaspoon salt
¼	teaspoon freshly ground black pepper
½	cup walnuts
5	tablespoons cider vinegar
3	tablespoons maple syrup
½	cup water
1	package (8½ ounces) precooked whole-grain pilaf
1	package (9 ounces) microwave-in-the-bag spinach

1. Rub chicken with oil, then rub with thyme, salt, and pepper. Let stand.

2. Meanwhile, in nonstick 12-inch skillet, toast walnuts over medium heat, stirring occasionally, 4 to 6 minutes or until golden and fragrant. Transfer walnuts to dish; return skillet to heat.

3. Add chicken to same skillet; cook, turning over frequently, 12 minutes or until chicken is golden brown and juices run clear when pierced with tip of knife. (Instant-read thermometer inserted horizontally into breast should reach 165°F.) Transfer chicken to clean plate; return skillet to heat.

4. To same skillet, add vinegar and cook, stirring, 1 minute. Add syrup and water; simmer, stirring occasionally, 6 to 7 minutes or until mixture has thickened.

5. Meanwhile, cook pilaf, then spinach, in microwave as labels direct.

6. Stir walnuts and any chicken juices into sauce. Divide pilaf and spinach among dinner plates. Top with chicken, and spoon maple-walnut sauce all around.

EACH SERVING: About 435 calories, 40g protein, 33g carbohydrate, 17g total fat (2g saturated), 10g fiber, 82mg cholesterol, 310mg sodium

HEART-SMART INGREDIENT: WALNUTS

We all know that walnuts provide delicious crunch, but did you know that one-quarter cup of walnuts contains almost 91% of the recommended daily value of omega-3 fatty acids? These fatty acids promote healthy cell function as well as the production of prostaglandin, hormone-type substances that help control many important bodily functions, including blood pressure and blood clotting.

CRISPY BALSAMIC CHICKEN

This easy chicken dish pops with Italian flavor, thanks to the luscious balsamic glaze and fresh arugula and basil salad. A coating of panko breadcrumbs plus a quick turn in the oven makes the cutlets crisp but light.

ACTIVE TIME: 10 minutes **TOTAL TIME:** 30 minutes

MAKES: 4 main-dish servings

1	pound carrots, peeled and thinly sliced at an angle
2	teaspoons extra-virgin olive oil
¼	teaspoon salt
½	teaspoon ground black pepper
1	cup panko (Japanese-style breadcrumbs)
1¼	pounds skinless, boneless, thin-sliced chicken breast cutlets
1	tablespoon Dijon mustard
½	cup plus 1 tablespoon balsamic vinegar
1	bag (5 ounces) baby arugula
½	cup fresh basil leaves, torn

1. Preheat oven to 450°F. On jelly-roll pan, toss carrots with oil and ⅛ teaspoon each salt and pepper. Roast 8 to 10 minutes or until crisp-tender. Transfer carrots to large bowl to cool.

2. While carrots cook, place panko on large plate. In medium bowl, toss chicken with mustard and ¼ teaspoon pepper until well coated. Coat chicken with panko, pressing so crumbs adhere. Arrange chicken on rack in jelly-roll pan. Bake 12 to 14 minutes or until thermometer inserted horizontally into cutlet registers 165°F.

3. Meanwhile, in 1-quart saucepan, bring ½ cup vinegar and remaining ⅛ teaspoon each salt and pepper to a boil over high heat; reduce heat and simmer 8 to 12 minutes, or until syrupy.

4. To same bowl as roasted carrots, add arugula, basil, and remaining tablespoon vinegar, tossing to mix. Serve salad with chicken and balsamic glaze.

EACH SERVING: About 370 calories, 33g protein, 37g carbohydrate, 9g total fat (1g saturated), 4g fiber, 78mg cholesterol, 440mg sodium

OVEN-BAKED TANDOORI-STYLE CHICKEN

Plain yogurt tenderizes the chicken, while the exotic spices add rich flavor. We use low-fat yogurt to keep things skinny.

ACTIVE TIME: 10 minutes **TOTAL TIME:** 40 minutes plus marinating
MAKES: 6 main-dish servings

2 to 3 limes
1 container (8 ounces) plain low-fat yogurt
½ small onion, chopped
1 tablespoon peeled, minced fresh ginger
1 tablespoon paprika
1 teaspoon ground cumin
1 teaspoon ground coriander
¾ teaspoon salt
¼ teaspoon cayenne (ground red) pepper
Pinch ground cloves
6 bone-in chicken breast halves (3 pounds), skin removed

1. From 1 or 2 limes, squeeze 2 tablespoons juice. Cut remaining lime into 6 wedges; set aside for garnish. In blender, puree lime juice, yogurt, onion, ginger, paprika, cumin, coriander, salt, cayenne, and cloves until smooth. Place chicken and yogurt marinade in medium bowl or in resealable plastic bag, turning to coat chicken. Cover bowl or seal bag and refrigerate chicken 30 minutes to marinate.

2. Preheat oven to 450°F. Arrange chicken on rack in medium roasting pan (14″ by 10″). Spoon half of marinade over chicken; discard remaining marinade.

3. Roast chicken until cooked through, about 30 minutes. (Instant-read thermometer inserted into thickest part of meat should reach 165°F.)

4. Transfer chicken to warm platter; garnish with lime wedges to serve.

EACH SERVING: About 200 calories, 36g protein, 5g carbohydrate, 3g total fat (1g saturated), 1g fiber, 88mg cholesterol, 415mg sodium

CHICKEN AND APPLE STEW IN SQUASH BOWLS

This warming main-dish stew is cleverly served in edible bowls. As you scoop up spoonfuls of stew, be sure to include a little squash in every bite.

TOTAL TIME: 25 minutes

MAKES: 4 main-dish servings

2   small acorn squash (1 pound each), cut crosswise in half and seeded
¼   teaspoon coarsely ground pepper
½   teaspoon salt
1   slice bacon, cut into ¼-inch pieces
1   onion, cut in half and thinly sliced
1½ cups apple cider
1   teaspoon cornstarch
1   Granny Smith apple, cut into thin wedges
½   teaspoon dried sage
8   ounces skinless, boneless cooked chicken breast, cut into ½-inch pieces (2 cups)

1. Sprinkle insides of squash halves with pepper and ¼ teaspoon salt. Place halves, cut sides down, on microwave-safe plate. Cook in microwave oven on High 8 minutes or until fork-tender. Keep warm.

2. Meanwhile, in 12-inch skillet, cook bacon and onion over medium heat 8 to 10 minutes or until browned. In small bowl, with wire whisk, mix cider and cornstarch until blended. Add cider mixture and apple to skillet; increase heat to medium-high heat. Cook 3 minutes or until mixture thickens slightly, stirring occasionally.

3. Add sage, chicken, and remaining ¼ teaspoon salt to skillet; cover and cook 3 minutes or until apple is tender and chicken is heated through (165°F). Spoon chicken mixture into centers of squash halves to serve.

EACH SERVING: About 300 calories, 20g protein, 39g carbohydrate, 8g total fat (3g saturated), 5g fiber, 55mg cholesterol, 410mg sodium

ROMAN CHICKEN SAUTÉ WITH ARTICHOKES

This light and tangy chicken dish, studded with sweet grape tomatoes and garlicky artichoke hearts, is served over a bed of spicy arugula.

ACTIVE TIME: 15 minutes **TOTAL TIME:** 30 minutes

MAKES: 6 main-dish servings

1¼ pounds chicken breast tenders, cut crosswise in half and then cut lengthwise in half

¼ teaspoon salt

¼ teaspoon ground black pepper

1 tablespoon olive oil

2 garlic cloves, thinly sliced

1 can (13 to 14 ounces) artichoke hearts, drained and cut into quarters

½ cup dry white wine

½ cup canned chicken broth

1 pint grape tomatoes

1 teaspoon grated fresh lemon peel, plus additional for garnish

1 bag (5 to 6 ounces) baby arugula

1. Sprinkle chicken with salt and pepper on all sides. In 12-inch skillet, heat 2 teaspoons oil over medium-high heat until very hot. Add chicken and cook, stirring occasionally, 8 minutes or until browned on the outside and no longer pink inside. With slotted spoon, transfer chicken to bowl.

2. To same skillet, add remaining 1 teaspoon oil. Reduce heat to medium and add garlic; cook 30 seconds or until golden. Stir in artichokes, and cook 3 to 4 minutes or until browned. Stir in wine and cook 1 minute over medium-high heat.

3. Add chicken broth and tomatoes; cover and cook 2 to 3 minutes or until most tomatoes burst. Remove skillet from heat. Return chicken to skillet; stir in lemon peel until combined. Arrange arugula on platter; top with sautéed chicken mixture. Garnish chicken with remaining lemon peel.

EACH SERVING: About 165 calories, 25g protein, 7g carbohydrate, 4g total fat (1g saturated), 1g fiber, 55mg cholesterol, 330mg sodium

TANGERINE CHICKEN STIR-FRY

Toss stir-fried chicken and mixed vegetables with a citrus-infused sauce for a quick and delicious meal.

ACTIVE TIME: 20 minutes **TOTAL TIME:** 30 minutes
MAKES: 4 main-dish servings

3	tangerines
¼	cup dry sherry
1	tablespoon grated, peeled fresh ginger
1	teaspoon Asian sesame oil
1	teaspoon plus 1 tablespoon cornstarch
2	tablespoons reduced-sodium soy sauce
1½	pounds skinless, boneless chicken breast halves, cut into ½-inch-wide strips
1	cup quick-cooking (10-minute) brown rice
4	teaspoons vegetable oil
1	bag (12 ounces) broccoli florets
2	carrots, peeled and thinly sliced diagonally
3	green onions, cut into 1-inch pieces
⅓	cup water

1. From 1 tangerine, with vegetable peeler, remove peel in strips. Using small knife, remove and discard any white pith from peel; set peel aside. Into 1-cup liquid measuring cup, squeeze ½ cup juice from tangerines. Stir in sherry, ginger, sesame oil, and 1 teaspoon cornstarch; set juice mixture aside.

2. In medium bowl, combine soy sauce and remaining 1 tablespoon cornstarch. Add chicken and toss to coat; set chicken mixture aside.

3. Cook rice as label directs. Meanwhile, in 12-inch skillet, heat 2 teaspoons vegetable oil over medium-high heat until hot. Add tangerine peel and cook 1 minute or until lightly browned. With tongs or slotted spoon, transfer peel to large bowl.

4. To same skillet, add broccoli, carrots, and green onions; stir to coat with oil. Add water; cover and cook 4 minutes, stirring once. Uncover and cook 1 minute longer or until vegetables are tender-crisp, stirring frequently (stir-frying). Transfer vegetables to bowl with peel.

5. To same skillet, add remaining 2 teaspoons vegetable oil; reduce heat to medium. Add chicken mixture and cook 6 to 7 minutes or until chicken is golden and loses its pink color throughout, stirring frequently. Transfer chicken to bowl with cooked vegetables.

6. Add juice mixture to skillet and bring to a boil over medium-high heat heat; boil 1 minute, stirring until browned bits are loosened. Return chicken and vegetables to skillet and cook 1 minute to heat through, stirring. To serve, spoon brown rice into 4 shallow dinner bowls; top with chicken and vegetables.

EACH SERVING: About 390 calories, 45g protein, 32g carbohydrate, 9g total fat (1g saturated), 5g fiber, 99mg cholesterol, 420mg sodium

CHICKEN WITH PEARS AND MARSALA

Fresh pears and a wine sauce spiked with sage transform basic chicken breasts into an elegant main course. Serve with steamed broccoli florets as shown in photo—just 6 grams of carbs per ½-cup serving.

ACTIVE TIME: 10 minutes **TOTAL TIME:** 25 minutes

MAKES: 4 main-dish servings

1	teaspoon vegetable oil
4	small skinless, boneless chicken breast halves (1 pound)
¼	teaspoon salt
⅛	teaspoon ground black pepper
2	Bosc or Anjou pears, each peeled, cored, and quartered
¾	cup canned chicken broth
½	cup dry Marsala wine
1	tablespoon cornstarch
2	teaspoons chopped fresh sage leaves

1. In nonstick 10-inch skillet, heat oil over medium heat. Add chicken; sprinkle with salt and pepper. Cook, turning once, until chicken loses pink color throughout, 10 to 12 minutes. (Instant-read thermometer inserted horizontally into center of breast should register 165°F.) Transfer to plate; keep warm.

2. To skillet, add pears and cook until browned on all sides, 3 to 5 minutes. Meanwhile, in cup, whisk broth, wine, cornstarch, and sage until blended.

3. Carefully add broth mixture to skillet; boil 1 minute to thicken slightly. Return chicken with any juices to skillet; heat through.

EACH SERVING: About 195 calories, 27g protein, 12g carbohydrate, 3g total fat (1g saturated), 2g fiber, 66mg cholesterol, 410mg sodium

PANKO-MUSTARD CHICKEN

This recipe for oven-baked chicken couldn't be simpler—or more delicious. The breasts are brushed with a zippy mustard mixture and then coated in panko breadcrumbs, which become brown and crispy in the oven.

ACTIVE TIME: 15 minutes **TOTAL TIME:** 30 minutes
MAKES: 4 main-dish servings

1	shallot, minced
2	tablespoons butter
2	tablespoons Dijon mustard with seeds
2	teaspoons chopped tarragon
½	cup panko (Japanese-style breadcrumbs)
4	medium skinless, boneless chicken breast halves (1¼ pounds)
¼	teaspoon salt

1. Preheat oven to 475°F.

2. In small microwave-safe bowl, place shallot and 2 teaspoons butter. Heat in microwave oven on High 1 minute to cook shallot slightly. Stir in mustard and tarragon.

3. In another small microwave-safe bowl, place remaining 4 teaspoons butter. Heat in microwave oven on High until melted, 15 to 20 seconds. Stir in panko until mixed.

4. Arrange chicken breasts in 15½" by 10½" jelly-roll pan; sprinkle with salt. Spread mustard mixture evenly over breasts; top with panko mixture, patting on gently. Bake in top third of oven until chicken loses pink color throughout, 12 to 15 minutes. (Instant-read thermometer inserted horizontally into center of breasts should register 165°F.)

EACH SERVING: About 270 calories, 35g protein, 7g carbohydrate, 10g total fat (5g saturated), 0g fiber, 107mg cholesterol, 383mg sodium

GRILLED CHICKEN & GREENS

Lighten up with seasonal watercress and asparagus, served with flash-grilled chicken breasts. The greens deliver antioxidants and fiber—and almost no calories. Hint: Once you've dressed the watercress, assemble and serve ASAP! Like other delicate greens, it starts to wilt as soon as you add the dressing.

TOTAL TIME: 30 minutes

MAKES: 4 main-dish servings

1 cup packed fresh mint leaves

1 to 2 lemons

2 garlic cloves, crushed with garlic press

1 tablespoon plus 2 teaspoons extra-virgin olive oil

¼ teaspoon plus pinch salt

¼ teaspoon plus pinch freshly ground black pepper

1 pound skinless, boneless chicken breast halves, pounded to even ⅓-inch thickness

1 pound asparagus, ends trimmed

1 pound radishes, trimmed and very thinly sliced

2 packages watercress (4 ounces each)

1. Preheat large grill pan or outdoor grill for direct grilling over medium-high heat.

2. Finely chop half of mint. From lemons, finely grate 1 teaspoon peel and squeeze 4 tablespoons juice. In 9-inch pie plate, combine chopped mint, lemon peel, 1 tablespoon lemon juice, half of garlic, 1 teaspoon oil, and ⅛ teaspoon each salt and pepper. Add chicken and rub with mint mixture to coat evenly.

3. On jelly-roll pan, toss asparagus with 1 teaspoon oil, pinch each salt and pepper, and remaining garlic. Grill, turning occasionally, 4 to 6 minutes or until charred in spots.

4. Meanwhile, in large bowl, toss radishes, watercress, and remaining mint, 3 tablespoons lemon juice, 1 tablespoon oil, and ⅛ teaspoon each salt and pepper. Divide among plates.

5. Place hot asparagus on top of greens. Place chicken on grill. Cook 2 to 3 minutes per side or until instant-read thermometer inserted horizontally into center of breast reaches 165°F. Divide hot chicken among plates with greens.

EACH SERVING: About 225 calories, 27g protein, 10g carbohydrate, 9g total fat (2g saturated), 5g fiber, 63mg cholesterol, 315mg sodium

SUMMER SQUASH AND CHICKEN

Toss these wholesome ingredients on the grill for a simple, satisfying summer meal.

ACTIVE TIME: 15 minutes **TOTAL TIME:** 25 minutes plus marinating

MAKES: 4 main-dish servings

1	lemon
1	tablespoon olive oil
½	teaspoon salt
¼	teaspoon coarsely ground black pepper
4	skinless, boneless chicken thighs (1¼ pounds)
4	medium yellow summer squash and/or zucchini (8 ounces each), cut lengthwise into 4 wedges
¼	cup snipped chives, for garnish

1. From lemon, grate 1 tablespoon peel and squeeze 3 tablespoons juice. In medium bowl, with wire whisk, whisk together lemon peel and juice, oil, salt, and pepper; transfer 2 tablespoons to cup and set aside.

2. Add chicken to bowl with lemon marinade; cover and let stand 15 minutes at room temperature or 30 minutes in the refrigerator.

3. Meanwhile, prepare grill for direct grilling over medium heat.

4. Discard chicken marinade. Place chicken and squash on hot grill rack. Cover and grill until chicken loses pink color throughout and squash is tender and browned, 10 to 12 minutes, turning each piece over once and removing pieces as they are done. (Instant-read thermometer inserted into thickest part of thighs should register 165°F.)

5. Transfer chicken and squash to cutting board. Cut chicken into 1-inch-wide strips; cut each squash wedge crosswise in half.

6. To serve, on large platter, toss squash with reserved lemon juice marinade, then toss with chicken and sprinkle with chives.

EACH SERVING: About 255 calories, 29g protein, 8g carbohydrate, 8g total fat (3g saturated), 3g fiber, 101mg cholesterol, 240mg sodium

CHICKEN THIGHS PROVENÇAL

The quintessentially Provençal combination of tomatoes, thyme, basil, fennel, and orange makes for sensational chicken.

ACTIVE TIME: 30 minutes **TOTAL TIME:** 1 hour 45 minutes

MAKES: 8 servings

2	pounds skinless, boneless chicken thighs, fat removed and cut into quarters
¾	teaspoon salt
3	teaspoons olive oil
2	red peppers, cut into ¼-inch-wide strips
1	yellow pepper, cut into ¼-inch-wide strips
1	jumbo onion (1 pound), thinly sliced
3	garlic cloves, crushed with garlic press
1	can (28 ounces) plum tomatoes
¼	teaspoon dried thyme
¼	teaspoon fennel seeds, crushed
3	strips (3" by 1" each) orange peel
½	cup loosely packed fresh basil leaves, chopped

1. Sprinkle chicken with ½ teaspoon salt. In nonreactive 5-quart Dutch oven, heat 1 teaspoon oil over medium-high heat until very hot. Add half of chicken and cook until golden brown, about 5 minutes per side. With tongs, transfer chicken pieces to bowl as they are browned. Repeat with 1 teaspoon oil and remaining chicken.

2. Reduce heat to medium. To drippings in Dutch oven, add remaining 1 teaspoon oil, red and yellow peppers, onion, and remaining ¼ teaspoon salt. Cook, stirring frequently, until vegetables are tender and lightly browned, about 20 minutes. Add garlic; cook 1 minute longer.

3. Return chicken to Dutch oven. Add tomatoes with their juice, thyme, fennel seeds, and orange peel; bring to a boil, breaking up tomatoes with side of spoon. Reduce heat; cover and simmer until chicken loses its pink color throughout, about 15 minutes.

4. Transfer to serving bowl and sprinkle with basil to serve.

EACH SERVING: About 204 calories, 24g protein, 12g carbohydrate, 7g total fat (1g saturated), 3g fiber, 94mg cholesterol, 480mg sodium

GRILLED MAPLE-GLAZED CHICKEN

This riff on grilled, soy-sauced teriyaki is still Asian-inspired, but there's pure maple syrup in the marinade—a flavor-enhancing switch.

ACTIVE TIME: 15 minutes **TOTAL TIME:** 30 minutes

MAKES: 4 main-dish servings

3	tablespoons pure maple syrup
2	tablespoons rice vinegar
1	tablespoon sugar
1	tablespoon lower-sodium soy sauce
1	teaspoon grated peeled fresh ginger
8	ounces French green beans (haricots verts) or regular green beans, trimmed
10	ounces frozen peas, thawed
1¼	pounds skinless, boneless chicken thighs
¼	cup fresh cilantro leaves

1. In 1-quart saucepan, whisk maple syrup, vinegar, sugar, soy sauce, and ginger; bring to a boil over medium-high heat. Boil 1 minute, or until reduced by half, whisking. Remove from heat; stir in ¼ teaspoon pepper. Cool slightly. Transfer 2 tablespoons to small bowl for brushing chicken.

2. Place beans and *3 tablespoons water* in 2-quart glass baking dish; cover with vented plastic wrap. Microwave on High 3 minutes or until tender. Stir in peas. Cover; microwave 3 minutes longer. Drain well; toss with 1 tablespoon sauce. Transfer to platter.

3. Heat grill pan over medium-high heat. Sprinkle chicken with ⅛ teaspoon salt. Grill chicken 4 minutes or until grill marks appear. Brush chicken with reserved 2 tablespoons sauce. Turn chicken over; grill 4 to 5 minutes longer or until cooked through (165°F). Place chicken on top of vegetables. Serve with remaining sauce and cilantro.

EACH SERVING: About 350 calories, 31g protein, 30g carbohydrate, 11g total fat (3g saturated), 5g fiber, 93mg cholesterol, 365mg sodium

COCONUT CHICKEN CURRY

Served over rice, this chicken curry's spice subtly builds, only to be soothed by the creamy touch of coconut milk. We chose light coconut milk to keep the fat in check.

ACTIVE TIME: 25 minutes **TOTAL TIME:** 45 minutes

MAKES: 6 main-dish servings

1	tablespoon canola oil
1½	pounds skinless, boneless chicken thighs, cut into 1½-inch chunks
¼	teaspoon plus sprinkle of salt
1	onion, sliced
1	red pepper, cut into ¾-inch chunks
2	tablespoons Thai green curry paste
2	teaspoons peeled, grated fresh ginger
1	cup reduced-sodium chicken broth
1	large sweet potato, peeled and cut into ¾-inch chunks
¾	cup light coconut milk
1	teaspoon cornstarch
2	cups sugar snap peas, trimmed
½	cup fresh cilantro leaves

White rice, for serving

1. In 6-quart Dutch oven, heat oil over medium-high heat. Add chicken; sprinkle with salt. Cook 5 minutes or until browned, stirring. Transfer chicken to bowl.

2. Add onion and red pepper to pot. Cook 3 minutes, stirring; stir in curry, ginger, and ¼ teaspoon salt. Add broth and potato. Bring to a boil over high heat. Cover; cook 5 minutes. Stir in chicken. Reduce heat to maintain simmer. Cover; cook 10 minutes or until chicken pieces are no longer pink at center (165°F) and vegetables are tender.

3. Whisk coconut milk and cornstarch until smooth; stir into pot along with peas. Bring to a boil over high heat. Cover; simmer over medium heat 3 minutes or until peas are hot. Serve, sprinkled with cilantro, over rice.

EACH SERVING (WITHOUT RICE): About 240 calories, 24g protein, 14g carbohydrate, 9g total fat (3g saturated), 3g fiber, 94mg cholesterol, 475mg sodium

CHICKEN THIGHS WITH PEAR AND CELERY SLAW

This pan-seared chicken dish pairs skinless, boneless thighs with a warm pear-and-celery slaw and can be prepared on the fly!

TOTAL TIME: 20 minutes

MAKES: 4 main-dish servings

1	teaspoon olive oil
1	pound skinless, boneless chicken thighs, cut into 1-inch-wide strips
½	teaspoon salt
¼	teaspoon freshly ground black pepper
2	medium Bartlett pears, not peeled
2	stalks celery
2	tablespoons fresh lemon juice
1	shallot, finely chopped
¾	cup apple cider
1	tablespoon Dijon mustard
1	tablespoon chopped fresh parsley leaves

1. In nonstick 12-inch skillet, heat oil over medium heat. Add chicken thighs to skillet and sprinkle with salt and pepper. Cook chicken, turning over once, 8 to 10 minutes, until instant-read thermometer inserted horizontally into thickest part of thigh reaches 165°F. Transfer chicken to warm plate.

2. Meanwhile, cut each pear lengthwise in half; discard core. Cut halves lengthwise into matchstick-thin strips. Thinly slice celery on the diagonal. In large bowl, toss pear and celery with lemon juice; set aside.

3. To same skillet, add shallot and cook, stirring constantly, until beginning to brown, 30 seconds to 1 minute. Add cider and bring to a boil over high heat; whisk in mustard. Pour warm dressing over pear mixture and toss to coat. Serve slaw with chicken. Sprinkle with parsley.

EACH SERVING: About 230 calories, 23g protein, 21g carbohydrate, 6g total fat (1g saturated), 3g fiber, 94mg cholesterol, 430mg sodium

QUICK CHICKEN MOLE

Our speedy mole, which coats rotisserie chicken, is a richly flavored sauce made with spices, nuts, and raisins. A crisp green salad—perhaps with avocado—would be a perfect complement.

TOTAL TIME: 25 minutes

MAKES: 4 main-dish servings

2	teaspoons olive oil
1	onion, chopped
2	garlic cloves, crushed with garlic press
2	teaspoons chili powder
2	teaspoons unsweetened cocoa powder
¼	teaspoon ground cinnamon
1¼	cups canned chicken broth
1	tablespoon creamy peanut butter
1	tablespoon tomato paste
¼	cup golden or dark seedless raisins
1	rotisserie chicken (2 to 2½ pounds), cut into 8 pieces, skin removed, if you like
¼	cup loosely packed fresh cilantro leaves, chopped
	Cooked brown or white rice (optional)
	Lime wedges, for serving

1. In nonstick 12-inch skillet, heat oil over medium heat until hot. Add onion and cook 5 minutes, stirring occasionally. Add garlic, chili powder, cocoa powder, and cinnamon; cook 1 minute, stirring constantly.

2. Stir in broth, peanut butter, and tomato paste. Add raisins; bring to a boil. Add chicken pieces to skillet. Reduce heat to medium-low; cover and simmer 8 to 10 minutes to blend flavors, turning chicken pieces over halfway through cooking to coat all sides with sauce.

3. Sprinkle chicken with cilantro. Serve chicken and sauce over rice, if you like. Garnish with lime wedges.

EACH SERVING (WITHOUT RICE): About 400 calories, 44g protein, 15g carbohydrate, 18g total fat (4g saturated), 3g fiber, 126mg cholesterol, 475mg sodium

CHICKEN-STUFFED SPUDS

This quick recipe takes advantage of the microwave and toaster oven to bake the potatoes, then spices things up with a zesty chicken filling. When you can't be home for dinner, it's a dish your family could easily reheat in the microwave and assemble themselves.

TOTAL TIME: 25 minutes

MAKES: 4 main-dish servings

4	baking potatoes, not peeled
1	tablespoon olive oil
1	bunch green onions, sliced (¼ cup), dark-green tops reserved
1	teaspoon fennel seeds
1	pound ground chicken
1	large red pepper, chopped
2	teaspoons Asian chili sauce (Sriracha)
½	teaspoon salt
¼	cup reduced-fat sour cream

1. Preheat toaster oven to 425°F. Pierce potatoes with fork and place on microwave-safe plate; microwave on High 14 to 16 minutes or until tender, turning once. Transfer to toaster oven; cook 5 to 7 minutes or until skin is crisp.

2. Meanwhile, in 12-inch nonstick skillet, heat oil over medium heat 1 minute. Add sliced green onions and fennel seeds; cook 2 minutes, stirring frequently. Add chicken, red pepper, chili sauce, and salt. Cook 8 minutes or until chicken loses pink color throughout, stirring occasionally.

3. To serve, cut a slit in each potato and fill with chicken mixture. Top with sour cream and green-onion tops.

EACH SERVING: About 405 calories, 30g protein, 60g carbohydrate, 6g total fat (2g saturated), 7g fiber, 71mg cholesterol, 445mg sodium

HEALTHY MAKEOVER "FRIED" CHICKEN

The crunchy coating is what seals in the juices, giving traditional Southern fried chicken its finger-licking flavor. Too bad it also absorbs so much fat. By stripping the bird of its skin, baking instead of frying, and ditching the batter for Japanese-style panko breadcrumbs, our crispy cheat carves off 240 calories and 22 grams of fat per serving.

ACTIVE TIME: 10 minutes **TOTAL TIME:** 45 minutes plus marinating

MAKES: 4 main-dish servings

1½ cups buttermilk
½ teaspoon cayenne (ground red) pepper
¾ teaspoon salt
1 (3-pound) cut-up chicken (8 pieces), skin removed from all pieces except wings
1½ cups panko (Japanese-style breadcrumbs)
1 teaspoon grated fresh lemon peel

1. In large zip-tight plastic bag, place buttermilk, cayenne pepper, and salt; add chicken pieces, turning to coat. Seal bag, pressing out excess air. Refrigerate chicken at least 1 hour or preferably overnight, turning bag over once.

2. Preheat oven to 425°F. Spray 15½″ by 10½″ jelly-roll pan with nonstick spray. In large bowl, combine panko and lemon peel.

3. Remove chicken from marinade, shaking off excess. Discard marinade. Add chicken pieces, a few at a time, to panko mixture, turning to coat. Place chicken in prepared pan.

4. Bake 30 to 35 minutes or until coating is crisp and juices run clear when thickest part of chicken is pierced with tip of knife. For browner coating, after chicken is cooked, turn oven to broil. Broil chicken 5 to 6 inches from source of heat, 1 to 2 minutes or until golden brown.

EACH SERVING: About 305 calories, 36g protein, 16g carbohydrate, 9g total fat (3g saturated), 1g fiber, 101mg cholesterol, 370mg sodium

LEANER MEATBALLS

Enjoy some of these tasty Italian-style meatballs with your favorite pasta and sauce, and freeze the rest. Let them cool in the pan on a wire rack, then transfer the meatballs to a jelly-roll pan and place in the freezer until frozen. Transfer them to large zip-tight plastic bags and freeze for up to one month.

ACTIVE TIME: 25 minutes **TOTAL TIME:** 40 minutes

MAKES: 24 meatballs

⅓   cup water
1½   cups fresh breadcrumbs (about 3 slices firm white bread)
1   pound lean ground beef
1   pound lean ground turkey meat
2   large egg whites
⅓   cup freshly grated Pecorino Romano or Parmesan cheese
3   tablespoons grated onion
2   tablespoons chopped fresh parsley
1   garlic clove, minced
1   teaspoon salt
¼   teaspoon coarsely ground black pepper

1. Preheat oven to 425°F. Line 15½″ by 10½″ jelly-roll pan with foil and lightly grease.

2. In large bowl, pour water over breadcrumbs. With hands, toss until bread is evenly moistened. Add ground beef, ground turkey, egg whites, grated cheese, onion, parsley, garlic, salt, and pepper; with hands, combine just until well blended but not overmixed.

3. Shape mixture into twenty-four 2-inch meatballs (for easier shaping, use slightly wet hands), handling meat as little as possible. Arrange meatballs in prepared pan and bake until lightly browned and cooked through, 15 to 20 minutes.

EACH MEATBALL: About 80 calories, 8g protein, 2g carbohydrate, 4g total fat (1g saturated), 0g fiber, 44mg cholesterol, 166mg sodium

LINGUINE WITH CARROT-TURKEY RAGU

Every forkful of this nutrient-packed pasta will turn back time: Lean ground turkey boosts collagen growth, and both the linguine's whole grains and the carrot curls' beta-carotene help keep your heart healthy. Cinnamon in the sauce adds savory depth of flavor and aids with inhibiting inflammation.

ACTIVE TIME: 20 minutes **TOTAL TIME:** 35 minutes

MAKES: 6 main-dish servings

- 1 tablespoon olive oil
- 1 large leek, white and light-green parts only, sliced and well-rinsed
- 2 stalks celery, finely chopped
- 2 garlic cloves, finely chopped
- 3/8 teaspoon salt
- 5/8 teaspoon freshly ground black pepper
- 1 pound lean (93%) ground turkey
- 1 teaspoon ground cinnamon
- 2 cans (14½ ounces each) no-salt-added diced tomatoes, including liquid
- 1 pound carrots
- 8 ounces whole-wheat linguine
- 1 tablespoon chopped fresh parsley

1. Bring a large pot of *salted water* to a boil over high heat.

2. In 12-inch skillet, heat oil over medium-high heat. Add leek, celery, garlic, and ⅛ teaspoon each salt and pepper. Cook 5 minutes, stirring occasionally.

3. Add turkey; cook, stirring and breaking into small pieces, 4 minutes or until meat loses pink color throughout. Stir in cinnamon; cook 2 minutes. Stir in tomatoes. Bring to a boil, then reduce heat and simmer 15 minutes, stirring.

4. Meanwhile, with vegetable peeler, shave carrots into thin ribbons (see Tip).

5. Cook pasta in *boiling salted water* as label directs. During last 1 minute of cooking, add carrots; cook along with pasta. Drain and return to pot. Add turkey ragu and remaining ¼ teaspoon salt and ½ teaspoon pepper. Stir gently until well mixed. Top with parsley.

EACH SERVING: About 335 calories, 23g protein, 46g carbohydrate, 8g total fat (2g saturated), 8g fiber, 43mg cholesterol, 325mg sodium

TIP

Carrots add crunch to this simmer-while-the-pasta-cooks sauce. A Y-style peeler makes short work of shaving ribbons from even the fattest carrots.

SWEET POTATO SHEPHERD'S PIE

Enjoy shepherd's pie Louisiana style—with collard greens, sweet potatoes, and Cajun spices. Swapping in ground turkey for beef and low-fat milk for heavy cream keeps it heart-smart.

ACTIVE TIME: 30 minutes **TOTAL TIME:** 1 hour 10 minutes
MAKES: 6 main-dish servings

2½ pounds sweet potatoes, not peeled
½ cup water
½ cup low-fat (1%) milk
½ teaspoon salt
¼ teaspoon ground black pepper
1 tablespoon plus 1 teaspoon canola oil
1 large onion (12 ounces), finely chopped
1 bunch (12 ounces) collard greens, stems discarded and leaves very thinly sliced
2 garlic cloves, chopped
1 pound lean (93%) ground turkey
2 teaspoons salt-free Cajun seasoning
2 tablespoons tomato paste
1 tablespoon finely chopped flat-leaf parsley leaves, for garnish

1. Preheat oven to 400°F.

2. In large microwave-safe bowl, combine sweet potatoes and ¼ cup water. Cover with vented plastic wrap and microwave on High 15 minutes or until tender. When cool enough to handle, discard peels. In large bowl, mash potatoes with milk and ⅛ teaspoon each salt and pepper.

3. Meanwhile, in 12-inch skillet, heat 1 tablespoon oil over medium-high heat. Add onion and cook 5 minutes or until browned, stirring occasionally. Add collard greens and ⅛ teaspoon each salt and pepper. Cook 1 minute or until just wilted, stirring. Transfer to medium bowl.

4. In same skillet, heat remaining teaspoon oil. Add garlic and cook 15 seconds. Add turkey and remaining ¼ teaspoon salt. Cook 3 minutes or until browned, breaking meat into small pieces and stirring. Reduce heat to medium and add Cajun seasoning. Cook 1 minute, stirring. Add tomato paste and remaining ¼ cup water. Cook 2 minutes, stirring.

5. In 8-inch square shallow baking dish, spread half of mashed sweet potatoes. Top with turkey mixture, then collard-greens mixture. Spread remaining sweet-potato mixture on top. Bake 30 minutes or until potatoes are golden on top. Garnish with parsley.

EACH SERVING: About 290 calories, 19g protein, 36g carbohydrate, 9g total fat (2g saturated), 7g fiber, 44mg cholesterol, 350mg sodium

HERB-GRILLED TURKEY CUTLETS

Super-lean turkey cutlets, seasoned with fresh herbs and served with fiber-rich bulgur and tomato salsa, deliver a flavorful meal that's light on fat, calories, and effort.

TOTAL TIME: 30 minutes

MAKES: 4 main-dish servings

1	lemon
1	large tomato, chopped
2	cups water
1	cup bulgur
¼	cup loosely packed fresh parsley leaves, chopped
⅜	teaspoon salt
⅜	teaspoon freshly ground black pepper
1	tablespoon chopped fresh oregano leaves
1	tablespoon chopped fresh mint leaves
2	teaspoons olive oil
1	pound turkey breast cutlets

1. Prepare outdoor grill for direct grilling over medium heat. From lemon, grate ¼ teaspoon peel and squeeze 2 tablespoons juice. In small bowl, stir together 1 tablespoon juice and tomato; set aside.

2. In 3-quart saucepan, bring water to a boil over high heat. Stir in bulgur and reduce heat to low; cover and simmer until all liquid has been absorbed, about 15 minutes. Stir in parsley, ⅛ teaspoon each salt and pepper, lemon peel, and remaining 1 tablespoon lemon juice.

3. Meanwhile, in small bowl, combine oregano, mint, and oil. Pat cutlets dry; rub with herb mixture on both sides. Sprinkle with remaining ¼ teaspoon each salt and pepper to season both sides. Grill turkey, turning over once, 3 to 4 minutes, or until instant-read thermometer inserted horizontally into cutlet reaches 165°F. Top turkey with tomato; serve with bulgur.

EACH SERVING: About 285 calories, 32g protein, 30g carbohydrate, 5g total fat (1g saturated), 7g fiber, 66mg cholesterol, 280mg sodium

TURKEY CUTLETS, INDIAN STYLE

A spicy yogurt marinade makes these cutlets tasty in a jiffy. Serve with a squeeze of fresh lime or, for a festive presentation, set out bowls of yogurt, store-bought mango chutney, fluffy basmati rice, and chopped fresh cilantro alongside the cutlets.

ACTIVE TIME: 15 minutes **TOTAL TIME:** 20 minutes

MAKES: 6 main-dish servings

2	large limes
1/3	cup plain low-fat yogurt
1	tablespoon vegetable oil
2	teaspoons peeled, minced fresh ginger
1	teaspoon ground cumin
1	teaspoon ground coriander
1	teaspoon salt
1	garlic clove, crushed with garlic press
1½	pounds turkey cutlets

1. Prepare outdoor grill for direct grilling over medium heat.

2. From 1 lime, grate 1 teaspoon peel and squeeze 1 tablespoon juice. Cut remaining lime into wedges; reserve.

3. In large bowl, mix lime peel, lime juice, yogurt, oil, ginger, cumin, coriander, salt, and garlic until blended.

4. Just before grilling, add turkey cutlets to bowl with yogurt mixture; stir to coat. (Do not let cutlets marinate in yogurt mixture; their texture will become mealy.)

5. Grill cutlets until they just lose their pink color throughout, 5 to 7 minutes. (Instant-read thermometer inserted horizontally into cutlet should reach 165°F.) Serve with lime wedges.

EACH SERVING: About 160 calories, 29g protein, 3g carbohydrate, 3g total fat (1g saturated), 0g fiber, 71mg cholesterol, 450mg sodium

SOUTHWESTERN TURKEY FAJITAS

Broiling the tomatillos adds a subtle smokiness to this luscious salsa. Drizzle it over your fajitas; serve any extra with tortilla chips. When you use mixed seasonings, such as the fajita seasoning we call for here, choose low-sodium mixes and add salt to taste if necessary.

ACTIVE TIME: 20 minutes **TOTAL TIME:** 50 minutes
MAKES: 6 main-dish servings

TOMATILLO SALSA

- 1   pound tomatillos, husked and rinsed
- 1   small poblano chile, cut in half, stems and seeds discarded
- 1   small shallot, chopped
- 3   tablespoons fresh lime juice
- ¾   teaspoon salt
- ¾   teaspoon sugar
- ⅓   cup packed fresh cilantro leaves, chopped

TURKEY AND ONION FAJITAS

- 2   whole turkey breast tenderloins (1¾ pounds)
- 2   tablespoons low-sodium fajita seasoning
- 4   teaspoons olive oil
- 3   large onions (12 ounces each), cut into ½-inch-thick slices
- 12   (6-inch) corn tortillas

Cilantro sprigs and red chiles, for garnish

1. Make salsa: Set oven rack 5 to 6 inches from heat source and preheat broiler. Place tomatillos in broiling pan without rack and broil 10 minutes, turning over once, until blistering and blackened in spots. When turning tomatillos, add poblano, skin side up, to pan and broil 5 to 6 minutes or until charred.

2. In blender or food processor with knife blade attached, pulse tomatillos, poblano, shallot, lime juice, salt, and sugar until chopped. Stir in cilantro. Cover and refrigerate salsa up to 3 days if not serving right away. Makes about 2 cups.

3. Prepare fajitas: Prepare outdoor grill for direct grilling over medium-high heat heat or preheat grill pan. In medium bowl, toss turkey with fajita seasoning and 2 teaspoons oil. Brush onion slices with remaining 2 teaspoons oil.

4. Place turkey and onions on hot grill rack. Cook turkey 15 to 20 minutes, turning over once, until instant-read thermometer inserted into center of tenderloin reaches 170°F. Cook onions 12 to 15 minutes, until tender and golden, turning over once.

5. While turkey is cooking, place several tortillas on same grill and heat just until lightly browned, removing to sheet of foil as they brown. Wrap tortillas in foil and keep warm.

6. To assemble fajitas: Transfer onions to bowl. Transfer turkey to cutting board and thinly slice. Top tortillas with equal amounts of turkey and onion; spoon some salsa on each; garnish with cilantro and red chiles, and fold over to eat with your hands. Serve any remaining onions and salsa alongside.

EACH SERVING WITHOUT SALSA: About 350 calories, 36g protein, 35g carbohydrate, 7g total fat (1g saturated), 5g fiber, 88mg cholesterol, 440mg sodium

---

EACH 1-TABLESPOON SERVING SALSA: About 10 calories, 0g protein, 2g carbohydrate, 0g total fat, 0g fiber, 0mg cholesterol, 55mg sodium

HEART-SMART INGREDIENT: ONIONS

When we think about the nutritional value of different ingredients, it's easy to overlook the onion. One cup of chopped onion is high in the mineral chromium, which is important to the regulation of your body's blood-sugar levels. It's also a good source of vitamin C and dietary fiber.

TURKEY THIGHS OSSO BUCO STYLE

Cooked in a manner usually reserved for veal shanks, turkey thighs—a much leaner choice—make an excellent stew. Serve with soft polenta or rice pilaf.

ACTIVE TIME: 20 minutes **TOTAL TIME:** 1 hour 50 minutes

MAKES: 4 main-dish servings

¼	teaspoon salt
¼	teaspoon ground black pepper
2	turkey thighs (1¼ pounds each), skin removed
2	teaspoons vegetable oil
2	onions, finely chopped
4	carrots, peeled and cut into ¾-inch pieces
2	stalks celery, cut into ½-inch pieces
4	garlic cloves, finely chopped
1	can (14½ ounces) tomatoes in puree
½	cup dry red wine
1	bay leaf
¼	teaspoon dried thyme

1. Preheat oven to 350°F. Sprinkle salt and pepper on turkey. In nonreactive 5-quart Dutch oven, heat oil over medium-high heat until very hot. Add 1 turkey thigh and cook, turning occasionally, until golden brown, about 5 minutes. With tongs, transfer thigh to plate; repeat with second thigh. Discard all but 1 tablespoon fat from Dutch oven.

2. Reduce heat to medium. Add onions and cook, stirring occasionally, 5 minutes. Add carrots, celery, and garlic; cook, stirring frequently, 2 minutes longer.

3. Stir in tomatoes with puree, wine, bay leaf, and thyme, breaking up tomatoes with side of spoon; bring to a boil. Add browned turkey; cover and place in oven. Bake until turkey is tender, about 1 hour 30 minutes. Discard bay leaf. Remove turkey meat from bones and cut into bite-size pieces; return meat to Dutch oven and stir well.

EACH SERVING: About 325 calories, 36g protein, 24g carbohydrate, 9g total fat (3g saturated), 0g fiber, 122mg cholesterol, 480mg sodium

WATERCRESS AND PEACH SALAD WITH TURKEY

The addition of deli turkey transforms this fresh and colorful summer salad into a meal.

TOTAL TIME: 20 minutes plus marinating

MAKES: 4 main-dish servings

2 to 3 limes

½ teaspoon Dijon mustard

2 tablespoons olive oil

½ teaspoon salt

¼ teaspoon coarsely ground black pepper

4 ripe large peaches (2 pounds), peeled, pitted, and cut into wedges

2 bunches watercress (7 to 8 ounces each), tough stems discarded

8 ounces sliced deli turkey, cut crosswise into ¼-inch strips

1. From limes, grate ½ teaspoon peel and squeeze 3 tablespoons juice.

2. In medium bowl, with wire whisk, mix ¼ teaspoon lime peel and 2 tablespoons lime juice with mustard, 1 tablespoon oil, ¼ teaspoon salt, and ⅛ teaspoon pepper. Gently stir in peaches; let stand 15 minutes.

3. Just before serving, in large bowl, toss watercress and turkey with remaining ¼ teaspoon lime peel, 1 tablespoon lime juice, 1 tablespoon oil, ¼ teaspoon salt, and ⅛ teaspoon pepper. Transfer watercress mixture to platter; top with peach mixture.

EACH SERVING: About 205 calories, 20g protein, 17g carbohydrate, 7g total fat (1g saturated), 3g fiber, 47mg cholesterol, 360mg sodium

SEARED DUCK BREAST WITH DRIED CHERRIES AND PORT

If you can only find the larger duck breasts, which weigh in at 12 to 13 ounces each, buy two of them and cook them on medium-low 20 minutes, skin side down; turn them over and continue cooking 4 minutes longer. To serve, slice the breasts as in step 4, but give each diner the slices from half a breast.

ACTIVE TIME: 15 minutes **TOTAL TIME:** 35 minutes

MAKES: 4 main-dish servings

4	boneless fresh or frozen (thawed) duck breast halves with skin (6 ounces each)
¼	teaspoon salt
⅛	teaspoon coarsely ground black pepper
1	large shallot, thinly sliced
1	clove garlic, crushed with garlic press
1	cup port wine
2	tablespoons balsamic vinegar
⅓	cup dried cherries

1. Pat duck breasts dry with paper towels. With sharp knife, cut 4 diagonal slashes, about ¼-inch deep, in skin and fat on each breast half. On sheet of waxed paper, evenly season duck breasts on both sides with salt and pepper.

2. In nonstick 12-inch skillet, cook breasts, skin side down, over medium heat 15 minutes or until skin is well browned and crispy. As breasts cook, spoon off and discard fat in skillet. Turn breasts over and cook on flesh side about 4 minutes for medium-rare or until desired doneness. Transfer breasts to cutting board; cover with foil to keep warm until ready to serve.

3. Discard all but 1 teaspoon duck fat remaining in skillet. Add shallot and cook over medium heat 2 to 3 minutes or until beginning to brown. Stir in garlic and cook, 1 minute. Add port wine, balsamic vinegar, and cherries; bring to a boil. Boil 3 minutes or until sauce is reduced to ¾ cup, stirring frequently.

4. To serve, thinly slice each breast and transfer to a dinner plate. Spoon port sauce over breasts.

EACH SERVING: About 315 calories, 28g protein, 19g carbohydrate, 13g total fat (4g saturated), 1g fiber, 155mg cholesterol, 245mg sodium

ROSEMARY ROAST TURKEY BREAST

When a whole turkey is too much, use just the breast. It will make white-meat fans very happy.

ACTIVE TIME: 20 minutes
TOTAL TIME: 2 hours, 50 minutes
MAKES: 10 main-dish servings

1   bone-in turkey breast (6 to 7 pounds)
1 ½ teaspoons dried rosemary, crumbled
1   teaspoon salt
¾   teaspoon coarsely ground black pepper
1   cup chicken broth

1. Preheat oven to 350°F. Rinse turkey breast with cold running water and drain well; pat dry with paper towels In cup, combine rosemary, salt, and pepper. Rub rosemary mixture on both inside and outside of turkey breast.

2. Place turkey, skin side up, on rack in small roasting pan (13″ by 9″). Tent loosely with foil. Roast turkey 1 hour 30 minutes. Remove foil; roast, occasionally basting with pan drippings, 45 to 60 minutes longer. Start checking for doneness during last 30 minutes of cooking. Turkey breast is done when temperature on meat thermometer inserted into thickest part of breast (not touching bone) reaches 170°F and juices run clear when thickest part of breast is pierced with tip of knife.

3. Transfer turkey to warm platter. Let stand 15 minutes to set juices for easier carving.

4. Meanwhile, pour broth into drippings in hot roasting pan; bring to a boil, stirring until browned bits are loosened from bottom of pan. Strain pan-juice mixture through sieve into 1-quart saucepan; let stand 1 minute. Skim and discard fat. Heat pan-juice mixture over medium heat until hot; serve with turkey. Remove skin before eating.

EACH SERVING WITHOUT SKIN AND PAN JUICES: About 251 calories, 55g protein, 0g carbohydrate, 2g total fat (0g saturated), 0g fiber, 152mg cholesterol, 428mg sodium

Chicken-Fried Steak (page 296)

6 | LEAN RED MEAT

If you're trying to cut back on red meat to lower your family's intake of saturated fat, you're not alone. The good news: You don't have to completely eliminate beef, pork, or even lamb (unless your doctor suggests it). Simply serve small portions of lean cuts like flank steak and pork tenderloin, and explore low-fat cooking methods, including grilling and roasting. Here, we've provided lots of recipes for lean but flavorful meaty mains—most of them rounded out with wholesome veggies or grains or served as part of a salad. So fire up your grill or preheat that oven: It's time to enjoy a little meat.

If you or your spouse love to sink your teeth into a nice steak or chop, our Beef Eye Round au Jus, served with new potatoes and carrots, or Grilled Pork Chops with Mango Sauce will allow you to indulge. Or heat up a skillet and stir-fry skinny slices of beef or pork with mixed veggies; Five-Spice Pork with Gingered Vegetables is a winner.

We also offer low-maintenance roasts and slow-cooker meals that make it a cinch to get a heart-healthy home-cooked dinner on the table. Pork loin recipes like Pork Roast with Salsa Verde and slow-cooked Cuban-Style Beef are famously easy on the cook and oh-so-good. Pasta with meat sauce is not off limits, either: By swapping in whole-wheat pasta and lean ground beef, you can dig into penne topped with a zesty beef and picadillo sauce. Or, for an even more heart-smart option, consider combining the lean ground beef with ground turkey or chicken (see "The Ground Roundup" on page 307 for details).

SOY-SCALLION FLANK STEAK

A marinade of Asian ingredients amps up the flavor of lean grilled steak. Pair with Grilled Vegetables with Thai Pesto (page 382).

ACTIVE TIME: 15 minutes **TOTAL TIME:** 35 minutes plus marinating

MAKES: 8 main-dish servings

⅓ cup soy sauce

3 garlic cloves, crushed with garlic press

2 tablespoons peeled, grated fresh ginger

2 tablespoons rice vinegar

1 tablespoon Asian sesame oil

1 tablespoon sugar

½ teaspoon cayenne (ground red) pepper

1 bunch green onions

2½ pounds beef flank steak

2 tablespoons hot water

1. In medium bowl, whisk soy sauce, garlic, ginger, vinegar, oil, sugar, and cayenne until sugar dissolves. Reserve 2 tablespoons marinade; cover and set aside. Transfer remaining marinade to large zip-tight plastic bag.

2. Thinly slice green onions; reserve ¼ cup for garnish. Add steak and remaining green onions to bag, turning to coat. Seal bag, pressing out excess air. Place bag on plate and refrigerate 2 hours or overnight, turning over several times.

3. Prepare outdoor grill for direct grilling over medium heat. Remove steak from marinade, scraping off excess solids, and place on hot grill grate. Discard marinade in bag. Cover grill and cook steak 12 to 14 minutes for medium-rare or until desired doneness, turning over once. Let steak stand 10 minutes to set juices for easier slicing.

4. In small bowl, combine hot water with reserved marinade; drizzle over steak to serve and sprinkle with reserved green onion.

EACH SERVING: About 260 calories, 34g protein, 1g carbohydrate, 12g total fat (5g saturated), 0g fiber, 60mg cholesterol, 315mg sodium

HEALTHY MAKEOVER BEEF AND PEPPER STIR-FRY

A Chinese restaurant favorite gets a makeover: Lean top round steak stays tender when flash-fried in a hot skillet, while tomatoes add a flavor twist (and extra antioxidants) to the traditional veggie combo. Instant brown rice cooks in ten minutes and delivers the fiber missing from white rice.

TOTAL TIME: 30 minutes

MAKES: 4 main-dish servings

1   cup instant short-grain brown rice (see Box)
12   ounces beef top round steak, thinly sliced across the grain
1   tablespoon plus 1 teaspoon reduced-sodium soy sauce
1   teaspoon sugar
½   teaspoon freshly ground black pepper
2   teaspoons vegetable oil
3   peppers (preferably red, yellow, and orange), thinly sliced
2   garlic cloves, crushed with garlic press
2   ripe tomatoes, cored and cut into ½-inch wedges

1. Prepare brown rice as label directs.

2. In bowl, combine beef, 1 teaspoon soy sauce, ½ teaspoon sugar, and ¼ teaspoon black pepper.

3. In 12-inch skillet, heat 1 teaspoon oil over medium-high heat. Add beef in single layer. Cook, without stirring, 1 minute. Transfer to plate; return skillet to medium-high heat without cleaning.

4. Add remaining 1 teaspoon oil to skillet. Add peppers and garlic; stir-fry 4 to 5 minutes, until tender-crisp. Add tomatoes and remaining ½ teaspoon sugar. Cook, stirring, 3 to 4 minutes, until saucy. Return beef to skillet; add remaining ¼ teaspoon black pepper and 1 tablespoon soy sauce. Cook 1 minute, stirring. Serve over rice.

EACH SERVING: About 285 calories, 26g protein, 28g carbohydrate, 16g total fat (5g saturated), 3g fiber, 59mg cholesterol, 305mg sodium

HEART-SMART INGREDIENT:
INSTANT BROWN RICE

We all know how healthy brown rice is, but it takes a lot longer to cook than white rice. The solution? Instant brown rice: It cooks in just ten minutes, and there's no appreciable difference in its nutritional profile from that of regular brown rice. Both are considered whole grains, and both are good sources of fiber, manganese (a mineral that helps produce energy), magnesium (which helps build bones), and selenium (key to a healthy immune system). So, enjoy instant brown rice as the base for the stir-fry opposite and in other healthy-in-a-hurry meals.

LONDON BROIL WITH GARLIC AND HERBS

Round steak, not the most tender of cuts, benefits from a quick marinade of vinegar, garlic, and oregano.

ACTIVE TIME: 10 minutes **TOTAL TIME:** 25 minutes plus marinating and standing

MAKES: 6 main-dish servings

- 2   tablespoons red wine vinegar
- 1   tablespoon olive oil
- 2   garlic cloves, crushed with garlic press
- ¾   teaspoon dried oregano
- ¾   teaspoon salt
- ½   teaspoon ground pepper
- 1   beef top round steak, 1-inch thick (1½ pounds)

1. Prepare outdoor grill for direct grilling over medium heat. In large resealable plastic bag, mix vinegar, oil, garlic, oregano, salt, and pepper. Add steak, turning to coat. Seal bag, pressing out excess air. Place bag on plate and marinate 15 minutes at room temperature.

2. Remove steak from marinade; discard marinade. Place steak on hot grill rack. Grill 7 to 8 minutes per side for medium-rare or to desired doneness. (Instant-read thermometer inserted horizontally into center of steak should register 145°F.)

3. Transfer steak to platter. Let stand 10 minutes to set juices for easier slicing. To serve, thinly slice steak across the grain.

EACH SERVING: About 200 calories, 26g protein, 1g carbohydrate, 10g total fat (3g saturated), 0g fiber, 72mg cholesterol, 340mg sodium

FILET MIGNON WITH ROQUEFORT

We switched the traditional rib-eye steak for a lean filet mignon and cooked it in only 2 teaspoons olive oil. The Roquefort cheese topping is so luxuriously flavorful that just a tablespoon per serving is enough.

ACTIVE TIME: 5 minutes **TOTAL TIME:** 15 minutes
MAKES: 4 main-dish servings

2   teaspoons olive oil
4   beef tenderloin steaks (1-inch thick), trimmed of fat (4 ounces each)
½   teaspoon salt
¼   teaspoon coarsely ground black pepper
1   ounce Roquefort cheese, crumbled (¼ cup)

1. In 12-inch skillet, heat oil over high heat until hot. On waxed paper, evenly season steaks, on both sides, with salt and pepper.

2. Add steaks to skillet and cook 10 minutes for medium-rare or until desired doneness, turning over once. Transfer steaks to 4 dinner plates; top with Roquefort.

EACH SERVING: About 205 calories, 25g protein, 0g carbohydrate, 11g total fat (4g saturated), 0g fiber, 63mg cholesterol, 470mg sodium

COOK'S TIP:
STEAK SUCCESS

The easiest way to check the doneness of steak is to cut into its center. You can also use the "touch test." The longer a steak cooks, the firmer the meat becomes as its juices evaporate. Press the steak in the center. If the steak is somewhat soft, it is medium-rare. If it bounces back slightly, the steak is medium. If firm, the steak is well-done.

ANGEL-HAIR BEEF SALAD, INDOCHINE

This healthy one-dish dinner was created by Ellie Mathews, finalist in the main-dish category of our second Cook Your Heart Out contest.

ACTIVE TIME: 35 minutes **TOTAL TIME:** 45 minutes

MAKES: 4 main-dish servings

1	teaspoon canola oil
1	pound (¾-inch thick) boneless top sirloin, trimmed of excess fat
8	ounces angel hair pasta
4	cups chiffonade of Napa cabbage or romaine lettuce
1	carrot, grated or shaved into curls
6	tablespoons chopped unsalted peanuts
4	lime slices or wedges, for serving
6	cherry tomatoes, halved, for serving

ASIAN PESTO

2	green onions, including 3 to 4 inches of green tops
1	garlic clove
½	cup packed fresh Thai basil leaves
1	cup packed fresh cilantro leaves
2	tablespoons fresh lime juice
1	tablespoon Asian fish sauce
1½	tablespoons toasted sesame oil
⅛	teaspoon Chinese five-spice powder
1½	teaspoons sugar
¼	teaspoon Asian chili sauce (Sriracha)

1. Make pesto: In container of small food processor, combine all ingredients up to and including chili sauce. Blend to smooth paste and set aside.

2. Heat large covered pot of *water* to a boil over high heat. Meanwhile, in large skillet, heat canola oil over medium-high, tilting pan to coat bottom. Cook steak in skillet for 8 to 10 minutes for medium-rare, or until desired doneness, turning over once. (Instant-read thermometer inserted horizontally into center of steak should reach 145°F.) Transfer steak to cutting board; let stand 10 minutes.

3. Cook pasta as label directs, drain, and return to pan. Add pesto and toss thoroughly. Thinly slice steak on a diagonal across the grain. Top a bed of cabbage on each serving plate with pasta, steak, and carrots. Garnish with chopped peanuts, lime wedges, cherry tomatoes, and serve.

EACH SERVING: About 500 calories, 32g protein, 53g carbohydrate, 19g total fat (4g saturated), 4g fiber, 57mg cholesterol, 429mg sodium

THAI BEEF SALAD

This hearty salad makes a great one-dish meal.

ACTIVE TIME: 30 minutes   **TOTAL TIME:** 40 minutes plus marinating

MAKES: 4 main-dish servings

2 tablespoons sugar-free Asian fish sauce
Zero-calorie sweetener (1 tablespoon equivalent)
1 beef round-top steak, ¾-inch thick (1 pound)
2 limes
3 tablespoons vegetable oil
¼ teaspoon crushed red pepper
¼ teaspoon coarsely ground black pepper
2 bunches watercress, tough stems discarded
1 cup loosely packed fresh mint leaves
1 cup loosely packed fresh cilantro leaves
1 bunch radishes, cut in half and thinly sliced
½ small red onion, thinly sliced

1. In 8- or 9-inch square glass baking dish, stir 1 tablespoon fish sauce and half of sweetener. Add steak, turning to coat; marinate 15 minutes at room temperature or 1 hour in refrigerator, turning occasionally.

2. Prepare outdoor grill for direct grilling over medium heat.

3. Meanwhile, from limes, with vegetable peeler, remove peel in 2" by ¾" strips. With sharp knife, cut enough peel crosswise into matchstick-thin strips to equal 1 tablespoon. Squeeze limes to equal 3 tablespoons juice. In small bowl, whisk lime juice, oil, crushed red pepper, black pepper, and the remaining 1 tablespoon fish sauce and half of sweetener until blended.

4. In large bowl, toss watercress, mint, cilantro, radishes, onion, and lime peel; cover and refrigerate until ready to serve.

5. Place steak on hot grill rack. Cover grill and cook steak 10 to 15 minutes or to desired doneness, turning over once. (Instant-read thermometer inserted horizontally into center of steak should register 145°F.) Transfer steak to cutting board; let stand 10 minutes. Cut steak diagonally into thin strips.

6. Add steak and dressing to watercress mixture and toss until well coated.

EACH SERVING: About 310 calories, 28g protein, 7g carbohydrate, 23g total fat (4g saturated), 2g fiber, 73mg cholesterol, 295mg sodium

SEARED STEAK WITH MINTED WATERMELON

Inspired by an enticing Chinese flavor combination, this dish is packed with watermelon, cucumber, and mint—a cool contrast to savory grilled steak. A bed of rice noodles soaks up the luscious juices.

ACTIVE TIME: 25 minutes **TOTAL TIME:** 30 minutes plus standing

MAKES: 4 main-dish servings

8	ounces thin rice noodles
1	pound boneless beef sirloin steak (1-inch thick)
¼	teaspoon salt
¼	teaspoon freshly ground black pepper
1	shallot, finely chopped
1	stalk lemongrass, yellow and pale-green part only, finely chopped (see Tip)
1	teaspoon sugar
¼	cup fresh lime juice
1	tablespoon reduced-sodium fish sauce
½	small watermelon, rind removed and cut into ½-inch cubes (3 cups)
½	seedless (English) cucumber, cut in half and thinly sliced
½	cup packed fresh mint leaves, finely chopped

1. Prepare outdoor grill for covered direct grilling over medium heat.

2. Prepare noodles as label directs. Drain, rinse under cold water, and drain again.

3. Season steak with salt and pepper. Place on hot grill; cover. Cook 12 to 13 minutes for medium-rare or until desired doneness, turning over once. (Instant-read thermometer should reach 145°F.) Transfer steak to cutting board; let rest 10 minutes.

TIP

Prized for its sour-lemon flavor and fragrance, lemongrass has a scallionlike base and long, thin gray-green leaves. If you can't find it at your grocery store, visit an Asian market.

4. Meanwhile, in large bowl, stir together shallot, lemongrass, sugar, lime juice, and fish sauce until sugar dissolves.

5. Thinly slice steak across the grain. Add to bowl, along with watermelon, cucumber, and mint. Toss gently until well mixed. Divide noodles among serving plates. Top with steak mixture and accumulated juices.

EACH SERVING: About 430 calories, 26g protein, 64g carbohydrate, 8g total fat (3g saturated), 2g fiber, 75mg cholesterol, 435mg sodium

CHICKEN-FRIED STEAK

Whole-wheat flour, reduced-fat milk, and canola oil (instead of lard or bacon fat) make this version of a Southern favorite just a little bit healthier. For photo, see page 284. Try pairing it with our Kale Salad with Glazed Onions and Cheddar (page 356).

ACTIVE TIME: 30 minutes **TOTAL TIME:** 35 minutes

MAKES: 4 main-dish servings

1	cup white whole-wheat or regular whole-wheat flour
½	teaspoon cayenne (ground red) pepper
⅝	teaspoon salt
1	teaspoon ground black pepper
1	large egg white
1	cup plus 2 tablespoons reduced-fat (2%) milk
4	sandwich-cut beef steaks, each ¼-inch thick (1 pound)
5	tablespoons canola oil

1. On plate, combine flour, cayenne, and ½ teaspoon each salt and black pepper. Set 2 tablespoons of mixture aside.

2. In shallow dish, beat egg white and 2 tablespoons milk until frothy.

3. Dip 1 steak in flour mixture; shake off excess, then dip in egg mixture and let excess drip off. Dip in flour mixture again until coated; transfer to waxed-paper-lined plate. Repeat with remaining steaks.

4. In 12-inch skillet, heat 4 tablespoons oil over medium-high heat until shimmering. Shake excess flour off 1 steak; carefully add to hot oil. Cook 2 to 4 minutes, until golden brown on both sides, turning over once. Transfer to paper towels. Reheat oil; add another steak. Repeat until all steaks are cooked. (Instant-read thermometer inserted horizontally into center of steak should reach 145°F.) Pour off and discard cooking oil; wipe out skillet.

5. In skillet, heat remaining 1 tablespoon oil over medium-low heat. Whisk in reserved flour mixture. Cook 1 minute or until fragrant, whisking. Gradually whisk in remaining 1 cup milk. Bring to a boil over medium heat, then cook 2 minutes or until thickened, whisking. Whisk in remaining ⅛ teaspoon salt and ½ teaspoon black pepper. Serve sauce with steaks.

EACH SERVING: About 405 calories, 34g protein, 20g carbohydrate, 21g total fat (5g saturated), 2g fiber, 88mg cholesterol, 395mg sodium

BEEF EYE ROUND AU JUS

Julienned carrots and leeks are roasted in red wine along with the beef. For the tenderest results, do not cook this cut to more than medium-rare. Serve with a side of Oven Fries (page 401) or Sautéed Spinach with Garlic and Lemon (page 386).

ACTIVE TIME: 30 minutes **TOTAL TIME:** 1 hour 40 minutes plus standing

MAKES: 12 main-dish servings

1½ teaspoons salt
½ teaspoon dried thyme
¼ teaspoon ground black pepper
1 beef eye round roast (4½ pounds), trimmed
2 tablespoons olive oil
1 pound carrots, peeled and cut into 2" by ¼" matchstick strips
1 pound leeks (3 medium), white and light-green parts only, well washed and cut into 2" by ¼" matchstick strips
4 garlic cloves, thinly sliced
1¼ cups dry red wine
½ cup water
1 bay leaf

1. Preheat oven to 450°F. In small bowl, combine salt, thyme, and pepper; use to rub on roast. In 10-inch skillet, heat oil over medium-high heat until very hot. Add beef and cook until browned on all sides, about 10 minutes. Transfer beef to nonreactive medium roasting pan (14" by 10").

2. Add carrots, leeks, and garlic to skillet and cook, stirring occasionally, until carrots are tender, about 7 minutes. Arrange vegetable mixture around beef.

3. Roast beef 25 minutes. Add wine, water, and bay leaf to roasting pan. Reduce oven temperature to 325°F and continue roasting until instant-read thermometer inserted in center of roast reaches 140°F, about 45 minutes longer. Internal temperature of meat will rise to 145°F (medium) upon standing. Remove and discard bay leaf.

4. When roast is done, transfer to warm large platter and let stand 15 minutes to set juices. Cut roast into thin slices and serve with vegetables.

EACH SERVING: About 230 calories, 33g protein, 6g carbohydrate, 8g total fat (2g saturated), 1g fiber, 76mg cholesterol, 358mg sodium

HEALTHY MAKEOVER BEEF BURGUNDY

We dropped the bacon—a classic ingredient in a French beef stew—but couldn't bear to trade juicy beef chuck for tougher round, even though chuck is a bit fattier. Instead, we added lots more vegetables, like fresh mushrooms, carrots, and frozen peas, to stretch the meat and ramp up the nutritional value.

ACTIVE TIME: 45 minutes **TOTAL TIME:** 2 hours 15 minutes

MAKES: 8 main-dish servings

1	tablespoon olive oil
2	pounds boneless beef chuck, trimmed of fat and cut into 1½-inch chunks
3	large carrots, peeled and cut into 1-inch pieces
3	garlic cloves, crushed with side of chef's knife
1	large onion (12 ounces), cut into 1-inch pieces
2	tablespoons all-purpose flour
2	tablespoons tomato paste
¾	teaspoon salt
½	teaspoon coarsely ground black pepper
2	cups dry red wine
4	sprigs fresh thyme
2	packages (10 ounces each) mushrooms, halved
1	bag (16 ounces) frozen peas

1. In 5- to 6-quart Dutch oven, heat oil over medium-high heat until hot. Pat beef dry with paper towels. Add beef, in two batches, and cook 5 to 6 minutes per batch, until well browned on all sides. With slotted spoon, transfer beef to medium bowl. Preheat oven to 325°F.

2. To drippings in Dutch oven, add carrots, garlic, and onion, and cook 10 minutes or until vegetables are browned and tender, stirring occasionally. Stir in flour, tomato paste, salt, and pepper; cook 1 minute, stirring. Add wine and bring to a boil, stirring until browned bits are loosened from bottom of Dutch oven.

3. Return meat and any meat juices in bowl to Dutch oven. Add thyme and mushrooms; bring to a boil. Cover and bake 1½ hours or until meat is fork-tender, stirring once. Discard thyme sprigs. Just before stew is done, cook peas as label directs. Stir in peas.

EACH SERVING: About 330 calories, 32g protein, 26g carbohydrate, 11g total fat (3g saturated), 7g fiber, 52mg cholesterol, 475mg sodium

BRISKET WITH MUSHROOMS

Humble beef brisket becomes a company dish when combined with a heady blend of fresh and dried mushrooms and served with a rich red wine sauce.

ACTIVE TIME: 1 hour **TOTAL TIME:** 4 hours
MAKES: 10 main-dish servings

¾	cup boiling water
½	ounce dried porcini mushrooms (½ cup)
8	ounces small shiitake mushrooms, stems removed
8	ounces white mushrooms, trimmed
¼	cup vegetable oil
1	fresh beef brisket (4 pounds), well trimmed
4	medium red onions, sliced
2	garlic cloves, sliced
3	tablespoons all-purpose flour
1	can (14½ ounces) beef broth
1	cup dry red wine
¼	cup brandy
4	large fresh sage leaves
1	bay leaf
1½	teaspoons fresh thyme
½	teaspoon salt
¼	teaspoon coarsely ground black pepper
¼	cup chopped fresh parsley

1. In small bowl, pour boiling water over porcini mushrooms; let stand 30 minutes.

2. With slotted spoon, remove porcini, reserving mushroom liquid. Strain liquid through sieve lined with paper towels; set aside. Rinse mushrooms to remove any grit, then chop.

3. Preheat oven to 325°F. In 8-quart Dutch oven, heat oil over medium-high heat until very hot. Add brisket and cook until browned, about 10 minutes. Transfer brisket to platter; set aside. Add onions to Dutch oven and cook over medium heat, stirring occasionally, until lightly browned, about 15 minutes. Stir in garlic and cook 30 seconds. Stir in flour and cook, stirring until golden brown, about 2 minutes.

4. Return brisket to Dutch oven. Stir in porcini mushrooms, mushroom liquid, shiitake and white mushrooms, broth, wine, brandy, sage leaves, bay leaf, thyme, salt, pepper, and 2 tablespoons parsley. Bring to a boil over high heat. Cover and place in oven. Bake until brisket is tender, about 2 hours 30 minutes.

5. Transfer meat from Dutch oven to warm platter; let stand 15 minutes. Skim and discard fat from liquid in Dutch oven. Discard sage leaves and bay leaf. Bring liquid in pot to a boil over high heat. Reduce heat to medium; cook, uncovered, until thickened, about 15 minutes.

6. Slice brisket thinly across the grain. Stir remaining 2 tablespoons parsley into brisket liquid. Spoon some over meat; pass remaining liquid separately.

EACH SERVING: About 278 calories, 40g protein, 10g carbohydrate, 11g total fat (3g saturated), 2g fiber, 112mg cholesterol, 369mg sodium

COOK'S TIP: COOKING BEEF

To cook a tender piece of beef, it's best to match the cut of meat to the right cooking technique.

Broiling, grilling, and panfrying: Choose porterhouse steak, T-bone steak, London broil (top round), top loin, rib-eye, sirloin steak, tenderloin, flank steak, skirt steak, cube steak, minute steak, and ground beef.

Braising and stewing: Choose chuck roast, brisket, short ribs, shin (shank cross cuts), and oxtails. Cubes for stew are usually cut from boneless chuck or bottom round, but chuck gives the moistest results. Bone-in cuts add flavor and body to stews.

Roasting: Choose standing rib roast, tenderloin, rib-eye, eye round, and tri-tip.

BRACIOLE WITH GRAPE TOMATOES

Braciole, an Italian rolled roast, is traditionally simmered slowly in tomato sauce. This recipe uses a quicker method: roasting the beef at high heat alongside tiny sweet grape tomatoes.

ACTIVE TIME: 15 minutes **TOTAL TIME:** 40 minutes plus standing

MAKES: 8 main-dish servings

½	cup Italian-style breadcrumbs
1	garlic clove, crushed with garlic press
¼	cup finely grated Pecorino Romano cheese
½	cup packed fresh flat-leaf parsley leaves, finely chopped
4	teaspoons olive oil
½	teaspoon ground black pepper
¼	teaspoon salt
1	beef flank steak (1¾ to 2 pounds)
2	pints grape tomatoes

1. Preheat oven to 475°F. In small bowl, combine breadcrumbs, garlic, Pecorino, parsley, 1 tablespoon oil, and ¼ teaspoon pepper.

2. On large sheet of waxed paper, with flat side of meat mallet or heavy skillet, pound steak to even ½-inch thickness. Spread crumb mixture over steak in even layer; press into meat. Starting at one long side, roll steak into cylinder about 2½ inches in diameter, to enclose filling. (Some breadcrumbs may spill out.) With butcher's twine or kitchen string, tie roll tightly at 1-inch intervals. Place roll in center of 18″ by 12″ jelly-roll pan. Rub salt and remaining 1 teaspoon oil and ¼ teaspoon pepper all over steak. Scatter tomatoes around steak.

3. Roast 25 to 27 minutes, until instant-read thermometer inserted into thickest part of roll reaches 130°F. Let steak stand in pan 10 minutes to set juices for easier slicing. Remove and discard twine; cut roll crosswise into ½-inch-thick slices. Transfer meat and tomatoes with their juices to serving platter.

EACH SERVING: About 255 calories, 22g protein, 10g carbohydrate, 14g total fat (5g saturated), 1g fiber, 54mg cholesterol, 290mg sodium

CUBAN-STYLE BEEF

Boneless beef chuck roast is slow-cooked with onions, bell peppers, crushed tomatoes, and spices, then shredded and tossed with pimiento-stuffed olives. Serve over rice, if you like.

ACTIVE TIME: 30 minutes **SLOW-COOK TIME:** 10 hours on Low
MAKES: 12 main-dish servings

1	boneless beef chuck roast (4 pounds), tied
1	teaspoon dried oregano
1	teaspoon ground cumin
1	teaspoon salt
½	teaspoon ground black pepper
2	teaspoons vegetable oil
1	large onion (12 ounces), sliced
1	large green pepper (10 ounces), sliced
1	large red pepper (10 ounces), sliced
2	garlic cloves, chopped
2	tablespoons water
1	can (28 ounces) crushed tomatoes
½	cup pimiento-stuffed green olives, sliced

Fresh parsley leaves, for garnish (optional)

1. Rub roast with oregano, cumin, and ½ teaspoon each salt and pepper. In 12-inch skillet, heat oil over medium-high heat until very hot. Brown roast on all sides. Transfer to 6- to 7-quart slow-cooker bowl.

2. To skillet, add onion, green and red peppers, garlic, water, and ¼ teaspoon salt; cook over medium-high heat, stirring, 2 to 4 minutes, until slightly softened. Add tomatoes. Simmer 4 minutes, stirring. Transfer vegetables and liquids to slow-cooker bowl.

3. Cover and cook, following manufacturer's instructions, for 10 hours on Low or until roast is tender.

4. Shred meat, discarding fat and gristle. With slotted spoon, transfer vegetables to large serving bowl. Stir in meat, olives, and remaining ¼ teaspoon salt. Garnish with parsley, if desired.

EACH SERVING: About 245 calories, 33g protein, 9g carbohydrate, 8g total fat (3g saturated), 2g fiber, 96mg cholesterol, 435mg sodium

STUFFED TOMATOES WITH LEAN GROUND BEEF

Make a meal from garden-fresh tomatoes and the traditional flavors of Greece: mint, cinnamon, and a crumble of feta cheese.

ACTIVE TIME: 25 minutes **TOTAL TIME:** 1 hour

MAKES: 6 main-dish servings

½   cup quick-cooking (10-minute) brown rice
1   tablespoon olive oil
1   medium onion (6 to 8 ounces), chopped
1¼ pounds lean (90%) ground beef
⅓   cup loosely packed fresh mint leaves, chopped, plus sprigs for garnish
½   teaspoon ground cinnamon
¼   teaspoon salt
¼   teaspoon ground black pepper
6   large tomatoes (10 ounces each)
½   cup crumbled feta cheese (2 ounces)
¼   cup panko (Japanese-style breadcrumbs)

1. Preheat oven to 425°F. In 3-quart saucepan, cook rice as label directs.

2. Meanwhile, in nonstick 12-inch skillet, heat oil over medium heat, 1 minute. Add onion, and cook 10 to 12 minutes or until lightly browned and tender. Stir in ground beef, half of chopped mint, cinnamon, salt, and pepper. Cook 5 to 6 minutes or until beef loses its pink color throughout, breaking up meat with spatula and stirring occasionally. Stir in remaining chopped mint.

3. While ground beef cooks, cut each tomato horizontally in half. With melon baller or spoon, scoop out tomato pulp; place in large bowl. Remove 1 cup tomato pulp from bowl and chop. Discard remaining pulp or save for another use. Return chopped pulp to bowl. Add rice, feta cheese, and beef mixture; stir until well blended.

4. In 15 ½" by 10 ½" jelly-roll pan, place hollowed-out tomato halves, cut sides up. Mound scant ½ cup beef filling in each tomato half; sprinkle with panko. Bake tomatoes 25 to 30 minutes or until crumbs are browned and filling is heated through. Garnish with mint sprigs.

EACH SERVING: About 270 calories, 26g protein, 21g carbohydrate, 10g total fat (3g saturated), 4g fiber, 50mg cholesterol, 285mg sodium

GLAZED MEAT LOAF

Adding ground turkey and oats to the traditional beef base makes this meat loaf lighter and healthier—but it's just as hearty and comforting as any old-fashioned recipe. This is great with Light Mashed Potatoes (page 399) and some roasted Brussels sprouts.

ACTIVE TIME: 35 minutes
TOTAL TIME: 1 hour 20 minutes

MAKES: 8 main-dish servings

1	cup quick-cooking oats, uncooked
½	cup nonfat (skim) milk
1	onion, finely chopped
2	pinches salt
1	large red pepper (10 ounces), finely chopped
3	garlic cloves, crushed with garlic press
2	teaspoons reduced-sodium soy sauce
¼	cup plus 2 tablespoons ketchup
1	pound lean (93%) ground beef sirloin
1	pound ground turkey breast
3	carrots, peeled and grated
2	tablespoons spicy brown mustard
¼	teaspoon ground black pepper

1. Preheat oven to 400°F. Line jelly-roll pan with foil; lightly coat with nonstick cooking spray. In medium bowl, stir together oats and milk until combined.

2. Coat bottom of 12-inch skillet with nonstick cooking spray; heat over medium heat. Add onion and pinch salt; cook 2 to 4 minutes, until onion softens, stirring occasionally. Add red pepper and garlic; cook 4 to 6 minutes, until pepper softens, stirring often. Transfer to medium bowl; refrigerate to cool.

3. Meanwhile, in small bowl, whisk together soy sauce and ¼ cup ketchup. Set aside.

4. In large bowl, with hands, combine beef, turkey, carrots, oat mixture, cooled vegetable mixture, mustard, remaining 2 tablespoons ketchup, remaining pinch salt, and pepper until well mixed.

5. Form mixture into 8″ by 4″ loaf on prepared pan. Brush top and sides with soy ketchup. Bake 45 to 50 minutes, until instant-read thermometer inserted in center registers 165°F.

EACH SERVING: About 240 calories, 25g protein, 17g carbohydrate, 8g total fat (3g saturated), 3g fiber, 65mg cholesterol, 360mg sodium

NUTRITIONAL NOTES:
THE GROUND ROUNDUP

Whether you're making meat loaf, burgers, or a ragu sauce, how do you choose which ground meat to use? The flavor profiles and nutritional values below provide some guidance. The meats with the lowest saturated fat are, of course, the most heart-healthy options; consider mixing a little ground beef or pork into ground turkey or chicken for added flavor.

MEAT	FLAVOR PROFILE	APPROXIMATE NUTRITIONAL VALUES	COOK-TO INTERNAL TEMPERATURE
Ground beef, chuck (80% lean)	Juicy, rich, bold, robust, hearty	307 calories, 20g fat (8g saturated), 103mg cholesterol	160°F (medium doneness)
Ground lamb	Unique, full flavored, firm texture, aromatic	321 calories, 22g fat (9g saturated), 102mg cholesterol	160°F (medium doneness)
Ground pork	Delicate, mild, good alternative to beef and poultry	336 calories, 24g fat (9g saturated), 107mg cholesterol	160°F (medium doneness)
Ground chicken	Lean, light texture, tender, subtle flavor, excellent choice for add-ins and toppings	172 calories, 11g fat (3g saturated), 65mg cholesterol	170°F (well-done)
Ground turkey	Moist, delicate flavor, denser texture than chicken	213 calories, 12g fat (3g saturated), 113mg cholesterol	170°F (well-done)

*Per 4-ounce cooked burger. Values vary among brands.

PENNE RIGATE WITH SWEET-AND-SPICY PICADILLO SAUCE

We've given this pasta a Spanish twist, with a meat sauce similar to the filling you might find in empanadas. Whole-wheat penne boosts the fiber, while lean ground beef and reduced-sodium tomatoes create a heart-healthier sauce.

ACTIVE TIME: 10 minutes **TOTAL TIME:** 25 minutes

MAKES: 6 main-dish servings

1   pound whole-wheat penne rigate, bow ties (farfalle), or radiatore
2   teaspoons olive oil
1   small onion, finely chopped
2   garlic cloves, crushed with garlic press
¼   teaspoon ground cinnamon
⅛ to ¼ teaspoon cayenne (ground red) pepper
¾   pound lean (90%) ground beef
½   teaspoon salt plus additional to taste
1   can (14¼ ounces) reduced-sodium tomatoes in puree
½   cup dark seedless raisins
¼   cup salad olives or chopped pimiento-stuffed olives, drained
Chopped fresh parsley, for garnish

1. Cook pasta in *boiling salted water* as package label directs.

2. Meanwhile, in nonstick 12-inch skillet, heat oil over medium heat until hot. Add onion and cook, stirring frequently, until tender, about 5 minutes. Stir in garlic, cinnamon, and cayenne; cook 30 seconds. Add beef and ½ teaspoon salt; cook, stirring frequently, until beef begins to brown, about 8 minutes. Spoon off any excess fat as necessary. Stir in tomatoes with their puree, raisins, and olives, breaking up tomatoes with side of spoon, and cook until sauce thickens slightly, about 5 minutes longer.

3. When pasta has reached desired doneness, set aside *1 cup pasta cooking water.* Drain pasta and return to saucepot. Add beef mixture and reserved cooking water; toss well to coat pasta. Season with salt to taste. Garnish with parsley to serve.

EACH SERVING: About 450 calories, 22g protein, 67g carbohydrate, 12g total fat (3g saturated), 9g fiber, 37mg cholesterol, 175mg sodium

VEAL AND MUSHROOM STEW

In this recipe, the veal is slowly simmered with mushrooms and a touch of Marsala wine until tender. Peas are added for their subtle sweetness and color.

ACTIVE TIME: 30 minutes **TOTAL TIME:** 1 hour 30 minutes

MAKES: 6 main-dish servings

1½	pounds boneless veal shoulder, cut into 1½-inch pieces
¾	teaspoon salt
¼	teaspoon ground black pepper
3	tablespoons vegetable oil
1	pound white mushrooms, trimmed and cut in half
4	ounces shiitake mushrooms, stems removed
½	cup water
⅓	cup dry Marsala wine
1	package (10 ounces) frozen peas, thawed

1. Preheat oven to 350°F. Pat veal dry with paper towels. Sprinkle veal with salt and pepper. In nonreactive 5-quart Dutch oven, heat 2 tablespoons oil over medium-high heat until very hot. Add half of veal and cook until browned, using slotted spoon to transfer meat to bowl as it browns. Repeat with remaining veal (without additional oil).

2. In Dutch oven, heat remaining 1 tablespoon oil over medium-high heat. Add mushrooms and cook, stirring occasionally, until lightly browned.

3. Return veal to Dutch oven; stir in water and Marsala, stirring until browned bits are loosened from bottom of pan. Heat veal mixture to a boil.

4. Cover Dutch oven and bake, stirring occasionally, until veal is tender, 60 to 75 minutes. Stir in peas and heat through.

EACH SERVING: About 249 calories, 26g protein, 12g carbohydrate, 11g total fat (2g saturated), 3g fiber, 94mg cholesterol, 448mg sodium

VEAL SCALOPPINE MARSALA

Elegant and scrumptious, this quintessential Italian dish is quick and easy to prepare. The purpose of pounding the cutlets is twofold: to tenderize the meat and to ensure even cooking. The bonus: A single pound of veal stretches to feed six people. Try pairing this with our Potato Gratin with Broccoli (page 398).

TOTAL TIME: 25 minutes

MAKES: 6 main-dish servings

1	pound veal cutlets
¼	cup all-purpose flour
¼	teaspoon salt
⅛	teaspoon coarsely ground black pepper
3	tablespoons butter
½	cup dry Marsala wine
½	cup chicken broth
1	tablespoon chopped fresh parsley

1. With meat mallet, pound cutlets to even ⅛-inch thickness. Cut veal into roughly 3-inch squares. On waxed paper, combine flour, salt, and pepper; use to coat both sides of veal pieces, shaking off excess.

2. In nonstick 10-inch skillet, melt butter over medium heat. Cook veal in batches until lightly browned, 45 to 60 seconds per side, using slotted spatula to transfer pieces to warm platter as they are browned; keep warm.

3. Stir Marsala and broth into veal drippings in pan; cook until syrupy, 4 to 5 minutes, stirring until browned bits are loosened from bottom of skillet. Pour sauce over veal and sprinkle with fresh parsley.

EACH SERVING: About 180 calories, 17g protein, 5g carbohydrate, 7g total fat (4g saturated), 0g fiber, 75mg cholesterol, 288mg sodium

COOK'S TIP: POUNDING CUTLETS

For even cooking, it's a good idea to pound veal, turkey, or chicken cutlets to a uniform thickness. Here's how: Place one piece of veal or other cutlet between two sheets of plastic wrap. With a meat mallet, rolling pin, or heavy skillet, pound three or four times until the cutlet is ¼-inch thick, or whatever thickness is specified in the recipe.

GRILLED PORK CHOPS WITH MANGO SAUCE

A smoky, but still sweet, mango sauce adds brilliant, sunny color and a kick of flavor to these simply grilled pork chops.

ACTIVE TIME: 20 minutes **TOTAL TIME:** 35 minutes

MAKES: 4 main-dish servings

1	tablespoon vegetable oil
1	small onion, finely chopped
1	chipotle chile in adobo, seeded using tip of paring knife, and finely chopped
¼	teaspoon dried oregano
2	large ripe mangoes, peeled and chopped
2	tablespoons water
1	tablespoon packed brown sugar
4	bone-in, ¾-inch-thick pork loin or rib chops (6 ounces each)
¼	teaspoon salt
½	teaspoon freshly ground black pepper
1	green onion, thinly sliced, for garnish
¼	cup fresh cilantro leaves, for garnish

1. Prepare outdoor grill for covered direct grilling over medium heat.

2. In 12-inch skillet, heat oil over medium-high heat. Add onion and cook 2 to 3 minutes, until browned, stirring occasionally. Add chipotle and oregano; cook 1 minute, stirring. Add mangoes, water, and sugar; cook 10 minutes or until mangoes are soft, stirring occasionally.

3. Meanwhile, sprinkle pork with salt and pepper to season both sides. Grill, covered, 8 to 9 minutes, until browned outside and still slightly pink inside, turning over once. (Instant-read thermometer inserted horizontally into center of pork should reach 145°F.)

4. Transfer pork chops to cutting board; let rest 5 minutes.

5. Spoon mango sauce over pork. Garnish with green onion and cilantro.

EACH SERVING: About 385 calories, 27g protein, 39g carbohydrate, 15g total fat (4g saturated), 4g fiber, 80mg cholesterol, 210mg sodium

BALSAMIC-GLAZED PORK CHOPS

Balsamic vinegar is very versatile; it's not just for salad dressing. Here it's turned into a sweet-tart sauce just made for tender pork.

TOTAL TIME: 35 minutes

MAKES: 4 main-dish servings

8	boneless pork loin chops, ½-inch thick (3 ounces each), trimmed
½	teaspoon salt
¼	teaspoon ground black pepper
1	tablespoon olive oil
3	tablespoons finely chopped shallot or onion
⅓	cup balsamic vinegar
¼	cup packed brown sugar

1. Pat pork dry with paper towels. Sprinkle chops with salt and pepper. In 12-inch skillet, heat oil over medium-high heat until hot. Cook pork 4 minutes on one side; turn and cook 3 minutes on second side. Transfer pork to platter; keep warm.

2. Increase heat to high. Stir shallot into pan juices; cook 1 minute. Stir in vinegar and sugar and cook 1 minute longer. Pour sauce over pork.

EACH SERVING: About 275 calories, 28g protein, 15g carbohydrate, 11g total fat (3g saturated), 0g fiber, 76mg cholesterol, 364mg sodium

GRILLED PORK AND APPLE SALAD

This main-dish salad will make the transition with you from summer into fall. Apples give the dish a touch of sweetness—take advantage of the season and use the best apples you can find.

ACTIVE TIME: 15 minutes **TOTAL TIME:** 35 minutes

MAKES: 4 main-dish servings

8	ounces green beans, trimmed (3½ cups)
2	pounds crisp, mild apples such as Gala (about 4), cored and cut into eighths
3	teaspoons maple syrup
2	teaspoons plus 1 tablespoon olive oil
1	pork tenderloin (1 pound)
⅜	teaspoon salt
⅜	teaspoon freshly ground black pepper
1	romaine lettuce heart (6 ounces)
2	tablespoons balsamic vinegar
1	teaspoon Dijon mustard
6	ounces baby spinach

1. Prepare outdoor grill for covered direct grilling over medium heat.

2. Place green beans on 16" by 12" sheet of heavy-duty foil. Fold in half; crimp foil edges to create sealed packet. Toss apples with 1 teaspoon each maple syrup and oil. Rub 1 teaspoon oil all over pork, then sprinkle with ¼ teaspoon each salt and pepper.

3. Place bean packet, apples, and pork on grill; cover. Grill apples 8 minutes, turning over once. Transfer apples to large bowl; cool. Grill beans 10 minutes. Transfer packet to plate; open and let cool. Grill pork 15 minutes or until instant-read thermometer inserted into center of pork registers 145°F, turning occasionally. Transfer to cutting board; let rest 10 minutes.

4. Chop lettuce. In very large bowl, whisk vinegar, mustard, remaining 1 tablespoon oil, 2 teaspoons syrup, and ⅛ teaspoon each salt and pepper. Add spinach, lettuce, beans, and apples; toss well. Thinly slice pork across grain. Serve with salad.

EACH SERVING: About 375 calories, 28g protein, 40g carbohydrate, 13g total fat (3g saturated), 8g fiber, 78mg cholesterol, 380mg sodium

SPICE-BRINE PORK LOIN

Brining pork in a blend of kosher salt, sugar, and spices infuses it with flavor and keeps it tender and juicy. Allow the pork to soak in the brine for 18 to 24 hours before roasting. Serve with a side of sautéed garlicky greens or broccoli.

ACTIVE TIME: 20 minutes **TOTAL TIME:** 1 hour 20 minutes plus brining and standing
MAKES: 12 main-dish servings

2	cups cold water
¼	cup kosher salt
2	tablespoons coriander seeds
2	tablespoons cracked black pepper
2	tablespoons fennel seeds
2	tablespoons cumin seeds
	Peel from 1 navel orange, pith removed
3	cups ice
1	boneless pork loin (3 pounds), trimmed
4	garlic cloves, crushed with side of chef's knife

1. In 2-quart saucepan, bring 1 cup water, salt, coriander, pepper, fennel, cumin, and orange peel to a boil over high heat. Reduce heat to low; simmer 2 minutes. Remove saucepan from heat; stir in ice until almost melted. Stir in remaining 1 cup water.

2. Place pork with garlic in large resealable plastic bag with brine. Seal bag, pressing out excess air. Place bag in bowl or small roasting pan and refrigerate 18 to 24 hours.

3. Preheat oven to 400°F. Remove pork from bag; discard brine (it's okay if some spices stick to pork). Place pork on rack in medium roasting pan (14" by 10"). Roast until thermometer inserted into thickest part of meat reaches 145°F, 60 to 75 minutes (temperature will rise 5°F to 10°F upon standing). Transfer pork to cutting board and let stand 10 minutes to set juices for easier slicing.

EACH SERVING: About 175 calories, 24g protein, 1g carbohydrate, 8g total fat (3g saturated), 0g fiber, 67mg cholesterol, 445mg sodium

PORK LOIN WITH LEMON AND CORIANDER

Brining the pork loin allows you a lot of leeway in how far ahead you start your recipe—anywhere from 18 to 48 hours. For the best flavor and texture, do not leave the meat in the brine longer than that.

ACTIVE TIME: 20 minutes **TOTAL TIME:** 1 hour 20 minutes plus brining and standing
MAKES: 16 main-dish servings

3   lemons
½   cup kosher salt
½   cup sugar
3   tablespoons coriander seeds
3   tablespoons cracked black peppercorns
3   cloves garlic, crushed with side of chef's knife
3   cups water
4   cups ice cubes
1   boneless pork loin roast (5 pounds), trimmed of fat
Cilantro sprigs, for garnish

1. Prepare brine: From 2 lemons, with vegetable peeler, remove peel in ¾-inch-wide strips. In 4-quart saucepan, bring lemon peel, salt, sugar, coriander, pepper, garlic, and 2 cups water to a boil on high heat. Reduce heat to medium-low and simmer 3 minutes, stirring to make sure salt and sugar dissolve. Remove saucepan from heat, add ice cubes, and stir until ice cubes almost melt; stir in remaining 1 cup water.

2. Place pork in very large (2- to 2½-gallon) zip-tight plastic bag with brine and seal, pressing out excess air. (If necessary, cut pork loin crosswise in half and use one or two 1-gallon bags.) Place bag in bowl, making sure that pork is completely covered with brine, and refrigerate at least 18 or up to 48 hours.

3. When ready to cook pork, preheat oven to 400°F. Remove pork from brine and place fat side up on rack in large roasting pan (17″ by 11½″). Strain brine through sieve, discarding liquid. Press spices from sieve onto top of pork; discard lemon peel and garlic.

4. Roast pork 55 to 65 minutes (pork loin will vary in length and thickness, which can affect cooking time; begin to check the internal temperature at 50 minutes) or until instant-read thermometer reaches 150°F (internal temperature will rise 5°F to 10°F upon standing). Transfer pork to large platter; cover and set aside at least 10 minutes to allow juices to set for easier slicing. Cut remaining lemon into wedges; use to garnish platter along with cilantro sprigs.

EACH SERVING: About 200 calories, 27g protein, 2g carbohydrate, 9g total fat (3g saturated), 1g fiber, 76mg cholesterol, 425mg sodium

COOK'S TIP: COOKING PORK

Since pork is usually tender, many cuts are perfectly suitable for these cooking methods.

Broiling, grilling, panfrying, and stir-frying: Many lean cuts lend themselves to these methods. Best Bets: Tenderloin, loin, rib and loin chops, sirloin chops and cutlets, blade chops, and sausages. Spareribs are good broiled or grilled if first precooked.

Braising and stewing: Many cuts of pork stand up well to long, slow cooking in liquid. Best Bets: Sirloin chops, blade chops, shoulder, spareribs, and pork cubes for stew.

Roasting: Use tender cuts from the loin. Best Bets: Rib crown roast, shoulder arm roast, arm picnic roast, fresh ham, whole boneless tenderloin, bone-in and boneless loin, spareribs, and country-style ribs.

CARAWAY-BRINED PORK LOIN

Brining meat in an aromatic mixture of spices, sugar, and salt ensures succulence. For the best flavor, allow the pork to soak in the brine for 24 hours. Green Beans with Mixed Mushrooms (page 385) would make a good side.

ACTIVE TIME: 20 minutes **TOTAL TIME:** 1 hour 20 minutes plus chilling and brining
MAKES: 24 main-dish servings

8½ cups cold water
½   cup packed light brown sugar
½   cup kosher salt
¼   cup caraway seeds, crushed
¼   cup coriander seeds, cracked
3   tablespoons cracked black pepper
Strips of peel from 2 lemons, pith removed
2   garlic cloves, crushed with side of chef's knife
2   boneless pork-loin roasts (2 pounds each), trimmed

1. In 1-quart saucepan, bring 1 cup water, sugar, salt, caraway, coriander, pepper, and lemon peel to a boil over high heat. Reduce heat to low; simmer 2 minutes. Transfer mixture to large bowl; stir in garlic and 7 cups cold water. Refrigerate 1 hour or freeze 30 minutes, until brine is cool.

2. Place pork roasts with brine in jumbo resealable plastic bag. Seal bag, pressing out excess air. Place bag in large bowl or roasting pan and refrigerate pork 18 to 24 hours.

3. When ready to cook, preheat oven to 400°F. Remove pork from bag; discard brine (it's okay if some seeds stick to meat). Place pork on rack set in large roasting pan (17″ by 11½″). Roast until meat thermometer inserted in thickest part of pork reaches 155°F, 1 hour to 1 hour 15 minutes. Transfer pork to cutting board and let stand 10 minutes to set juices for easier slicing. Internal temperature of meat will rise to 160°F during this time.

4. Meanwhile, remove rack from roasting pan. Add remaining ½ cup water to pan and bring to a boil over medium-high heat, stirring until browned bits are loosened from bottom of pan, 2 minutes. Pour pan drippings through sieve into small bowl. Let stand until fat separates from pan juices; skim and discard fat. Spoon pan juices over sliced meat.

EACH SERVING: About 205 calories, 22g protein, 1g carbohydrate, 12g total fat (4g saturated), 0g fiber, 68mg cholesterol, 345mg sodium

FIVE-SPICE PORK WITH GINGERED VEGETABLES

In this simple meal, gingery veggies and bulgur pair perfectly with lean pork medallions seasoned with five-spice powder.

ACTIVE TIME: 15 minutes
TOTAL TIME: 25 minutes

MAKES: 4 main-dish servings

1½ cups bulgur

1 tablespoon plus 1 teaspoon canola oil

¾ teaspoon five-spice powder

⅜ teaspoon salt

1 pork tenderloin (1 pound), cut into 1-inch medallions

5 carrots, peeled and very thinly sliced at an angle

8 ounces stringless snap peas

1 tablespoon peeled, grated fresh ginger

¼ cup water plus additional if necessary

1. Prepare bulgur as label directs.

2. Meanwhile, in 12-inch skillet, heat oil over medium-high heat. Sprinkle ½ teaspoon five-spice powder and ¼ teaspoon salt on pork medallions to season all sides. Add medallions to hot oil in single layer. Cook, turning over once, 6 to 7 minutes, until instant-read thermometer inserted horizontally into pork medallion reaches 145°F. Transfer to plate.

3. To same skillet, add carrots, peas, ginger, ¼ cup water, and remaining ¼ teaspoon five-spice powder and ⅛ teaspoon salt. Cook, stirring, 2 minutes or until carrots are just tender, adding 1 tablespoon water if pan seems too dry. Serve vegetables over bulgur with pork.

EACH SERVING: About 405 calories, 32g protein, 53g carbohydrate, 8g total fat (1g saturated), 13g fiber, 74mg cholesterol, 345mg sodium

HOISIN PORK TENDERLOIN WITH GRILLED PINEAPPLE

When choosing a pineapple, pick one that is slightly soft with a deep, sweet fragrance. Pineapples are harvested ripe and will not get any sweeter with time.

ACTIVE TIME: 10 minutes **TOTAL TIME:** 30 minutes

MAKES: 4 main-dish servings

¼	cup hoisin sauce
1	tablespoon honey
1	tablespoon grated, peeled fresh ginger
1	teaspoon Asian sesame oil
1	pork tenderloin (1½ pounds), trimmed
½	medium pineapple
2	tablespoons brown sugar

1. Prepare outdoor grill for covered direct grilling over medium heat. In small bowl, combine hoisin sauce, honey, ginger, and sesame oil.

2. Place pork on hot grill rack over medium heat. Cover grill and cook pork, turning occasionally, until an instant-read thermometer inserted in thickest part of tenderloin registers 155°F, 18 to 20 minutes. Pork will be browned on the outside and still slightly pink in the center.

3. Meanwhile, with serrated knife, cut pineapple half into 4 wedges. Rub cut sides of pineapple with brown sugar.

4. Grill pineapple on rack with pork until browned on both sides, about 5 minutes, turning over once. While pineapple is grilling, brush pork with hoisin-honey glaze and turn frequently.

5. Transfer pork to cutting board; let stand 5 minutes to allow juices to set for easier slicing. Transfer pineapple to platter. Thinly slice pork and serve with pineapple wedges.

EACH SERVING: About 275 calories, 31g protein, 23g carbohydrate, 6g total fat (2g saturated), 2g fiber, 92mg cholesterol, 245mg sodium

PORK TENDERLOIN WITH ROASTED GRAPES

If you've never had roasted grapes, try this recipe. They are absolutely delicious and a perfect match for the pork.

ACTIVE TIME: 15 minutes **TOTAL TIME:** 30 minutes
MAKES: 4 main-dish servings

1	teaspoon fennel seeds, crushed
½	teaspoon salt
½	teaspoon coarsely ground black pepper
1	pork tenderloin (1 pound)
2	teaspoons extra-virgin olive oil
3	cups seedless red and green grapes (about 1 pound)
½	cup canned or homemade chicken broth

1. Preheat oven to 475°F. In cup, with fork, stir fennel seeds, salt, and pepper. Rub mixture all over pork.

2. In 12-inch skillet with oven-safe handle, heat oil over medium-high heat until very hot. Add pork and cook 5 minutes, turning to brown all sides.

3. Add grapes and broth to skillet; bring to a boil. Cover and place in oven. Roast until instant-read thermometer inserted in center of roast reaches 150°F, 15 to 18 minutes. Internal temperature of meat will rise to 160°F upon standing. Transfer pork to warm platter.

4. Meanwhile, bring grape mixture to a boil over high heat; boil until liquid has thickened slightly, about 1 minute. Slice pork; serve with grapes and pan juices.

EACH SERVING: About 245 calories, 25g protein, 22g carbohydrate, 7g total fat (2g saturated), 2g fiber, 74mg cholesterol, 475mg sodium

PORK MEDALLIONS WITH ASPARAGUS SALAD

Herbed tenderloin is served atop a seasonal, fiber-rich salad.

ACTIVE TIME: 20 minutes **TOTAL TIME:** 40 minutes

MAKES: 4 main-dish servings

½   cup packed fresh flat-leaf parsley, finely chopped
1   tablespoon fresh rosemary, finely chopped
1   pork tenderloin (12 ounces)
2   large carrots, peeled
1   pound asparagus, ends trimmed
¼   teaspoon salt
¼   teaspoon freshly ground black pepper
1   teaspoon plus 1 tablespoon extra-virgin olive oil
1   bunch radishes, trimmed and cut into thin wedges
1   green onion, thinly sliced
1   package (5 ounces) baby greens and herbs mix
¼   cup balsamic vinegar

1. Preheat oven to 400°F. Bring large saucepot of water to a boil over high heat.

2. Rub 2 tablespoons parsley and rosemary on pork; let stand while oven heats.

3. Add carrots to boiling water. Cook 5 minutes. With tongs, transfer to a bowl of *ice water*. When cool, remove to cutting board. Add asparagus to boiling water. Cook 3 minutes. Transfer with tongs to ice water. When cool, drain well.

4. Sprinkle ⅛ teaspoon each salt and pepper over pork. In ovenproof 12-inch skillet, heat 1 teaspoon oil on medium-high heat. Add pork; cook 6 to 8 minutes, browning on all sides. Transfer to oven. Roast 8 to 10 minutes or until instant-read thermometer inserted in thickest part registers 145°F; let rest 5 minutes.

5. Meanwhile, cut carrots into 2-inch-long matchsticks. Cut asparagus into 2-inch-long pieces. In large bowl, toss carrots, asparagus, radishes, green onion, baby greens, and remaining parsley with remaining ⅛ teaspoon each salt and pepper and 1 tablespoon oil. Add vinegar; toss to combine. Divide salad among plates. Slice pork; arrange on salads.

EACH SERVING: About 235 calories, 26g protein, 14g carbohydrate, 8g total fat (2g saturated), 5g fiber, 62mg cholesterol, 255mg sodium

PORK ROAST WITH FENNEL AND GARLIC

Our flavorful secret is a spice paste. For greater flavor absorption, rub the meat ahead of time and refrigerate for up to 24 hours.

ACTIVE TIME: 20 minutes **TOTAL TIME:** 2 hours 55 minutes
MAKES: 8 main-dish servings

4   garlic cloves, finely chopped
2½ teaspoons fennel seeds, crushed
1   teaspoon salt
½   teaspoon ground black pepper
2   teaspoons olive oil
1   bone-in pork loin roast (4 pounds), trimmed
⅓   cup dry white wine
⅔   cup chicken broth

1. Preheat oven to 450°F. In cup, combine garlic, fennel seeds, salt, pepper, and oil to make paste.

2. Place roast in small roasting pan (13″ by 9″) and rub fennel paste on outside of pork and between bones. Roast pork 45 minutes. Reduce oven temperature to 350°F, tent meat loosely with foil, and roast until instant-read thermometer inserted in thickest part of roast (not touching bone) reaches 155°F, about 45 minutes longer. Internal temperature of meat will rise to 160°F upon standing. When roast is done, transfer to warm platter and let stand 15 minutes to set juices for easier carving.

3. Meanwhile, add wine to roasting pan and bring to a boil over high heat, stirring until browned bits are loosened from bottom of pan. Add broth and bring to a boil. Remove from heat; skim and discard fat. Serve sauce with roast.

EACH SERVING: About 270 calories, 35g protein, 1g carbohydrate, 13g total fat (4g saturated), 0g fiber, 99mg cholesterol, 440mg sodium

PORK ROAST WITH FRESH SAGE

Prepare as above but substitute ¼ **cup fresh parsley, 2 tablespoons chopped fresh sage**, and ½ **teaspoon dried thyme** for fennel seeds.

BALSAMIC ROASTED PORK WITH BERRY SALAD

Satisfying and slimming, this salad pairs roasted pork tenderloin with potassium-rich produce—including strawberries, blackberries, and baby spinach—to help keep blood pressure in check.

ACTIVE TIME: 25 minutes **TOTAL TIME:** 35 minutes

MAKES: 4 main-dish servings

4	tablespoons balsamic vinegar
2	tablespoons extra-virgin olive oil
3	teaspoons Dijon mustard
2	teaspoons packed fresh oregano leaves, finely chopped
2	medium bulbs fennel (1½ pounds each), cut into ¼-inch-thick slices
1	small red onion, thinly sliced
1	pork tenderloin (1 pound)
⅛	teaspoon freshly ground black pepper
⅜	teaspoon salt
1	pound strawberries
¼	cup packed fresh basil leaves
5	ounces baby spinach
½	pint (6 ounces) blackberries

1. Preheat oven to 450°F.

2. In large bowl, with wire whisk, stir together 3 tablespoons balsamic vinegar, 1 tablespoon oil, 2 teaspoons mustard, and oregano. Add fennel, tossing until well coated. Arrange on outer edges of 18″ by 12″ jelly-roll pan. To same bowl, add onion, tossing until well coated. Arrange onion in center of pan. Add pork to same bowl and toss until coated; place on top of onion slices.

3. Sprinkle pork and vegetables with pepper and ¼ teaspoon salt. Roast 18 to 22 minutes, until instant-read thermometer inserted in thickest part of pork reaches 140°F. Let pork stand 5 minutes; temperature will rise to 145°F or 150°F.

4. While pork roasts, hull and slice strawberries. Finely chop basil; place in large bowl.

5. In bowl with basil, whisk together remaining 1 tablespoon vinegar,

1 tablespoon oil, 1 teaspoon mustard, and ⅛ teaspoon salt until well combined. Thinly slice pork. Add fennel, onion, spinach, and strawberries to bowl with dressing, tossing until well mixed. Divide among serving plates. Top with blackberries and pork.

EACH SERVING: About 315 calories, 26g protein, 30g carbohydrate, 11g total fat (2g saturated), 10g fiber, 62mg cholesterol, 480mg sodium

CURRIED PORK AND APPLES

Tender slices of pork and tart apples are flavored with curry, then tossed with baby carrots in this simple skillet dinner. Serve with shredded cabbage sautéed in olive oil and apple cider vinegar.

ACTIVE TIME: 5 minutes **TOTAL TIME:** 15 minutes
MAKES: 4 main-dish servings

- 1   bag (16 ounces) peeled baby carrots
- 1   tablespoon olive oil
- 1   medium Gala or Golden Delicious apple, unpeeled, cored, and cut into ½-inch cubes
- 2   teaspoons curry powder
- 1   garlic clove, crushed with garlic press
- 1   pork tenderloin (1 pound), trimmed and cut into ¾-inch-thick slices
- ½   teaspoon salt
- ¼   cup apple cider or apple juice

1. Place carrots in covered microwavable dish with *¼ cup water*. Cook in microwave oven on High until carrots are tender, about 6 minutes.

2. Meanwhile, in nonstick 12-inch skillet, heat oil over medium-high heat. Add apple, curry powder, and garlic; cook, stirring, 1 minute.

3. Add pork and salt, and cook until pork is still slightly pink in center, 6 to 8 minutes. (An instant-read thermometer inserted horizontally into pork should register 145°F.) Add cider and cooked carrots with any liquid, and bring to a boil; cook 1 minute.

EACH SERVING: About 250 calories, 25g protein, 17g carbohydrate, 9g total fat (2g saturated), 3g fiber, 71mg cholesterol, 390mg sodium

PORK ROAST WITH SALSA VERDE

Tomatillos, also called Mexican green tomatoes, are the main ingredient in salsa verde. They bring a bright, lemony hint of flavor to this set-it-and-forget-it slow-cooker dish featuring pork-shoulder roast and red new potatoes.

ACTIVE TIME: 10 minutes **SLOW-COOK TIME:** 8 hours on Low or 5 hours on High

MAKES: 8 main-dish servings

1	large bunch cilantro
3	garlic cloves, sliced
2	pounds small red potatoes (about 8), cut into quarters
1	bone-in pork-shoulder roast (about 3 pounds), well trimmed
1	jar (16 to 18 ounces) salsa verde (green salsa)

1. From bunch of cilantro, remove 15 large sprigs and set aside. Remove enough leaves from remaining cilantro to equal ½ cup, loosely packed; set aside in refrigerator.

2. In 4½- to 6-quart slow-cooker pot, combine cilantro, garlic, and potatoes. Place pork on top of potato mixture. Pour salsa over and around pork. Cover and cook as manufacturer directs on Low 8 to 10 hours or on High 5 to 5½ hours.

3. Transfer pork to cutting board and slice. Transfer pork and potatoes to warm deep platter. Skim and discard fat and cilantro from cooking liquid. Spoon cooking liquid over pork and potatoes. Sprinkle with reserved cilantro leaves.

EACH SERVING: About 300 calories, 25g protein, 27g carbohydrate, 9g total fat (3g saturated), 2g fiber, 79mg cholesterol, 295mg sodium

FRESH HAM WITH SPICED APPLE GLAZE

A whole ham will provide enough meat for your grandest dinner party. A fragrant blend of cinnamon, cloves, and nutmeg—ideal with pork—is rubbed on before roasting. Serve with several kinds of mustard.

ACTIVE TIME: 15 minutes **TOTAL TIME:** 5 hours plus standing
MAKES: 24 main-dish servings

1	whole pork leg (fresh ham, 15 pounds), trimmed
2	teaspoons dried thyme
2	teaspoons ground cinnamon
2	teaspoons salt
1	teaspoon coarsely ground black pepper
½	teaspoon ground nutmeg
½	teaspoon ground cloves
1	jar (10 ounces) apple jelly
¼	cup balsamic vinegar

1. Preheat oven to 350°F. With knife, remove skin and trim excess fat from pork leg, leaving only a thin layer of fat.

2. In cup, combine thyme, cinnamon, salt, pepper, nutmeg, and cloves. Use to rub on pork. Place pork, fat side up, on rack in large roasting pan (17" by 11½"). Roast pork 3 hours. Tent pork loosely with foil. Continue roasting until instant-read thermometer inserted into thickest part of pork (not touching bone) registers 150°F, about 1 more hour.

3. Meanwhile, in 1-quart saucepan, bring apple jelly and vinegar to a boil over high heat; boil 2 minutes. Set aside.

4. When pork has reached 150°F, remove foil and brush pork with glaze. Continue roasting pork, brushing occasionally with remaining glaze, until temperature reaches 165°F. (Meat near bone will be slightly pink.) Internal temperature of pork will rise to 170°F upon standing.

5. When roast is done, transfer to warm large platter; let stand 20 minutes to set juices for easier carving.

EACH SERVING: About 298 calories, 38g protein, 6g carbohydrate, 12g total fat (4g saturated), 0g fiber, 123mg cholesterol, 232mg sodium

OVEN-BAKED PEPPER BACON

The perfect way to make bacon for a crowd: in the oven! This method works best when using lean bacon, but if the bacon renders an excessive amount of fat, pour it off before switching racks.

ACTIVE TIME: 10 minutes **TOTAL TIME:** 35 minutes

MAKES: 12 main-dish servings

1½ pounds sliced lean bacon
2½ teaspoons coarsely ground black pepper

1. Preheat oven to 400°F. Arrange bacon slices in 2 jelly-roll or roasting pans, overlapping the lean edge of each bacon slice with fat edge of the next. Sprinkle pepper evenly over bacon. Bake until golden brown and crisp, about 25 minutes, rotating pans between upper and lower oven racks halfway through baking.

2. Transfer bacon to paper towels. Keep warm until ready to serve.

EACH SERVING: About 93 calories, 5g protein, 0g carbohydrate, 8g total fat (3g saturated), 0g fiber, 13mg cholesterol, 254mg sodium

GLAZED ROSEMARY LAMB CHOPS

These rosemary-scented lamb chops are broiled with an apple-jelly and balsamic-vinegar glaze. Keep this glaze in mind for pork, too. New potatoes tossed with fresh herbs and a little olive oil would be nice on the side.

ACTIVE TIME: 10 minutes **TOTAL TIME:** 20 minutes

MAKES: 4 main-dish servings

8	lamb loin chops, 1-inch thick (4 ounces each)
1	large garlic clove, cut in half
2	teaspoons chopped fresh rosemary, or ½ teaspoon dried rosemary, crumbled
¼	teaspoon salt
¼	teaspoon coarsely ground black pepper
¼	cup apple jelly
1	tablespoon balsamic vinegar

1. Place oven rack at position closest to heat source; preheat broiler. Rub both sides of each lamb chop with garlic; discard garlic. Sprinkle lamb with rosemary, salt, and pepper. In cup, combine apple jelly and balsamic vinegar.

2. Place chops on rack in broiling pan; broil 4 minutes. Brush chops with half of apple-jelly mixture; broil 1 minute. Turn chops over and broil 4 minutes longer. Brush chops with remaining jelly mixture and broil 1 minute longer for medium-rare or until desired doneness. (Instant-read thermometer inserted horizontally into chop should reach 145°F.)

3. Transfer lamb to warm platter. Skim and discard fat from drippings in pan. Serve chops with pan juices or drizzle them with additional balsamic vinegar.

EACH SERVING: About 240 calories, 26g protein, 14g carbohydrate, 8g total fat (3g saturated), 0g fiber, 82mg cholesterol, 223mg sodium

BUTTERFLIED LAMB WITH MOROCCAN FLAVORS

Start the meal with our Roasted Red Pepper Dip (page 100) and serve the lamb with basmati rice or roasted new potatoes and tomatoes.

ACTIVE TIME: 15 minutes **TOTAL TIME:** 30 minutes plus marinating

MAKES: 12 main-dish servings

1/3 cup loosely packed fresh cilantro leaves, chopped

1/4 cup olive oil

2 tablespoons dried mint, crumbled

2 teaspoons ground coriander

1 teaspoon ground ginger

1 teaspoon salt

1/2 teaspoon coarsely ground black pepper

1/2 teaspoon chili powder

1 butterflied boneless leg of lamb (3 1/2 pounds), trimmed (see Tip)

1. In small bowl, stir cilantro, oil, mint, coriander, ginger, salt, pepper, and chili powder.

2. Place lamb in 13" by 9" glass or ceramic baking dish. Rub cilantro mixture on lamb to coat completely. Cover and refrigerate at least 1 hour or up to 4 hours.

3. Prepare outdoor grill for covered direct grilling over medium-low heat.

4. Place lamb on hot grill rack; cover and cook, turning over occasionally, 15 to 25 minutes for medium-rare or until desired doneness. (Instant-read thermometer inserted into thickest part of meat should reach 145°F.) Thickness of butterflied lamb will vary throughout; cut off sections as they are cooked and transfer to cutting board. Let stand 10 minutes to allow juices to set for easier slicing. Thinly slice lamb to serve.

EACH SERVING: About 225 calories, 28g protein, 1g carbohydrate, 12g total fat (3g saturated), 0g fiber, 88mg cholesterol, 270mg sodium

TIP

Ask your butcher to bone a 4 1/2-pound lamb-leg shank half and slit the meat lengthwise so that it spreads open like a thick steak.

Ginger-Spiced Carrot Soup (page 342)

7 | SOUPS, SALADS & SIDES

We've provided our favorite recipes for heart-smart mains; now it's time to pair them with simple, healthy sides and first-course soups and salads. These recipes are all great ways to sneak extra vegetables into a meal—and if you fill up on soup or salad, you'll be less likely to overindulge when it comes to the main event (or dessert).

Kick-start any heart-healthy meal with one of our light soups, from a classic Manhattan Clam Chowder to an inventive Ginger-Spiced Carrot Soup. Or choose from our side salads, including a healthier Caesar, Mesclun with Pears and Pumpkin Seeds, and a Warm Peas and Carrots Salad that'll appeal to the kids. All could be served for lunch or as a light dinner; just pair them with crusty bread or toss in some protein, such as beans, poached salmon, or grilled chicken breast.

If your main dish doesn't include grains, why not introduce some of their cholesterol-lowering goodness to the meal by serving our satisfyingly chewy Barley-Cherry Salad, Jalapeño Cornbread, or Vegetable-Herb Stuffing, which is made with multigrain bread? Potatoes are not off limits: Dig into our creamy Yukon Gold mashed potatoes, made lighter with fat-free half-and-half, or nibble on our golden oven-baked fries. These sides are the perfect match for our healthier Chicken-Fried Steak (page 296) or Mini Barbecued Pork Sandwiches (page 84). Just be sure to include some greens in the mix!

TURKEY SOUP

What's the Friday after Thanksgiving without turkey soup? Use your favorite vegetables to personalize this simple recipe.

ACTIVE TIME: 15 minutes **TOTAL TIME:** 5 hours 15 minutes plus overnight chilling

MAKES: about 13 cups or 12 first-course servings

6	carrots, peeled
3	stalks celery

Roasted turkey carcass, plus 2 cups cooked turkey meat, finely chopped

2	medium onions, each cut into quarters
5	parsley sprigs
1	garlic clove, peeled
¼	teaspoon dried thyme
½	bay leaf
6	quarts water
1¼	teaspoons salt
1	cup regular long-grain rice, cooked as label directs
2	tablespoons fresh lemon juice or 1 tablespoon dry sherry

1. Cut 2 carrots and 1 stalk celery into 2-inch pieces. In 12-quart stockpot, combine turkey carcass, carrot and celery pieces, onions, parsley sprigs, garlic, thyme, bay leaf, and 6 quarts water or enough water to cover; bring to a boil over high heat. Skim foam from surface. Reduce heat and simmer, skimming occasionally, 4 hours.

2. Strain broth through colander set over large bowl; discard solids. Strain again through sieve into several containers; cool. Cover and refrigerate overnight.

3. Remove and discard fat from surface of broth; measure broth and pour into 5-quart saucepot. If necessary, boil broth over high heat until reduced to 10 cups, to concentrate flavor.

4. Cut remaining 4 carrots and remaining 2 stalks celery into ½-inch pieces; add to broth with salt. Bring to a boil. Reduce heat and simmer until vegetables are tender, about 15 minutes. Stir in cooked rice and turkey; heat through, about 5 minutes. Remove from heat and stir in lemon juice.

EACH SERVING: About 113 calories, 10g protein, 12g carbohydrate, 2g total fat (1g saturated), 21mg cholesterol, 355mg sodium

LENTIL SOUP WITH TUBETTINI

This soup is so hearty and satisfying—the perfect antidote to a cold winter's day. Top with some cheese, if you like, or a drizzle of flavorful olive oil.

ACTIVE TIME: 20 minutes   **TOTAL TIME:** 50 minutes

MAKES: 6 first-course servings

2	tablespoons olive oil
2	medium carrots, peeled and diced
1	medium onion, chopped
2	garlic cloves, minced
1	can (16 ounces) tomatoes in puree
1	can (14½ ounces) vegetable broth
¾	cup lentils, rinsed and picked through
½	teaspoon salt
½	teaspoon coarsely ground black pepper
½	teaspoon dried thyme
6	cups water
½	small head (10 ounces) escarole, torn into 2-inch pieces (4 cups firmly packed)
¼	package (16 ounces) tubettini pasta
¾	cup freshly grated Parmesan cheese (optional)

1. In 5-quart Dutch oven or saucepot, heat oil over medium-high heat until hot. Add carrots, onion, and garlic, and cook until onion is tender and golden, about 10 minutes. Add tomatoes with their puree, broth, lentils, salt, pepper, thyme, and water; bring to a boil over high heat, stirring to break up tomatoes. Reduce heat to low; cover and simmer until lentils are almost tender, about 20 minutes.

2. Stir in escarole and tubettini; bring to a boil over high heat. Reduce heat to medium; cook until tubettini is tender, about 10 minutes. Sprinkle with Parmesan to serve, if you like.

EACH SERVING: About 260 calories, 12g protein, 42g carbohydrate, 6g total fat (1g saturated), 8g fiber, 0mg cholesterol, 345mg sodium

CHILLED BUTTERMILK AND CORN SOUP

This refreshing refrigerator soup—bursting with the summery flavors of corn, ripe tomatoes, cucumber, and basil—is both low in fat and satisfying.

TOTAL TIME: 20 minutes plus chilling

MAKES: about 4½ cups or 6 first-course servings

1	quart low-fat buttermilk
4	ripe medium tomatoes (1½ pounds), seeded and chopped
1	small cucumber, peeled, seeded, and chopped
2	cups corn kernels cut from cobs (about 4 ears)
½	teaspoon salt
¼	teaspoon coarsely ground black pepper
10	fresh basil sprigs

1. In large bowl, combine buttermilk, tomatoes, cucumber, corn, salt, and pepper. Cover and refrigerate until very cold, at least 2 hours.

2. To serve, set aside 6 small basil sprigs; pinch 12 large basil leaves from remaining sprigs and thinly slice. Spoon soup into bowls; garnish with sliced basil and small basil sprigs.

EACH SERVING: About 135 calories, 8g protein, 24g carbohydrate, 2g total fat (1g saturated), 2g fiber, 6mg cholesterol, 365mg sodium

HONEYDEW AND LIME SOUP

This chilled soup starts a summer meal off with a refreshing mix of surprising flavors. Choose a melon that is fully ripe to achieve a smooth consistency.

TOTAL TIME: 10 minutes plus chilling

MAKES: about 6 cups or 6 first-course servings

1	honeydew melon (5 pounds), chilled and cut into 1-inch chunks (8 cups)
¼	cup fresh lime juice
¼	cup loosely packed fresh cilantro leaves
1	teaspoon jalapeño hot sauce
⅛	teaspoon salt

In blender, pulse melon with lime juice, cilantro, hot sauce, and salt until pureed. Transfer soup to large bowl or pitcher; cover and refrigerate 2 hours or until chilled. Stir before serving.

EACH SERVING: About 85 calories, 1g protein, 23g carbohydrate, 0g total fat, 2g fiber, 0mg cholesterol, 80mg sodium

GINGER-SPICED CARROT SOUP

With one and a half pounds of carrots and two cups of peas, this creamy-smooth vegetable soup is supercharged with vitamin A, a vision-enhancing nutrient. Subbing ginger-steeped green tea for stock slashes the sodium, too. For photo, see page 336.

ACTIVE TIME: 25 minutes **TOTAL TIME:** 55 minutes

MAKES: 6 first-course servings

4	green onions
1	(1-inch) piece fresh ginger
5	cups water
3	bags green tea
1	tablespoon olive oil
1	onion, finely chopped
1½	pounds carrots, peeled and cut into ¾-inch-thick pieces
1	all-purpose potato, peeled and chopped
½	teaspoon salt
¼	teaspoon ground black pepper
2	cups frozen peas

1. From green onions, cut off white and pale-green parts and place in 5-quart saucepot. Thinly slice dark-green onion parts; set aside. From ginger, cut 4 slices; set aside. Peel remaining piece of ginger and grate enough to make 1 teaspoon; set aside.

2. To saucepot, add sliced ginger and water. Bring to a boil over high heat. Add tea bags. Cover, remove from heat, and let stand 10 minutes.

3. While tea steeps, in 12-inch skillet, heat oil over medium-high heat. Add onion, carrots, potato, and ¼ teaspoon each salt and pepper. Cook, stirring, 6 minutes or until golden. Add grated ginger; cook 1 minute, stirring.

4. With slotted spoon, remove ginger, tea bags, and green-onion pieces from pot and discard after squeezing excess liquid back into pot. Bring ginger tea to a boil over high heat; stir in carrot mixture. Reduce heat to maintain simmer. Cook 10 minutes or until vegetables are tender, stirring.

5. Transfer half of soup to blender; keep remaining soup simmering. With center part of lid removed to allow steam to escape (drape with clean kitchen towel to avoid splatter), blend mixture until pureed; return to pot. Stir in peas and remaining ¼ teaspoon salt. Cook 3 minutes or until peas are bright green and hot. Divide among soup bowls; garnish with sliced green onions.

EACH SERVING: About 135 calories, 5g protein, 25g carbohydrate, 3g total fat (1g saturated), 6g fiber, 0mg cholesterol, 275mg sodium

COOK'S TIP: PEELING FRESH GINGER

Use a vegetable peeler to peel ginger; be careful to remove only the very top layer of skin because the flesh directly beneath is the youngest and most delicate. Then, chop, slice, or shred the ginger as directed with a sharp knife or box grater. A ginger grater works best for fine grating because it yields plenty of juice with minimal fiber.

CARROT AND DILL SOUP

Combine sweet carrots with fresh orange, dill, and a touch of milk for a refreshing, creamy soup without the cream.

ACTIVE TIME: 25 minutes **TOTAL TIME:** 1 hour 10 minutes

MAKES: 10 1/2 cups or 10 first-course servings

1	tablespoon olive oil
1	large onion (12 ounces), chopped
1	medium stalk celery, chopped
2	large oranges
2	bags (16 ounces each) carrots, peeled and chopped
1	can (14 1/2 ounces) vegetable broth
1	tablespoon sugar
3/4	teaspoon salt
1/4	teaspoon ground black pepper
4	cups water
1	cup milk
1/4	cup chopped fresh dill

Dill sprigs, for garnish

1. In 5-quart Dutch oven, heat oil over medium-high heat. Add onion and celery; cook until tender and golden, about 15 minutes, stirring occasionally.

2. Meanwhile, with vegetable peeler, remove 4 strips of peel (3" by 1" each) from 1 orange, and squeeze 1 cup juice from both oranges.

3. Add orange-peel strips to Dutch oven and cook 2 minutes longer, stirring. Add orange juice, carrots, broth, sugar, salt, pepper, and water; bring to a boil over high heat. Reduce heat to low; cover and simmer until carrots are very tender, about 25 minutes.

4. Remove strips of orange peel from soup. In blender, with center part of cover removed to allow steam to escape, blend soup in small batches until smooth. Pour pureed soup into large bowl after each batch.

5. Return soup to Dutch oven, and stir in milk and chopped dill; heat just to simmering over medium heat. Garnish each serving with dill sprigs.

EACH SERVING: About 95 calories, 3g protein, 16g carbohydrate, 3g total fat (1g saturated), 3g fiber, 3mg cholesterol, 380mg sodium

NUTRITIONAL NOTE:
THE SKINNY ON SOUP

Looking to lose a few pounds? Embrace soup. Research shows that the best way to start a meal may be with a broth- or water-based soup. It fills you up—even more so than salad or other low-calorie foods—so you'll end up eating less during the meal. Or make soup a meal in itself. Veggie- and grain-based soups provide fiber to keep you feeling fuller longer. Look for soups containing 5 grams or more of fiber per serving.

MANHATTAN CLAM CHOWDER

Substitute cherrystone clams, if you like; there's no need to chop them.

ACTIVE TIME: 30 minutes **TOTAL TIME:** 1 hour 20 minutes

MAKES: 12 cups or 12 first-course servings

5	cups water
36	chowder or cherrystone clams, scrubbed (see directions, page 219)
5	slices bacon, finely chopped
1	large onion (12 ounces), finely chopped
2	large carrots, peeled and finely chopped
2	stalks celery, finely chopped
1	pound all-purpose potatoes (about 3 medium), peeled and finely chopped
½	bay leaf
1¼	teaspoons dried thyme
¼	teaspoon ground black pepper
1	can (28 ounces) plum tomatoes
2	tablespoons chopped fresh parsley

Salt, to taste

1. In nonreactive 8-quart saucepot, bring 1 cup water to a boil over high heat. Add clams; return to a boil. Reduce heat to medium; cover and simmer until clams open, 5 to 10 minutes, transferring clams to bowl as they open. Discard any unopened clams.

2. When cool enough to handle, remove clams from shells and coarsely chop. Strain clam broth through sieve lined with paper towels into bowl. Set aside.

3. Rinse saucepot and place over medium heat; cook bacon until browned; add onion and cook until tender, about 5 minutes. Add carrots and celery; cook 5 minutes.

4. Add clam broth to bacon mixture in saucepot. Add potatoes, remaining 4 cups water, bay leaf, thyme, and pepper; bring to a boil. Reduce heat; cover and simmer 10 minutes. Add tomatoes with their liquid, breaking up with side of spoon, and simmer 10 minutes longer.

5. Stir in clams and heat through. Discard bay leaf and sprinkle with parsley.

EACH SERVING: About 115 calories, 5g protein, 12g carbohydrate, 6g total fat (2g saturated), 0g fiber, 12mg cholesterol, 342mg sodium

HEALTHY NEW ENGLAND CLAM CHOWDER

To slim this dish—by more than half the calories and cholesterol—we trimmed the bacon, swapped reduced-fat milk for cream, and added in flour in place of several starchy potatoes.

ACTIVE TIME: 20 minutes **TOTAL TIME:** 55 minutes

MAKES: 6 first-course servings

1½ cups water plus more for broth

12   large cherrystone or chowder clams, scrubbed (see directions, page 219, but don't shuck)

2   slices bacon, chopped

1   medium onion, chopped

1   medium carrot, chopped

1   stalk celery, chopped

2   tablespoons all-purpose flour

1   large potato (12 ounces), peeled and cut into ½-inch chunks

2   cups reduced-fat (2%) milk

⅛   teaspoon ground black pepper

1   tablespoon finely chopped fresh chives

1. In 4-quart saucepan, bring water to a boil over high heat. Add clams; return to a boil. Reduce heat to medium-low; cover and simmer until clams open, 5 to 10 minutes, transferring clams to bowl as they open. Discard any unopened clams.

2. Into 4-cup liquid measuring cup, strain clam broth through sieve lined with paper towel. Add water to broth to equal 2½ cups total.

3. Rinse saucepan to remove any grit. In same saucepan, cook bacon on medium until browned. With slotted spoon, transfer bacon to paper towels to drain, leaving bacon fat in pan. Add onion, carrot, and celery to pan, and cook 9 to 10 minutes or until tender, stirring occasionally. Meanwhile, remove clams from shells and coarsely chop.

4. Stir flour into vegetable mixture; cook 1 minute, stirring. Gradually stir in clam broth. Add potato; bring to a boil. Cover; simmer on low 12 minutes or until potato is tender, stirring occasionally. Stir in milk, clams, pepper, and bacon; heat through (do not boil). Sprinkle with chives to serve.

EACH SERVING: About 180 calories, 8g protein, 20g carbohydrate, 9g total fat (4g saturated), 2g fiber, 21mg cholesterol, 155mg sodium

SQUASH SOUP WITH CUMIN

This healthful soup has two delicious variations.

ACTIVE TIME: 25 minutes **TOTAL TIME:** 35 minutes

MAKES: 10 cups or 5 first-course servings

2	medium butternut squash, cut in half
1	tablespoon olive oil
2	medium stalks celery, chopped
1	medium onion, chopped
1	teaspoon ground cumin
¼	teaspoon chipotle chile powder
½	teaspoon salt
¼	teaspoon freshly ground black pepper
2	cans chicken broth (3½ cups)
2	cups water

Roasted salted pumpkin seeds (pepitas)

Fresh chives, for garnish

1. Preheat oven to 450°F. Line 15½" by 10½" jelly-roll pan with foil. Place squash halves, cut sides down, in lined pan, and roast about 45 minutes or until very tender when pierced with knife. Cool until easy to handle, then, with spoon, scoop squash from skins and place in large bowl. Discard skins.

2. Meanwhile, in 5- to 6-quart saucepot, heat oil over medium heat until hot. Add celery and onion, and cook 10 minutes. Stir in cumin, chipotle chile powder, salt, and pepper; cook 30 seconds, stirring.

3. Add broth, water, and squash to saucepot; cover and bring to a boil over high heat. Reduce heat to low, and simmer 10 minutes.

4. In batches, ladle squash mixture into blender. With center part of blender cover removed to allow steam to escape, blend squash mixture until pureed. Pour soup into large bowl. Return all soup to saucepot and heat through. Garnish each serving with pumpkin seeds and chives.

EACH CUP: About 109 calories, 3g protein, 22g carbohydrate, 2g total fat (0g saturated), 6g fiber, 2mg cholesterol, 473mg sodium

SQUASH SOUP WITH ROSEMARY

Prepare squash as in step 1. In step 2, omit cumin and chipotle chile powder, and add **1 teaspoon chopped fresh rosemary leaves** along with the salt and pepper. Complete recipe as in steps 3 and 4, but omit garnish, and top each serving with several **Pecorino Romano shavings** if you like. Makes five 1-cup servings.

EACH 1-CUP SERVING: About 90 calories, 3g protein, 19g carbohydrate, 2g total fat (0g saturated), 3g fiber, 0mg cholesterol, 350mg sodium

SQUASH SOUP WITH CURRIED PEAR

Prepare squash as in step 1. In step 2, omit cumin and chipotle chile powder. Add **2 Bartlett or Anjou pears**, peeled, cored, and chopped, **1 tablespoon curry powder**, and **salt and pepper** to saucepot after celery and onion have cooked 8 minutes. Cook 5 minutes longer. Complete recipe as in steps 3 and 4, but garnish each serving with a drizzle of **low-fat yogurt**. Makes five 1-cup servings.

EACH 1-CUP SERVING: About 85 calories, 2g protein, 19g carbohydrate, 1g total fat (0g saturated), 3g fiber, 0mg cholesterol, 270mg sodium

LENTIL STEW WITH BUTTERNUT SQUASH

Here's a hearty vegetarian meal that's packed with fiber and low in sodium. A slow cooker makes it a cinch to prepare.

ACTIVE TIME: 20 minutes **SLOW-COOK TIME:** 8 hours on Low

MAKES: 8 first-course servings

3 large stalks celery, cut into ¼-inch-thick slices

1 large onion (12 ounces), chopped

1 large butternut squash (2½ pounds), peeled, seeded, and cut into 1-inch chunks

1 pound brown lentils

4 cups water

1 can (14½ ounces) vegetable broth

½ teaspoon dried rosemary

¾ teaspoon salt

¼ teaspoon ground black pepper

1 ounce Parmesan or Pecorino Romano cheese, shaved with vegetable peeler

¼ cup loosely packed fresh parsley leaves, chopped

1. In 4½- to 6-quart slow-cooker bowl, combine celery, onion, squash, lentils, water, broth, rosemary, salt, and pepper. Cover and slow-cook on Low, 8 hours.

2. To serve, spoon lentil stew into bowls; top with cheese shavings and sprinkle with chopped parsley.

EACH SERVING: About 285 calories, 20g protein, 51g carbohydrate, 2g total fat (1g saturated), 20g fiber, 3mg cholesterol, 420mg sodium

HEART-SMART INGREDIENT: BUTTERNUT SQUASH

This sweet orange vegetable contains numerous heart-healthy phytonutrients. It's one of the most concentrated plant sources for the omega-6 fatty acid alpha-linolenic acid, which also contributes to cardiovascular health. Butternut squash provides more than 100% of the daily requirement for vitamin A, which supports lung function.

APPLE AND SQUASH SOUP

This big-batch soup makes enough for a crowd—or simply freeze half for later. To fry sage leaves for garnish, heat about ¼ inch oil in a small saucepan until hot and "shimmering." Add 5 or 6 medium-sized leaves at a time and stir 5 seconds. With a slotted spoon, transfer leaves to paper towels to drain. The leaves will crisp as they cool.

ACTIVE TIME: 20 minutes **TOTAL TIME:** 1 hour 35 minutes

MAKES: 16 cups or 12 first-course servings

2	medium butternut squash (3 pounds), each cut in half lengthwise and seeds removed
1	tablespoon vegetable oil
1	medium onion, chopped
1	stalk celery, chopped
4	large Granny Smith apples (2 pounds), peeled, cored, and cut into 1-inch chunks
1	carton (32 ounces) vegetable broth
4	cups water
½	teaspoon salt
	Fried sage leaves, for garnish

1. Preheat oven to 450°F. Line 15½″ by 10½″ jelly-roll pan with foil. Place squash halves, cut sides down, in lined pan and roast until very tender when pierced with paring knife, 40 to 45 minutes. Cool until easy to handle, then, with spoon, scoop squash from skins and place in large bowl. Discard skins.

2. Meanwhile, in 5- to 6-quart saucepot, heat oil over medium heat until hot. Add onion and celery; cover and cook 10 minutes. Add apples; cover and cook until vegetables and apples are very tender, about 10 minutes longer.

3. Add broth, water, salt, and squash to saucepot; cover and bring to a boil over high heat. Reduce heat to low and simmer 10 minutes.

4. In blender, with center part of cover removed to allow steam to escape, blend soup in small batches until smooth. Pour into large bowl.

5. Return soup to saucepot and heat through. Garnish each serving with a fried sage leaf.

EACH SERVING: About 95 calories, 2g protein, 21g carbohydrate, 1g total fat (0g saturated), 3g fiber, 0mg cholesterol, 385mg sodium

BLENDER TOMATO SOUP

Here's a sensational way to use ripe summer tomatoes at their peak. Serve it cold or hot. For a creamier version, stir in a little low-fat plain yogurt.

ACTIVE TIME: 20 minutes **TOTAL TIME:** 1 hour 30 minutes
MAKES: 8 first-course servings

1	tablespoon butter
1	onion, diced
1	stalk celery, diced
1	carrot, peeled and diced
1	garlic clove, crushed with garlic press
2	teaspoons fresh thyme leaves
4	pounds ripe tomatoes, chopped
1	can (14½ ounces) reduced-sodium chicken broth
½	teaspoon salt
¼	teaspoon coarsely ground black pepper
1	bay leaf
½	cup water

Snipped chives, for garnish

1. In 5-quart Dutch oven, melt butter over low heat. Add onion, celery, and carrot; cook 10 minutes or until tender. Stir in garlic and thyme; cook 1 minute.

2. Add tomatoes, broth, salt, pepper, bay leaf, and water; bring to a boil over high heat. Reduce heat to medium-low and cook, uncovered, 45 minutes or until tomatoes are broken up and mixture has thickened slightly. Discard bay leaf.

3. In blender, with center part of cover removed to allow steam to escape (drape with clean kitchen towel to avoid splatter), blend tomato mixture in small batches until pureed. Pour into large bowl after each batch. Repeat until all soup has been pureed. Refrigerate soup to serve cold, or reheat soup in same Dutch oven to serve hot. Sprinkle with chives to serve.

EACH SERVING: About 80 calories, 3g protein, 13g carbohydrate, 3g total fat (1g saturated), 3g fiber, 0mg cholesterol, 210mg sodium

HOMEMADE VEGETABLE BROTH

This broth is delicious, nutritious, and great in soups, risottos, and sauces.

ACTIVE TIME: 25 minutes **TOTAL TIME:** 2 hours 25 minutes

MAKES: 6 cups

4 large leeks
2 to 4 garlic cloves, not peeled
13 cups water
Salt
1 large all-purpose potato, peeled, cut lengthwise in half, and thinly sliced
1 small fennel bulb, trimmed and chopped (optional)
3 parsnips, peeled and thinly sliced (optional)
2 large carrots, peeled and thinly sliced
3 stalks celery with leaves, thinly sliced
4 ounces mushrooms, trimmed and thinly sliced
10 parsley sprigs
4 thyme sprigs
2 bay leaves
1 teaspoon whole black peppercorns, plus additional ground black pepper as needed

1. Cut off roots and trim dark green tops from leeks. Thinly slice leeks and rinse them in large bowl of *cold water,* swishing to remove sand. Transfer to colander to drain, leaving sand in bottom of bowl.

2. In 6-quart saucepot, combine leeks, garlic, 1 cup water, and pinch salt; bring to a boil. Reduce heat to medium; cover and cook 15 minutes.

3. Add potato, fennel if using, parsnips if using, carrots, celery, mushrooms, parsley and thyme sprigs, bay leaves, peppercorns, and remaining 12 cups water. Bring to a boil; reduce heat and simmer, uncovered, at least 1 hour 30 minutes.

4. Taste and continue cooking if flavor is not concentrated enough. Season with salt and pepper to taste. Strain broth through fine-mesh sieve into containers, pressing on solids with back of wooden spoon to extract liquid; cool. Cover and refrigerate to use within 3 days, or freeze up to 4 months.

EACH 1-CUP SERVING: About 20 calories, 1g protein, 4g carbohydrate, 0g total fat, 0g fiber, 0mg cholesterol, 9mg sodium

HOMEMADE CHICKEN BROTH

Nothing beats the rich flavor of homemade chicken broth. It serves as a base for many of our soups and stews. Make large batches and freeze it in sturdy containers for up to four months. Bonus: The cooked chicken can be used in casseroles and salads.

ACTIVE TIME: 30 minutes **TOTAL TIME:** 40 minutes plus cooling
MAKES: 5 1/2 cups

1   chicken (3 to 3 1/2 pounds), including neck (reserve giblets for another use)
2   carrots, peeled and cut into 2-inch pieces
1   stalk celery, cut into 2-inch pieces
1   onion, unpeeled, cut into quarters
5   parsley sprigs
1   garlic clove, unpeeled
1/2 teaspoon dried thyme
1/2 bay leaf
3   quarts water, plus more if needed

1. In 6-quart saucepot, combine chicken, chicken neck, carrots, celery, onion, parsley, garlic, thyme, bay leaf, and water. If necessary, add more water to cover broth ingredients; bring to a boil over high heat. With slotted spoon, skim foam from surface. Reduce heat to low; cover and simmer, turning chicken once and skimming foam occasionally, 1 hour.

2. Remove from heat; transfer chicken to large bowl. When chicken is cool enough to handle, remove skin and bones and reserve meat for another use. Return skin and bones to pot and return to a boil over high heat. Skim foam; reduce heat to low and simmer, uncovered, 3 hours.

3. Strain broth through colander into large bowl; discard solids. Strain again though fine mesh sieve into containers; cool. Cover and refrigerate to use within 3 days, or freeze up to 4 months.

4. Discard fat from surface of chilled broth before use.

EACH 1-CUP SERVING: About 35 calories, 3g protein, 4g carbohydrate, 1g total fat (1g saturated), 0g fiber, 3mg cholesterol, 91mg sodium

KALE SALAD WITH GLAZED ONIONS AND CHEDDAR

With glazed onions, dried cherries, pine nuts, and crunchy kale, the flavor of this salad is as bright as it is colorful.

ACTIVE TIME: 30 minutes **TOTAL TIME:** 40 minutes

MAKES: 6 side-dish servings

- 1 bunch curly kale (8 ounces), tough ribs and stems removed and discarded, leaves very thinly sliced
- 1 tablespoon fresh lemon juice
- 2 teaspoons extra-virgin olive oil
- 1/8 teaspoon salt
- 1/8 teaspoon freshly ground black pepper
- 8 ounces frozen pearl onions, thawed
- 1 tablespoon butter
- 2 tablespoons water
- 2 teaspoons Worcestershire sauce
- 1 teaspoon sugar
- 1 tablespoon cider vinegar
- 1/3 cup dried tart cherries
- 3 tablespoons pine nuts
- 1 ounce extra-sharp white Cheddar cheese, shredded (1/4 cup)

1. In large bowl, toss kale with lemon juice, oil, salt, and pepper; set aside.

2. In 12-inch skillet, combine pearl onions, butter, 1 tablespoon water, Worcestershire sauce, and sugar. Cook over medium heat 8 to 10 minutes, until onions are tender and almost all liquid has evaporated, stirring occasionally.

3. Add vinegar to skillet. Increase heat to medium-high. Cook 3 to 4 minutes, until onions are browned, stirring frequently. Add remaining 1 tablespoon water. Cook 1 minute longer, swirling pan constantly. (Onions can be refrigerated, covered, up to overnight.) Transfer onions to bowl with kale.

4. To kale, add cherries and pine nuts; toss vigorously to combine. Add Cheddar; toss. Transfer to serving platter.

EACH SERVING: About 130 calories, 3g protein, 13g carbohydrate, 8g total fat (1g saturated), 3g fiber, 3mg cholesterol, 130mg sodium

MESCLUN WITH PEARS AND PUMPKIN SEEDS

Instead of the pecans we used to include in this recipe, we've swapped in toasted pumpkin seeds, or pepitas, which have become supermarket staples in recent years. They're also great on-the-go snacks.

TOTAL TIME: 10 minutes

MAKES: 12 side-dish servings

¼   cup pumpkin seeds (pepitas)
3   tablespoons cider vinegar
1   tablespoon Dijon mustard
2   teaspoons pure honey
¼   cup extra-virgin olive oil
3   ripe red pears, cored and thinly sliced
2   packages (5 ounces each) mixed baby greens
¼   teaspoon salt
¼   teaspoon freshly ground black pepper

1. In small skillet, heat pumpkin seeds over medium heat until all are toasted and some start to pop, 2 to 3 minutes. Cool completely. Toasted seeds can be stored in airtight container up to 1 week.

2. In small bowl, with wire whisk, stir vinegar, mustard, and honey until blended. Continue whisking and add oil in slow, steady stream. Whisk until well blended and emulsified. Dressing can be made ahead. Cover tightly and refrigerate up to 3 days.

3. In large bowl, combine sliced pears, greens, toasted pumpkin seeds, dressing, salt, and pepper. Toss until evenly coated.

EACH SERVING: About 100 calories, 1g protein, 9g carbohydrate, 7g total fat (1g saturated), 2g fiber, 0mg cholesterol, 85mg sodium

---

TIP
You can combine the dressing and pears up to 1 hour before serving to prevent the sliced pears from turning brown. When ready to serve, toss with the greens, pumpkin seeds, and seasonings.

SNAP PEA SALAD

This yummy double-pea salad is easy to prepare for company. Use any leftover fresh dill in your next mayonnaise-based salad.

ACTIVE TIME: 10 minutes **TOTAL TIME:** 15 minutes
MAKES: 8 side-dish servings

1	pound sugar snap peas, strings removed
1	package (10 ounces) frozen peas
½	cup minced red onion
2	tablespoons white wine vinegar
2	tablespoons vegetable oil
2	tablespoons chopped fresh dill
1	tablespoon sugar
½	teaspoon salt
¼	teaspoon coarsely ground black pepper

1. In 5- to 6-quart saucepot, bring *2 inches water* to a boil over high heat. Add snap peas and frozen peas; cook 1 minute. Drain vegetables; rinse under cold running water to stop cooking. Drain again; pat dry between layers of paper towels.

2. In large bowl, stir onion, vinegar, oil, dill, sugar, salt, and pepper until mixed. Add peas; toss to coat. If not serving right away, cover and refrigerate up to 4 hours.

EACH SERVING: About 100 calories, 4g protein, 13g carbohydrate, 4g total fat (0g saturated), 4g fiber, 0mg cholesterol, 245mg sodium

MIXED GREENS WITH PEARS AND PECANS

The sweetness of ripe pears and the crunchiness of buttery pecans make this salad irresistible.

TOTAL TIME: 45 minutes

MAKES: 10 side-dish servings

3	tablespoons red wine vinegar
2	teaspoons Dijon mustard
½	teaspoon salt
½	teaspoon coarsely ground black pepper
⅓	cup olive oil
3	ripe medium pears, peeled, cored, and cut into 16 wedges
1	wedge (4 ounces) Parmesan cheese
2	small radicchio, cored and torn into large pieces
2	small heads Belgian endive, separated into leaves
2	small bunches (4 ounces each) arugula, trimmed
½	cup pecans, toasted (see Tip) and coarsely chopped

1. Prepare dressing: In very large bowl, with wire whisk, mix vinegar, mustard, salt, and pepper. In thin, steady stream, whisk in oil until blended. Add pears, tossing to coat.

2. With vegetable peeler, remove enough shavings from wedge of Parmesan to measure 1 cup, loosely packed.

3. Add radicchio, endive, and arugula to pears; toss until mixed and coated with dressing. Top salad with Parmesan shavings and pecans.

EACH SERVING: About 166 calories, 4g protein, 11g carbohydrate, 13g total fat (2g saturated), 3g fiber, 4mg cholesterol, 244mg sodium

COOK'S TIP: TOASTING NUTS

To toast a small amount of nuts or seeds, cook them in a dry, ungreased skillet over low heat until lightly browned, 3 to 5 minutes, shaking or stirring often.

SPINACH AND NECTARINE SALAD

If you're packing this spinach salad for lunch, toss the nectarines with the dressing and store them separately from the greens.

TOTAL TIME: 15 minutes

MAKES: 2 first-course servings

2	tablespoons orange marmalade
1	large shallot, thinly sliced
2	tablespoons white balsamic vinegar
2	teaspoons olive oil
¼	teaspoon salt
¼	teaspoon ground black pepper
¼	cup slivered almonds
1	package (7 ounces) baby spinach
2	ripe nectarines, pitted and cut into wedges

1. In microwave-safe small bowl or 1-cup liquid measuring cup, combine marmalade and shallot. Cover with vented plastic wrap and cook in microwave oven on High, 1 minute. Stir in vinegar, oil, salt, and pepper.

2. In small skillet, cook almonds over medium heat until toasted, about 5 minutes, stirring. Set aside to cool, about 2 minutes.

3. To serve, toss spinach, nectarines, and marmalade mixture until combined. Place on 2 dinner plates; scatter almonds on top.

EACH SERVING: About 285 calories, 8g protein, 37g carbohydrate, 14g total fat (1g saturated), 14g fiber, 0mg cholesterol, 420mg sodium

COOK'S TIP:
HOW SAFE IS PREWASHED SALAD?

Packaged greens seem like the perfect shortcut to a healthy meal—until you hear media reports linking them to high bacteria levels or even outbreaks of deadly food-borne illnesses. Can you really trust the greens without washing them first?

Branded, pre-washed salad blends sold in hermetically sealed, clear bags are processed with rinse water that contains sanitizing agents such as chlorine. Even this careful process doesn't remove *all* microorganisms, but the bacteria commonly found in bagged lettuce cause food spoilage, not disease. If the salad isn't refrigerated properly or is not eaten before its "use by" date, these bacteria will cause it to turn brown and slimy, alerting you to discard it—before bacteria multiply to unsafe levels. Although bagged blends have an excellent safety record, don't assume all are ready to eat. Always read the small print. Salads from large manufacturers say washed and ready-to-eat right on the package, but we have found other greens—like watercress, spinach, and shredded cabbage—that looked salad-ready or even had the word *washed* on the front of the bag, but stated *rinse before using* on the back.

The truth is, when it comes to food-borne illnesses like *E. coli* and salmonella, even the most vigorous washing won't help. If the contamination is present, the only thing that will kill it is cooking it to a temperature of 160°F or more.

HEALTHY MAKEOVER CAESAR SALAD

In this lighter take on the Caesar, we coated the croutons with cooking spray instead of olive oil, then replaced the egg yolk with light mayonnaise to keep the classic dressing's creamy texture—without the classic guilt.

ACTIVE TIME: 15 minutes **TOTAL TIME:** 25 minutes

MAKES: 6 first-course servings

4	ounces Italian bread
1	garlic clove, cut in half
	Nonstick olive oil cooking spray
¼	cup light mayonnaise
¼	cup freshly grated Parmesan cheese
3	tablespoons fresh lemon juice
1	tablespoon olive oil
1	teaspoon anchovy paste
¼	teaspoon coarsely ground black pepper
1	package (18 ounces) hearts of romaine lettuce, torn into bite-size pieces

1. Preheat oven to 400°F.

2. Cut bread into ½-inch-thick slices. Rub bread slices, on both sides, with cut sides of garlic. Cut bread into ½-inch cubes; place in jelly-roll pan. Spray bread liberally with cooking spray. Bake 10 minutes or until golden-brown and crisp. Cool croutons in pan.

3. Meanwhile, in large salad bowl, with wire whisk, mix together mayonnaise, Parmesan, lemon juice, olive oil, anchovy paste, and pepper.

4. Add lettuce and croutons to dressing in bowl; toss to coat.

EACH SERVING: About 140 calories, 4g protein, 13g carbohydrate, 8g total fat (2g saturated), 2g fiber, 7mg cholesterol, 280mg sodium

WARM PEAS AND CARROTS SALAD

This is the perfect salad for kids who love their peas and carrots.

TOTAL TIME: 15 minutes

MAKES: 4 side-dish servings

1	cup frozen peas
3	carrots, peeled
1	small onion, peeled
1	tablespoon vegetable oil
½	teaspoon salt
1	tablespoon fresh lemon juice
1	head romaine lettuce

1. Place frozen peas in small bowl; cover with *boiling water* and let stand 5 minutes.

2. Meanwhile, thinly slice carrots and onion. In nonstick 10-inch skillet, heat oil over medium-high heat until hot. Add carrots, onion, and salt, and cook, stirring occasionally, until vegetables are tender and lightly browned.

3. Drain peas; stir into vegetable mixture, along with lemon juice. Remove skillet from heat.

4. Cut enough lettuce leaves crosswise into ¼-inch-wide strips to measure 4 cups loosely packed; reserve remaining lettuce for another use. Toss lettuce with carrot mixture to mix well.

EACH SERVING: About 95 calories, 3g protein, 14g carbohydrate, 4g total fat (0g saturated), 5g fiber, 0mg cholesterol, 350mg sodium

BARLEY-CHERRY SALAD

This sweet-and-savory salad is the perfect summer starter. Barley has a satisfyingly creamy, chewy texture—and lots of heart-healthy fiber.

ACTIVE TIME: 20 minutes **TOTAL TIME:** 25 minutes

MAKES: 6 first-course servings

1	cup pearl barley
12	ounces cherries, pitted and chopped (3 cups)
3	stalks celery
¼	cup chopped fresh mint leaves
2	tablespoons cider vinegar
½	teaspoon salt
½	head green-leaf lettuce, for serving

1. Cook pearl barley as label directs. Drain, rinse until cool, and drain again.

2. Toss barley with cherries, celery, mint, vinegar, and salt until mixed. Place in lettuce-lined bowl to serve.

EACH SERVING: About 135 calories, 4g protein, 30g carbohydrate, 1g total fat (0g saturated), 7g fiber, 0mg cholesterol, 226mg sodium

NUTRITIONAL NOTE: BARLEY BASICS

Barley is one of the oldest grains in cultivation. The fiber in barley may be even more effective than the fiber in oats at lowering cholesterol, so it's worth your while to work it into your diet.

Pearl barley has been polished (milled) to remove its outer hull, which omits some of the bran. It has a creamy, chewy texture and is a great choice for soups. Hulled barley has had only the hull removed; it's chewier and more nutritious than pearl barley because it contains all of the bran, but it takes longer to cook. Use it as a base for stews or in casseroles.

CITRUS SALAD

Serve this bright and refreshing side salad for brunch alongside our Crustless Tomato and Ricotta Pie (page 56).

TOTAL TIME: 25 minutes

MAKES: 6 side-dish servings

2	oranges
2	red or pink grapefruits
2	tablespoons fresh lemon juice
1	tablespoon white wine vinegar
2	teaspoons Dijon mustard
¼	teaspoon salt
¼	teaspoon freshly ground black pepper
3	tablespoons extra-virgin olive oil
1	bunch upland cress or watercress (3 ounces), trimmed
1	head Boston lettuce, torn
¼	cup packed fresh basil leaves, torn if large

1. Cut off and discard peel and white pith from oranges. Holding orange over medium bowl, slice on either side of membranes and allow each segment to fall into bowl. Repeat with grapefruits, placing segments in same bowl. Segments can be covered and refrigerated up to 3 days.

2. In small bowl, whisk lemon juice, vinegar, mustard, and salt and pepper. Whisk in oil until emulsified. Dressing can be covered and refrigerated up to 3 days; whisk well before using.

3. In large bowl, gently toss cress, lettuce, and basil with dressing until well coated. Top with citrus segments.

EACH SERVING: About 125 calories, 2g protein, 16g carbohydrate, 7g total fat (1g saturated), 2g fiber, 0mg cholesterol, 145mg sodium

SEAWEED SALAD

If you've never considered eating seaweed, you should! Ounce for ounce, it is higher in vitamins and minerals than any other class of food. It is particularly prized as a rich source of iodine. This recipe features dried hijiki, commonly used in Japanese home cooking and found in natural food stores or online.

ACTIVE TIME: 5 minutes **TOTAL TIME:** 30 minutes
MAKES: 4 side-dish servings

½ cup dried hijiki seaweed
5 cups warm water
1 large carrot, peeled
3 tablespoons thinly sliced green onion
3 tablespoons seasoned rice vinegar
1 teaspoon sugar
½ teaspoon toasted sesame oil
Pinch ground black pepper

1. Place seaweed in medium bowl and cover with water. Soak 25 minutes.

2. Meanwhile, grate carrot. Place carrot and green onion in medium bowl.

3. Drain seaweed and pat dry. Add to bowl with carrot and green onion. Mix in vinegar, sugar, sesame oil, and pepper until well combined. Serve at room temperature, or cover and refrigerate up to 3 days.

EACH SERVING: About 35 calories, 0g protein, 7g carbohydrate, 0g total fat, 2g fiber, 0mg cholesterol, 276mg sodium

CHUNKY GREEK SALAD

This salad is a great big bowl of goodness—pieces of tomato, cucumber, red pepper, olives, and feta tossed with a citrus dressing and a generous handful of refreshing chopped mint.

TOTAL TIME: 30 minutes

MAKES: 12 side-dish servings

2	tablespoons extra-virgin olive oil
2	tablespoons fresh lemon juice
¾	teaspoon salt
½	teaspoon coarsely ground pepper
1	pint grape tomatoes, cut in half
6	Kirby (pickling) cucumbers (1½ pounds), not peeled, cut into 1" by ½" chunks
1	large red pepper (8 to 10 ounces), cut into 1-inch pieces
1	green onion, thinly sliced
½	cup Kalamata olives, pitted and coarsely chopped
½	cup loosely packed fresh mint leaves, chopped
3	ounces feta cheese (¾ cup), crumbled (optional)

1. In large serving bowl, with fork, combine oil, lemon juice, salt, and black pepper.

2. Add tomatoes, cucumbers, red pepper, green onion, olives, and mint. Toss until mixed and evenly coated with dressing. If not serving right away, cover and refrigerate up to 6 hours. Sprinkle with feta to serve, if you like. Toss before serving.

EACH SERVING: About 45 calories, 1g protein, 5g carbohydrate, 3g total fat (0g saturated), 2g fiber, 0mg cholesterol, 195mg sodium

NUTRITIONAL NOTE: OLIVES

Olives are high in vitamin E and iron, and contain a variety of phytonutrients that protect cells against the damage caused by free radicals.

CREAMY CUCUMBER-DILL SALAD

This cool, crunchy salad is a summertime classic. Don't skip the salting step, or the cucumbers will be limp, not crisp.

TOTAL TIME: 35 minutes plus standing and chilling

MAKES: 5 cups or 10 side-dish servings

8	large (about 5 pounds) cucumbers
1	teaspoon salt
6	large radishes
1	container (8 ounces) plain low-fat yogurt
½	cup reduced-fat sour cream
½	cup loosely packed fresh dill, chopped
2	tablespoons fresh lime juice
¼	teaspoon ground black pepper
1	small garlic clove, crushed with garlic press

1. With vegetable peeler, remove several strips of peel from each cucumber. Cut each cucumber lengthwise in half; with teaspoon, scoop out seeds. With knife or in food processor fitted with slicing blade, thinly slice cucumber halves crosswise. In large bowl, toss cucumbers with salt; let stand 30 minutes.

2. Meanwhile, thinly slice radishes; transfer to serving bowl. Add yogurt, sour cream, dill, lime juice, pepper, and garlic. Stir until combined.

3. Transfer sliced cucumbers to a colander. Place colander in sink and, with hands, press cucumbers to remove as much liquid as possible. Pat cucumbers dry with paper towels.

4. Add cucumbers to bowl with yogurt mixture. Toss until evenly coated. Cover and refrigerate at least 1 hour or overnight to blend flavors.

EACH SERVING: About 60 calories, 3g protein, 9g carbohydrate, 2g total fat (1g saturated), 2g fiber, 6mg cholesterol, 180mg sodium

CANTALOUPE & CUCUMBER SALAD

Juicy, ripe cantaloupes and crunchy English cucumbers are a tempting duo.

TOTAL TIME: 20 minutes

MAKES: 8 ½ cups or 10 side-dish servings

¼   cup fresh lime juice

¼   teaspoon salt

⅛   teaspoon freshly ground black pepper

1   large English (seedless) cucumber (1 pound), peeled in alternating strips and coarsely chopped

2   ripe cantaloupes, flesh removed from rind and seeds discarded, coarsely chopped

3   green onions, thinly sliced

½   cup loosely packed fresh cilantro leaves, chopped

In large bowl, whisk lime juice, salt, and pepper until blended. Add cucumber, cantaloupe, green onion, and cilantro; toss to coat.

EACH SERVING: About 45 calories, 6g protein, 25g carbohydrate, 5g total fat (1g saturated), 5g fiber, 0mg cholesterol, 160mg sodium

NECTARINE & BERRY SALAD

Summer fruits are pleasing practically unadorned. Crystallized ginger and fresh lime juice add a bit of sweetness and tang to this seasonal combo.

TOTAL TIME: 15 minutes

MAKES: 8 side-dish servings

3   tablespoons fresh lime juice (from 2 limes)

2   tablespoons finely chopped crystallized ginger

1   tablespoon sugar

2   pounds nectarines (6 medium), pitted and chopped

1   pint blackberries

In large bowl, stir lime juice, ginger, and sugar until sugar dissolves. Add nectarines and berries, and toss until coated. If not serving immediately, spoon into storage container with tight-fitting lid and refrigerate for up to 4 hours.

EACH SERVING: About 85 calories, 1g protein, 21g carbohydrate, 1g total fat (0g saturated), 4g fiber, 0mg cholesterol, 0mg sodium

BULGUR AND GRAPE SALAD WITH DRIED FIGS AND ALMONDS

Try this irresistible riff on the Middle Eastern bulgur salad, tabbouleh, dreamed up by Barbara Estabrook, finalist in the side-dish category of our second Cook Your Heart Out contest. It's tossed with sweet grapes and figs and crunchy roasted almonds and dressed with a shallot-and-parsley vinaigrette.

ACTIVE TIME: 15 minutes **TOTAL TIME:** 1 hour

MAKES: 6 side-dish servings

1	cup uncooked bulgur
2	cups water
3	tablespoons extra-virgin olive oil
3	tablespoons champagne or white wine vinegar
¼	cup shallots, finely chopped
1	small garlic clove, grated
¼	teaspoon salt
¼	teaspoon cracked black pepper
1½	cups champagne grapes or black grapes, halved
⅓	cup dried Calimyrna figs, tiny stems removed, sliced
3	tablespoons chopped fresh flat-leaf parsley
3	tablespoons coarsely chopped roasted almonds (skin on)
1	tablespoon chopped fresh mint

1. Place bulgur in large bowl. Bring water to a boil in microwave or small pan. Pour boiling water over bulgur, cover, and seal top of bowl with foil. Let bulgur stand 30 minutes or until water is absorbed. Uncover and fluff with fork. Let stand 15 to 20 minutes more.

2. Meanwhile, in small bowl, whisk together oil, vinegar, shallots, garlic, salt, and pepper. When bulgur is ready, add grapes, figs, and parsley to bowl; gently toss to combine. Gradually add vinaigrette to bulgur mixture while tossing to coat. Stir in almonds, then scatter mint over top of salad and serve.

EACH SERVING: About 215 calories, 5g protein, 33g carbohydrate, 9g total fat (1g saturated), 6g fiber, 0mg cholesterol, 104mg sodium

MINTED CORN AND BROWN RICE SALAD

Here's a fresh-from-the-garden salad—the sweetness of corn, the tangy flavor of crispy radishes, and the refreshing bright taste of mint—combined with toothsome brown rice.

ACTIVE TIME: 35 minutes **TOTAL TIME:** 55 minutes plus cooling
MAKES: 12 side-dish servings

1	cup long-grain brown rice
1¼	teaspoons salt
¼	cup fresh lemon juice
3	tablespoons olive oil
¼	teaspoon freshly ground black pepper
8	medium ears corn, husks and silk removed
1	bunch radishes, chopped (1¼ cups)
¾	cup shelled fresh peas or thawed frozen peas
½	cup loosely packed fresh mint leaves, thinly sliced
2	tablespoons snipped fresh chives

1. Prepare rice as label directs, but do not add butter and use only ½ teaspoon salt.

2. While rice is cooking, prepare dressing: In large bowl, with wire whisk, mix lemon juice, oil, pepper, and remaining ¾ teaspoon salt until blended.

3. Add hot rice to dressing and toss to coat. Cool slightly, about 30 minutes, tossing occasionally.

4. Meanwhile, in 5-quart Dutch oven, bring *3 quarts water* to a boil over high heat. Add corn and cook 5 minutes. Drain. When corn is cool enough to handle, cut kernels from cobs (you should have about 4 cups).

5. Add corn to rice with radishes, peas, mint, and chives. Toss until evenly mixed. If not serving right away, cover and refrigerate up to 8 hours.

EACH SERVING: About 140 calories, 3g protein, 25g carbohydrate, 4g total fat (1g saturated), 4g fiber, 0mg cholesterol, 255mg sodium

MILLET WITH CORN AND GREEN CHILES

Millet has a mild flavor that is greatly enhanced by pan-toasting it first. For an extra shot of flavor, serve this topped with a dollop of reduced-fat sour cream and your favorite salsa.

ACTIVE TIME: 25 minutes **TOTAL TIME:** 50 minutes

MAKES: 8 side-dish servings

1 cup millet
2 cups fresh corn (cut from 4 ears) or frozen corn kernels
2 teaspoons vegetable oil
1 medium onion, chopped
1 garlic clove, crushed with garlic press
1 teaspoon ground cumin
3½ cups water
1 can (4½ ounces) diced green chiles, drained
½ teaspoon salt
¼ cup lightly packed fresh cilantro leaves, chopped (optional)

1. In large skillet, cook millet over medium heat until toasted, about 5 minutes, stirring frequently. Pour millet into bowl and set aside.

2. Add corn to dry skillet and cook over high heat until corn browns, about 5 minutes, stirring frequently. Transfer corn to plate.

3. In same skillet, heat oil over medium heat. Add onion; cook until softened, about 5 minutes. Stir in garlic and cumin and cook until fragrant, about 1 minute. Add water, green chiles, and salt. Bring to a boil. Stir in millet. Reduce heat; cover and simmer until millet is tender and water is absorbed, 25 to 30 minutes.

4. Remove skillet from heat, stir in corn; cover and let stand 5 minutes to heat through. Stir in cilantro, if using.

EACH SERVING: About 150 calories, 4g protein, 29g carbohydrate, 3g total fat (0g saturated), 4g fiber, 0mg cholesterol, 200mg sodium

BASIL AND BALSAMIC BEETS

Fresh chopped basil is a cool counterpart to sweet, roasted beets in this easy-to-prepare side dish. Serve with roasted chicken for a delicious, diet-friendly dinner.

ACTIVE TIME: 5 minutes **TOTAL TIME:** 1 hour 5 minutes plus cooling
MAKES: 4 side-dish servings

2	pounds beets
1	tablespoon olive oil
2	tablespoons chopped fresh basil
2	tablespoons balsamic vinegar
1	tablespoon brown sugar
¼	teaspoon salt

1. Preheat oven to 450°F. In 13" by 9" roasting pan, toss beets with oil. Roast 1 hour or until tender. Cool beets; peel and discard skins.

2. Cut beets into ¼-inch pieces; toss with basil, vinegar, brown sugar, and salt.

EACH SERVING: About 120 calories, 2g protein, 19g carbohydrate, 4g total fat (0.5g saturated), 4g fiber, 0mg cholesterol, 260mg sodium

HEART-SMART: EAT YOUR BEETS

Just 1 cooked cup of this superveggie packs 34 percent of your daily need for folate (which can help lower levels of heart-threatening homocysteine), 15 percent of potassium (which reduces blood pressure levels), and 27 percent of manganese (which helps maintain your bones).

SHREDDED BEETS WITH CELERY AND DATES

This simple salad features raw grated beets, which lend the salad high crunch appeal and a rich garnet color.

TOTAL TIME: 10 minutes

MAKES: 4 cups or 8 side-dish servings

1	pound beets, peeled
3	stalks celery, thinly sliced
½	cup pitted dried dates, chopped
3	tablespoons fresh lemon juice
¼	teaspoon salt
¼	teaspoon coarsely ground black pepper

1. Cut beets into quarters. In food processor with shredding blade attached, shred beets; transfer to large bowl.

2. Stir in celery, dates, lemon juice, salt, and pepper. If not serving right away, cover and refrigerate up to 4 hours.

EACH SERVING: About 50 calories, 1g protein, 13g carbohydrate, 0g total fat, 2g fiber, 0mg cholesterol, 110mg sodium

GRILLED EGGPLANT CAPONATA SALAD

Eggplant simply inhales the smoky goodness from the grill. This delicious salad will be a recipe you go back to again and again.

ACTIVE TIME: 25 minutes **TOTAL TIME:** 35 minutes

MAKES: 16 side-dish servings

2   small red onions, cut into ½-inch-thick slices
2   small eggplants (1 to 1¼ pounds each), cut into ¾-inch-thick slices
Nonstick cooking spray
4   medium stalks celery
½   teaspoon salt
2   tablespoons red wine vinegar
2   tablespoons extra-virgin olive oil
1   teaspoon sugar
¼   teaspoon coarsely ground black pepper
6   ripe medium plum tomatoes (1½ pounds), cut into ½-inch chunks
1   cup Kalamata, Gaeta, or green Sicilian olives, pitted and chopped
¼   cup golden raisins
3   tablespoons drained capers
½   cup loosely packed fresh flat-leaf parsley leaves

1. Prepare outdoor grill for covered direct grilling over medium heat.

2. Meanwhile, for easier handling, insert metal skewers through onion slices, if you like. Lightly spray both sides of eggplant slices with cooking spray. Sprinkle onions, eggplant, and celery with salt.

3. Place onions, eggplant, and celery on hot grill rack over medium heat. Cover grill and cook vegetables until tender and lightly browned, 8 to 10 minutes, turning once and transferring to plate as they are done. Cool slightly until easy to handle.

4. Cut eggplant and celery into ¾-inch chunks; coarsely chop onions. In large bowl, mix vinegar, oil, sugar, and pepper until blended. Stir in tomatoes, olives, raisins, capers, and parsley. Add eggplant, onions, and celery, and gently toss to coat.

5. Serve salad at room temperature, or cover and refrigerate up to 1 day.

EACH SERVING: About 75 calories, 1g protein, 11g carbohydrate, 3g total fat (1g saturated), 2g fiber, 0mg cholesterol, 240mg sodium

GRILLED EGGPLANT WITH FETA AND FRESH MINT

We love the combination of smoky, grilled eggplant and tangy feta cheese.

ACTIVE TIME: 10 minutes
TOTAL TIME: 20 minutes

MAKES: 4 side-dish servings

1 large eggplant (2¼ to 2½ pounds)
2 tablespoons olive oil
¼ cup crumbled feta cheese
2 tablespoons chopped fresh mint
Orange wedges, for garnish

1. Cut eggplant into ½-inch-thick slices; brush each slice with oil.

2. Place on hot, ridged grill pan over medium-high heat; cook eggplant slices until tender, 4 to 6 minutes per side. Transfer to platter.

3. Sprinkle with feta and mint. Garnish with orange wedges.

EACH SERVING: About 105 calories, 3g protein, 9g carbohydrate, 7g total fat (2g saturated), 4g fiber, 8mg cholesterol, 110mg sodium

NUTRITIONAL NOTE: EGGPLANT

Eggplant is rich in nutrients, including potassium and vitamin B_1 (both important for muscle and nerve activity) and bone-building manganese and magnesium. Since it's high in dietary fiber (and 1 cup of cooked eggplant is only 28 calories), it's also a great choice when you're watching your weight.

A GUIDE TO GRILLED VEGETABLES

Preheat the grill to medium-high. Brush vegetables with seasoning and grill as directed.

MAKES: 4 servings

VEGETABLE	PREPARATION	SEASONING	GRILLING TIME
8 ears corn	Soak 15 minutes, then remove silk (leave husks on) or remove husks and silk	Brush with 1 tablespoon oil	20 minutes, turning occasionally
1½-pound eggplant	Cut crosswise into ½-inch-thick slices	Brush with 4 teaspoons oil	11 to 13 minutes per side
4 yellow squash or zucchini (8 ounces each)	Cut lengthwise into ¼-inch-thick slices	Brush with 4 teaspoons oil	5 minutes per side
8 ounces large white mushrooms	Trim and thread onto skewers	Brush with 2 teaspoons oil	20 minutes, turning several times
4 large portobello mushrooms (about 1 pound)	Remove stems	Brush with 4 teaspoons oil	15 minutes per side
4 bell peppers	Cut lengthwise into quarters	no seasonings	10 to 12 minutes per side
4 medium red or white onions	Cut crosswise into ½-inch-thick slices; secure with toothpicks	Brush with 4 teaspoons oil	12 to 14 minutes per side

GRILLED VEGETABLES WITH THAI PESTO

Fresh lime and sweet chili sauce add zip to this Thai-inspired pesto. Grilled peppers, eggplant, zucchini, and other vegetables make healthy and delicious dippers. Serve this as a side or a starter at your next barbecue.

ACTIVE TIME: 25 minutes **TOTAL TIME:** 35 minutes

MAKES: 4 side-dish servings

THAI PESTO

1   large lime
½   cup walnuts
1   cup packed fresh basil leaves
1   tablespoon Thai sweet chili sauce
3   tablespoons water
¼   teaspoon salt

GRILLED VEGETABLES

4   plum tomatoes, cut lengthwise in half
2   yellow peppers, cut into quarters, seeded, and stemmed
½   medium eggplant, cut crosswise into ¾-inch-thick slices
1   large zucchini, cut diagonally into ½-inch-thick slices
½   large sweet onion, cut through root end into 6 wedges
Olive oil nonstick cooking spray
¼   teaspoon salt

1. Prepare pesto: From lime, grate ½ teaspoon peel and squeeze 2 tablespoons juice. In skillet, toast walnuts over medium heat about 5 minutes, stirring, until fragrant. Set aside.

2. In food processor with knife blade attached, blend nuts, basil, chili sauce, water, lime peel and juice, and salt. Store covered in refrigerator up to 2 days. Makes about ⅔ cup.

3. Prepare vegetables: Prepare outdoor grill for direct grilling over medium heat, or preheat large ridged grill pan over medium heat. Lightly spray tomatoes, peppers, eggplant, zucchini, and onion with cooking spray. Place vegetables on hot grill grate, cover, and cook until tender, turning each vegetable over once during cooking time. Cook tomatoes and zucchini 6 to 8 minutes, peppers and onion 8 to 10 minutes, and eggplant 10 to 12 minutes. As vegetables finish cooking, transfer to serving plate. Sprinkle with salt and serve with pesto.

EACH SERVING: About 205 calories, 6g protein, 28g carbohydrate, 11g total fat (1g saturated), 7g fiber, 0mg cholesterol, 365mg sodium

GREEN BEANS WITH MIXED MUSHROOMS

Inspired by a favorite casserole, this features caramelized onions, earthy cremini and shiitake mushrooms, and fresh green beans.

ACTIVE TIME: 30 minutes **TOTAL TIME:** 45 minutes

MAKES: 12 side-dish servings

2	tablespoons olive oil
4	sprigs fresh thyme
2	large onions (12 ounces each), thinly sliced
1	garlic clove, crushed with garlic press
8	ounces cremini mushrooms, thinly sliced
4	ounces shiitake mushrooms, stems discarded, thinly sliced
2½	teaspoons salt
½	teaspoon ground black pepper
3	pounds green beans, trimmed

1. Bring covered 7- to 8-quart saucepot of *water* to a boil over high heat.

2. Meanwhile, in 12-inch skillet, heat oil over medium-high heat. Add thyme and onions; cook 10 to 12 minutes, until browned and very tender, stirring occasionally. Stir in garlic and cook 1 minute. Add all mushrooms and cook 5 minutes or until tender, stirring occasionally. Stir in ½ teaspoon each salt and pepper. Remove and discard thyme.

3. Add green beans and remaining 2 teaspoons salt to boiling water. Cook, uncovered, 8 to 9 minutes, until tender, stirring occasionally. Drain and rinse with cold water. If making ahead, transfer mushroom mixture to medium bowl. Cover; refrigerate up to overnight. Transfer beans to resealable plastic bag; refrigerate up to overnight.

4. When ready to serve, return green beans to saucepot and add mushroom mixture, stirring to combine. Cook over medium heat until beans are heated through, stirring occasionally.

EACH SERVING: About 80 calories, 3g protein, 14g carbohydrate, 3g total fat (0g saturated), 4g fiber, 0mg cholesterol, 125mg sodium

SAUTÉED SPINACH WITH GARLIC AND LEMON

This simple sauté is packed with folate, iron, calcium, and vitamins A and C.

ACTIVE TIME: 5 minutes **TOTAL TIME:** 10 minutes

MAKES: 4 side-dish servings

- 1   tablespoon olive oil
- 2   garlic cloves, crushed
- 2   bags (10 ounces each) spinach
- 1   tablespoon fresh lemon juice
- ¼   teaspoon salt

In 6-quart saucepot, heat oil over medium-high heat. Rinse spinach and set within reach of stovetop; leave water clinging to leaves. Add garlic to hot oil and cook 1 minute or until golden, stirring. Add spinach to pot in three batches; cook 2 minutes or until spinach fits in pot. Cover and cook 2 minutes longer or just until spinach wilts, stirring once. Stir in lemon juice and salt and serve.

EACH SERVING: About 45 calories, 4g protein, 1g carbohydrate, 4g total fat (1g saturated), 12g fiber, 0mg cholesterol, 305mg sodium

GREEN BEANS WITH CARAMELIZED ONIONS

Caramelized onions make everything better. And this green-bean side dish—a lighter take on a beloved holiday casserole—is no exception.

ACTIVE TIME: 30 minutes **TOTAL TIME:** 1 hour 10 minutes

MAKES: 14 cups or 16 side-dish servings

3   pounds green beans, trimmed

1½   pounds red onions (about 3 medium), cut in half and then sliced

3   tablespoons butter

1   tablespoon fresh thyme leaves, chopped

1½   teaspoons salt

½   teaspoon ground black pepper

1. Fill large bowl with *ice water* to cool beans quickly after cooking; set aside. Bring 6- to 8-quart saucepot of *salted water* to a boil over high heat. Add beans in 2 batches and cook each batch 4 minutes or until beans are tender-crisp, making sure water returns to boiling before adding each batch of beans. With slotted spoon or sieve, transfer beans to bowl of ice water. Drain beans thoroughly.

2. In nonstick 12-inch skillet, combine onions, butter , thyme, salt, and pepper. Cook over medium heat 15 minutes or until onions start to brown, stirring occasionally. Reduce heat to medium-low and cook 5 to 7 minutes longer or until onions turn dark brown, stirring frequently. Stir beans into onion mixture; heat through before serving.

EACH SERVING: About 60 calories, 2g protein, 9g carbohydrate, 2g total fat (0g saturated), 3g fiber, 0mg cholesterol, 250mg sodium

TIP

If you'd like to make this dish ahead of time, (up to two days in advance), blanch, cool, and drain beans. Cook onion mixture and cool. Refrigerate each component separately in sealed plastic bags. To reheat, toss beans and onion mixture in 4-quart microwave-safe glass bowl. Microwave on High about 8 minutes, stirring halfway through heating.

TARRAGON PEAS AND PEARL ONIONS

Fresh tarragon adds a perky licorice flavor to these lightly cooked peas and pearl onions.

ACTIVE TIME: 10 minutes **TOTAL TIME:** 15 minutes

MAKES: 8 side-dish servings

1   tablespoon butter
1   bag (16 ounces) frozen pearl onions
1   bag (16 ounces) frozen peas
¼   cup water
½   teaspoon salt
¼   teaspoon ground black pepper
1   tablespoon chopped fresh tarragon leaves

1. In nonstick 12-inch skillet, melt butter over medium heat. Add frozen pearl onions and cook 7 to 9 minutes or until browned.

2. Add frozen peas, water, salt, and pepper to skillet; stir to combine. Cover and cook 3 to 4 minutes longer or until onions and peas are tender. Stir tarragon into vegetables and spoon into serving bowl.

EACH SERVING: About 75 calories, 3g protein, 12g carbohydrate, 2g total fat (0g saturated), 4g fiber, 0mg cholesterol, 202mg sodium

APPLE CIDER–BRAISED GREENS

Our easy Apple Cider–Braised Greens make an excellent side dish for holidays or any day.

ACTIVE TIME: 30 minutes **TOTAL TIME:** 1 hour 5 minutes
MAKES: 8 cups or 16 side-dish servings

1	pound mustard greens
1	pound collard greens
1	pound Swiss chard
2	tablespoons olive oil
3	large garlic cloves, thinly sliced
1	cup apple cider
1	tablespoon cider vinegar
1	teaspoon salt
2	red cooking apples, such as Gala or Rome Beauty, unpeeled and cut into ¾-inch chunks

1. Remove stems from mustard greens; discard stems. Trim stem ends from collard greens and Swiss chard; remove stems from leaves. Cut stems into 1-inch pieces; cut leaves into 2-inch pieces. Rinse leaves and stems; drain well.

2. In 8-quart saucepot, heat oil over high heat until hot. Add garlic and cook 30 seconds to 1 minute or until golden, stirring constantly. Add as many leaves and stems as possible, cider, vinegar, and salt, stirring to wilt greens. Add remaining greens in batches.

3. Reduce heat to medium. Cover saucepot and cook greens 15 minutes. Stir in apples; cook, partially covered, 10 minutes longer or until stems are very tender and most of liquid evaporates, stirring occasionally. With slotted spoon, transfer to serving bowl.

EACH SERVING: About 60 calories, 2g protein, 10g carbohydrate, 2g total fat (0g saturated), 3g fiber, 0mg cholesterol, 310mg sodium

TIP
To make this dish ahead, spoon cooked greens into microwave-safe bowl; cover with plastic wrap and refrigerate up to 2 days. When ready to serve, vent plastic wrap and microwave on High 8 minutes or until hot, stirring halfway through.

MAPLE SQUASH

In the vegetable department, nothing evokes the fall season like butternut squash. Here we toss it with a mix of maple syrup and spices, then roast it to concentrate its natural sweetness.

ACTIVE TIME: 5 minutes **TOTAL TIME:** 35 minutes
MAKES: 8 side-dish servings

1   package (2 pounds) peeled and cubed butternut squash
1   tablespoon olive oil
¼   teaspoon salt
⅓   cup maple syrup
½   teaspoon pumpkin pie spice
Pinch cayenne (ground red) pepper

1. Preheat oven to 425°F. Line 15 ½″ by 10 ½″ jelly-roll pan with foil. Place squash in pan; drizzle with oil, sprinkle with salt, and toss to combine. Spread cubes into single layer and roast 15 minutes.

2. Meanwhile, in 1-cup liquid measuring cup, stir maple syrup with pumpkin pie spice and cayenne. Toss squash with maple mixture. Continue roasting until fork-tender, 15 to 20 minutes longer. Spoon squash, along with any pan juices, into serving dish.

EACH SERVING: About 100 calories, 1g protein, 22g carbohydrate, 2g total fat (0g saturated), 2g fiber, 0mg cholesterol, 80mg sodium

CARROT AND ZUCCHINI RIBBONS

Southwestern seasonings make this quick side salad a great complement to summertime's grilled foods.

TOTAL TIME: 20 minutes

MAKES: 4 side-dish servings

1	tablespoon fresh lime juice
1	teaspoon vegetable oil
⅛	teaspoon chipotle chile powder (see Tip)
¼	teaspoon salt
¼	teaspoon pepper
3	carrots, peeled
1	large zucchini
¼	cup fresh cilantro leaves

1. In large bowl, whisk together lime juice, oil, chile powder, salt, and pepper.

2. Use vegetable peeler to cut carrots into long ribbons. Stop peeling when you reach core; discard core. Shave zucchini into ribbons; stop peeling when you reach seeds; discard seeds. Cut ribbons in half to make them more manageable, if you like.

3. Add ribbons and cilantro leaves to bowl with dressing; toss until evenly coated.

EACH SERVING: About 40 calories, 1g protein, 7g carbohydrate, 1g total fat (0g saturated), 2g fiber, 0mg cholesterol, 183mg sodium

> **TIP**
> Chipotle chile peppers are a type of hot pepper that can be found dried, pickled, or canned in adobo sauce. Here we use the dried powdered form to add both heat and a subtle smoky flavor to this side dish.

CRUNCHY PEANUT BROCCOLI

Toasted peanuts partner with shallots and soy in this kid-friendly side.

ACTIVE TIME: 20 minutes **TOTAL TIME:** 30 minutes
MAKES: 4 side-dish servings

1¼ teaspoons salt
1 pound broccoli flowerets
2 tablespoons vegetable oil
¼ cup roasted unsalted peanuts, chopped
1 small shallot, finely chopped
1 teaspoon reduced-sodium soy sauce
¼ teaspoon freshly ground black pepper
1 green onion (green parts only) thinly sliced

1. Bring large covered saucepot of *water* to a boil over high heat. Fill large bowl with *ice and water*.

2. Add 1 teaspoon salt, then broccoli, to boiling water. Cook, uncovered, 3 to 4 minutes, until bright green and tender-crisp. Drain, then transfer to bowl of ice water. When cool, drain well. Place between paper towels to dry completely. Broccoli can be refrigerated in airtight container or resealable plastic bag up to overnight.

3. In 12-inch skillet, combine oil and peanuts. Cook over medium heat 4 to 5 minutes, until nuts are golden, stirring occasionally. Stir in shallot and cook , 1 minute. Stir in soy sauce, then broccoli. Sprinkle with pepper and remaining ¼ teaspoon salt. Cook, stirring and tossing, 2 minutes or until broccoli is heated through and evenly coated with nut mixture. Garnish with sliced green onion.

EACH SERVING: About 150 calories, 6g protein, 9g carbohydrate, 12g total fat (1g saturated), 4g fiber, 0mg cholesterol, 300mg sodium

HEART-SMART INGREDIENT: BROCCOLI

Broccoli serves up heart-healthy folate, vitamin B₆, omega-6 fatty acids, and potassium, as well as calcium, vitamin C (which helps with the absorption of calcium), and sleep-promoting tryptophan.

JALAPEÑO CORNBREAD

What's not to love about a pan of homemade cornbread hot from the oven? We gave this version some sass by throwing a chopped jalapeño into the batter. It can be made with either regular milk or soy milk.

ACTIVE TIME: 10 minutes **TOTAL TIME:** 40 minutes

MAKES: 12 servings

1 cup frozen corn
2 cups cornmeal
¾ cup all-purpose flour
1 teaspoon baking powder
1 teaspoon baking soda
½ teaspoon salt
2 cups milk or soy milk
1 tablespoon cider vinegar
⅓ cup canola oil
2 tablespoons honey
1 jalapeño chile, seeded and finely chopped

1. Preheat oven to 350°F. Line 13" by 9" baking pan with parchment paper and spray with nonstick cooking spray.

2. Rinse corn in colander with warm water to defrost. Drain thoroughly and set aside.

3. Meanwhile, in large bowl, sift together cornmeal, flour, baking powder, baking soda, and salt.

4. In medium bowl, whisk milk, vinegar, oil, and honey until mixture begins to foam, about 1 minute. Pour wet ingredients into dry and stir until just combined. Fold in corn and jalapeño.

5. Spread batter evenly into prepared pan. Bake until toothpick inserted in center comes out clean, 30 to 35 minutes. Cut into squares.

EACH SERVING: About 220 calories, 4g protein, 33g carbohydrate, 7g total fat (0g saturated), 2g fiber, 0mg cholesterol, 270mg sodium

DOUBLE CORNBREAD

Corn and jalapeños enhance the texture and flavor of this hearty cornbread.

ACTIVE TIME: 20 minutes **TOTAL TIME:** 30 minutes
MAKES: 24 pieces

1½ cups all-purpose flour
1½ cups yellow cornmeal
¼ cup sugar
4 teaspoons baking powder
½ teaspoon baking soda
1 teaspoon salt
2½ cups buttermilk
3 large eggs
2 cups fresh corn kernels or 1 package (10 ounces) frozen corn, thawed
6 tablespoons butter, melted
2 jalapeño chiles, seeds and membranes discarded, finely chopped

1. Preheat oven to 450°F. Grease 13" by 9" baking pan. In large bowl, combine flour, cornmeal, sugar, baking powder, baking soda, and salt. In medium bowl, with wire whisk or fork, beat buttermilk and eggs until blended.

2. Add corn, melted butter, and jalapeños to buttermilk mixture, then add to flour mixture. Stir until ingredients are just mixed.

3. Pour batter into prepared pan. Bake 22 to 25 minutes or until golden at edges and toothpick inserted in center comes out clean. Cut lengthwise into 4 strips, then cut each strip crosswise into 6 pieces. Serve warm.

EACH SERVING: About 125 calories, 4g protein, 19g carbohydrate, 4g total fat (2g saturated), 1g fiber, 36mg cholesterol, 255mg sodium

WHOLE-WHEAT SESAME BISCUITS

We blended whole-wheat flour with toasted sesame seeds to make these light golden rounds.

ACTIVE TIME: 15 minutes **TOTAL TIME:** 30 minutes
MAKES: 12 biscuits

2   tablespoons sesame seeds
1   cup whole-wheat flour
1   cup all-purpose flour
1   tablespoon baking powder
¾   teaspoon salt
4   tablespoons cold butter
¾   cup plus 3 tablespoons milk

1. In small skillet, toast sesame seeds over medium heat until lightly browned, about 5 minutes, stirring occasionally.

2. Preheat oven to 425°F. Lightly grease large cookie sheet.

3. In large bowl, mix whole-wheat and all-purpose flours, baking powder, salt, and 5 teaspoons toasted sesame seeds. With pastry blender or two knives used scissor-fashion, cut in butter until mixture resembles coarse crumbs. Stir in ¾ cup plus 2 tablespoons milk, stirring just until mixture forms a soft dough that leaves sides of bowl.

4. Turn dough onto lightly floured surface; knead 8 to 10 strokes to mix thoroughly. With floured rolling pin, roll dough ½-inch thick.

5. With floured 2½-inch round biscuit cutter, cut out biscuits. Place biscuits about 2 inches apart on cookie sheet. Press trimmings together; roll out and cut again.

6. Brush tops of biscuits with remaining 1 tablespoon milk; sprinkle with remaining 1 teaspoon sesame seeds. Bake until golden, 12 to 15 minutes.

EACH BISCUIT: About 125 calories, 3g protein, 17g carbohydrate, 6g total fat (1g saturated), 2g fiber, 3mg cholesterol, 285mg sodium

VEGETABLE-HERB STUFFING

At 86 fewer calories and 4 grams less fat per serving than classic bread stuffing, this recipe is a win-win. The secret? We replaced the butter with a smaller amount of heart-healthy olive oil and increased the ratio of vegetables and fresh herbs to bread.

ACTIVE TIME: 20 minutes **TOTAL TIME:** 1 hour 20 minutes
MAKES: 12 cups or 24 side-dish servings

1½ pounds sliced firm multigrain bread
1   tablespoon olive oil
2   carrots, peeled and finely chopped
2   stalks celery, finely chopped
1   onion, finely chopped
½   cup loosely packed fresh parsley leaves, coarsely chopped
¾   teaspoon poultry seasoning
½   teaspoon salt
¼   teaspoon ground black pepper
2½ cups canned chicken broth

1. Preheat oven to 400°F. Grease shallow 3- to 3½-quart baking dish; set aside.

2. Arrange bread slices on two large cookie sheets and toast in oven 16 to 17 minutes, until golden and dry, turning slices over halfway through toasting.

3. Meanwhile, in nonstick 12-inch skillet, heat oil over medium heat until hot. Add carrots, celery, and onion and cook, stirring occasionally, until vegetables are tender and lightly browned, about 12 minutes.

4. Remove skillet from heat; stir in parsley, poultry seasoning, salt, and pepper.

5. With serrated knife, cut toasted bread into ½-inch cubes, then place in very large bowl. Reduce oven temperature to 325°F.

6. Add broth and vegetable mixture to bread in bowl and toss until bread is evenly moistened.

7. Spoon stuffing into prepared baking dish. Cover with foil and bake 30 minutes. Remove foil and bake 15 to 20 minutes longer, until heated through and lightly browned on top.

EACH ½-CUP SERVING: About 90 calories, 3g protein, 16g carbohydrate, 2g total fat (1g saturated), 2g fiber, 0mg cholesterol, 203mg sodium

POTATO GRATIN WITH BROCCOLI

We've trimmed the fat from a family favorite by choosing creamy Yukon Gold potatoes for the base of this dish—their creamy texture makes the traditional use of heavy cream and milk unnecessary. Broccoli flowerets add color—and lots of vitamins.

ACTIVE TIME: 10 minutes **TOTAL TIME:** 30 minutes
MAKES: 8 side-dish servings

1   pound broccoli flowerets
1   pound Yukon Gold potatoes, peeled and cut into 1-inch chunks
2   cups water
Pinch ground nutmeg
¾   cup freshly grated Parmesan cheese
½   teaspoon salt
¼   teaspoon coarsely ground black pepper

1. In 4-quart saucepan, place broccoli, potatoes, and water. Cover and bring to a boil over high heat. Reduce heat to medium-low; cover and cook until potatoes and broccoli are very tender, 17 to 20 minutes, stirring once halfway through cooking.

2. Meanwhile, set oven rack 6 inches from source of heat and preheat broiler.

3. Drain vegetables in colander set over large bowl, reserving ¼ *cup cooking water*. Return vegetables to saucepan. With potato masher or slotted spoon, coarsely mash vegetables, adding some reserved vegetable cooking liquid if mixture seems dry. Stir in nutmeg, ¼ cup Parmesan, salt, and pepper.

4. In shallow, broiler-safe 1- to 1½-quart baking dish, spread vegetable mixture; sprinkle with remaining ½ cup Parmesan. Place dish in oven and broil until Parmesan is browned, 2 to 3 minutes.

EACH SERVING: About 95 calories, 6g protein, 13g carbohydrate, 3g total fat (2g saturated), 2g fiber, 6mg cholesterol, 305mg sodium

LIGHT MASHED POTATOES

Fat-free half-and-half gives these potatoes the same silky texture you'd get with heavy cream but without the extra fat and cholesterol.

ACTIVE TIME: 15 minutes **TOTAL TIME:** 30 minutes
MAKES: 6 side-dish servings

2   pounds Yukon Gold potatoes, peeled and cut into 1-inch pieces
1   tablespoon butter
¾   teaspoon salt
½   cup fat-free half-and-half, warmed

1. In 4-quart saucepan, combine potatoes with *water to cover* and bring to a boil over high heat. Reduce heat to low; cover and simmer 8 to 10 minutes, until potatoes are fork-tender. Reserve *¼ cup cooking water.* Drain potatoes and return to saucepan.

2. Add butter and salt to potatoes and mash. Gradually add half-and-half, continuing to mash until mixture is smooth and well blended; add some of reserved cooking water if necessary.

EACH SERVING: About 145 calories, 3g protein, 29g carbohydrate, 2g total fat (0g saturated), 2g fiber, 0mg cholesterol, 345mg sodium

SWEET POTATOES WITH "MARSHMALLOW" MERINGUE

To modernize this crowd-pleaser, we microwaved the potatoes before mashing them and topped them with meringue mounds—a less-sugary substitute for the mini marshmallows made popular in the 1950s.

ACTIVE TIME: 30 minutes **TOTAL TIME:** 50 minutes

MAKES: 12 side-dish servings

3	pounds sweet potatoes
2	tablespoons pure maple syrup
1	tablespoon packed dark brown sugar
1	tablespoon fresh lemon juice
1/8	teaspoon ground allspice
1/4	teaspoon salt
3	large egg whites
1/4	teaspoon cream of tartar
1/3	cup granulated sugar

1. Preheat oven to 400°F. Pierce sweet potatoes all over with tip of knife; place in large microwave-safe bowl. Cover with vented plastic wrap and microwave on High 15 to 17 minutes, until very tender when pierced with fork; drain. When cool enough to handle, peel potatoes and return to bowl.

2. To bowl with sweet potatoes, add maple syrup, brown sugar, lemon juice, allspice, and salt. Mash potatoes with potato masher until smooth. Transfer to 2-quart casserole dish. (If making ahead, cover and refrigerate up to overnight, then bake in 400°F oven for 15 minutes or until heated through before proceeding.)

3. In large bowl, with mixer on high speed, beat egg whites and cream of tartar until soft peaks form. Sprinkle in granulated sugar, 2 tablespoons at a time, beating until sugar dissolves and meringue stands in stiff, glossy peaks when beaters are lifted.

4. Transfer meringue to large piping bag fitted with 1/2-inch plain tip or to heavy-duty gallon-size resealable plastic bag with one corner cut to form 1/2-inch hole. Starting at one side of casserole dish, pipe meringue in small mounds onto sweet potatoes, covering entire surface. Bake 6 to 8 minutes, until meringue is golden.

EACH SERVING: About 100 calories, 2g protein, 23g carbohydrate, 0g total fat, 2g fiber, 0mg cholesterol, 90mg sodium

OVEN FRIES

You won't miss the fat in these hand-cut "fries." They bake beautifully in a jelly-roll pan with a spritz of nonstick cooking spray and a sprinkle of salt and pepper.

ACTIVE TIME: 10 minutes **TOTAL TIME:** 30 minutes
MAKES: 4 side-dish servings

Nonstick cooking spray
3   medium baking potatoes (8 ounces each), not peeled
½   teaspoon salt
¼   teaspoon coarsely ground black pepper

1. Preheat oven to 500°F. Spray two 15½" by 10½" jelly-roll pans or two large cookie sheets with nonstick cooking spray.

2. Scrub potatoes well and cut each lengthwise in half. Arrange each potato half cut side down and cut lengthwise into ¼-inch-thick slices. Place slices in medium bowl and toss with salt and pepper.

3. Divide potatoes between pans and spray with nonstick cooking spray. Roast potatoes until tender and lightly browned, about 20 minutes, rotating pans between upper and lower racks halfway through.

EACH SERVING: About 130 calories, 4g protein, 28g carbohydrate, 1g total fat (0g saturated), 3g fiber, 0mg cholesterol, 280mg sodium

ROSEMARY AND GARLIC OVEN FRIES

Prepare potatoes as directed, but in step 2 sprinkle with ½ **teaspoon dried rosemary**, crumbled, and **2 garlic cloves**, crushed with garlic press.

CONFETTI RICE PILAF

Tender rice cooked with a festive mix of peas, carrots, and green onions—it's a great way to sneak additional veggies into a meal.

ACTIVE TIME: 10 minutes **TOTAL TIME:** 30 minutes
MAKES: 12 side-dish servings

3	tablespoons butter
2	carrots, peeled and diced
2	cups regular long-grain white rice
1	can (14½ ounces) chicken broth
1	small bay leaf
½	teaspoon salt
¼	teaspoon coarsely ground black pepper
2	cups water
1	package (10 ounces) frozen peas
2	green onions, sliced

1. In 3-quart saucepan, melt butter over medium heat. Add carrots and cook 2 to 3 minutes, until slightly softened, stirring occasionally. Add rice and cook 1 minute, stirring until grains are coated. Stir in broth, bay leaf, salt, pepper, and water; bring to a boil over high heat. Reduce heat to low; cover and simmer 15 to 20 minutes, until all liquid is absorbed and rice is tender.

2. Discard bay leaf. Stir in peas and green onions; heat through.

EACH SERVING: About 165 calories, 4g protein, 29g carbohydrate, 3g total fat (0g saturated), 0g fiber, 0mg cholesterol, 260mg sodium

GARLIC AND HERB BREAD

We used olive oil instead of butter and just one tablespoon of Parmesan to keep this loaf heart smart. We use dried oregano in this recipe, but you can swap in one tablespoon chopped fresh oregano if you have it on hand.

ACTIVE TIME: 5 minutes **TOTAL TIME:** 20 minutes
MAKES: 10 slices

1   loaf Italian bread
2   tablespoons olive oil
2   garlic cloves, finely chopped
1   teaspoon dried oregano
1   tablespoon freshly grated Parmesan cheese

Preheat oven to 350°F. Slice loaf lengthwise in half. Sprinkle cut sides of bread with oil, garlic, oregano, and Parmesan. Press halves of bread together again and wrap loaf in foil; bake 15 minutes or until top of bread is lightly browned.

EACH SLICE: About 110 calories, 3g protein, 16g carbohydrate, 4g total fat (1g saturated), 1g fiber, 0mg cholesterol, 188mg sodium

Apple-Pear Crisp with Peanut Butter (page 424)

8 | SWEET & FRUITY DESSERTS

If you're worried that eating heart-healthy means you'll have to pass on sweet treats, relax! In this chapter, we've selected an assortment of irresistible desserts that put the spotlight on fruit. We've already discussed the nutritional benefits of blueberries (see page 16), which top the list of fruits and veggies with antioxidants (and strawberries are a close runner-up). Apples contain both antioxidant nutrients and heart-healthy dietary fiber. In fact, if you eat seasonal fruits throughout the year, you'll get a rotating roster of good nutrition. Don't forget that frozen and dried fruit count, too! Use them to sweeten up your desserts and you'll need less added sugar.

Enjoy fruit in baked goods like Apple-Berry Hand Pies, Apple-Pear Crisp with Peanut Butter (the kids will love it), and Healthy Makeover Strawberry Shortcake, which includes coarsely ground oatmeal in the flour blend. Or savor it in creamy puddings and frozen treats like Blueberry-Lemon Tiramisu, Peachy Frozen Yogurt, and Healthy Makeover Strawberry Ice Cream. Finish the meal with a dessert that's all about the fruit: Try luscious Sliced Citrus with Lime Syrup or our Summer Salsa with Sweet Tortilla Chips.

And, of course, we share recipes that include dark chocolate, which contains flavonols that lower LDL cholesterol and blood pressure, too (see page 16 for details). Guilt-free treats for the chocoholics among you include our healthy makeover brownies and chewy chocolate chip cookies, which include heart-smart oatmeal in the mix.

WHEAT-FREE ALMOND BUTTER COOKIES

The almond butter, flaxseeds, and sliced almonds in these treats are all loaded with omega-3 fatty acids. Plus, they're gluten- and dairy-free, so everyone can enjoy them.

ACTIVE TIME: 10 minutes **BAKE TIME:** 11 minutes per batch
MAKES: about 36 cookies

1   tablespoon ground flaxseeds or flaxseed meal (see Tip)
3   tablespoons water
1   cup smooth almond butter
1   cup packed brown sugar
1   teaspoon baking soda
½   teaspoon vanilla extract
Pinch salt
½   teaspoon pumpkin pie spice
Sliced almonds, for topping (optional)

1. Preheat oven to 350°F. Line two cookie sheets with parchment paper.

2. In small bowl, mix flaxseeds with water. Let stand 5 minutes.

3. In mixer bowl, combine almond butter, brown sugar, baking soda, vanilla, salt, pumpkin pie spice, and soaked flaxseeds; mix on low speed until thoroughly combined. Using tablespoon measure, form dough into balls and place 1½ inches apart on prepared baking sheets. If desired, top balls with almonds.

4. Bake until slightly golden, 11 to 12 minutes, rotating cookie sheets between upper and lower oven racks halfway through baking. Set sheets on wire racks to cool. Repeat with remaining dough.

5. Store cookies in airtight container up to 3 days, or freeze up to 3 months.

EACH SERVING: About 70 calories, 1g protein, 8g carbohydrate, 4g total fat (0g saturated), 13g fiber, 0mg cholesterol, 72mg sodium

> **TIP**
> Flaxseeds can be found in the natural food section of most supermarkets.

HEALTHY MAKEOVER OATMEAL CHOCOLATE-CHIP COOKIES

Revamped, these gems are still ooey-gooey good—plus, they're only 80 calories each (with a gram of healthy fiber per cookie). We've also cut out half the fat you'd find in this treat's calorie-laden cousins.

ACTIVE TIME: 15 minutes **BAKE TIME:** 12 minutes per batch

MAKES: about 48 cookies

½ cup packed brown sugar

½ cup granulated sugar

½ cup vegetable oil spread (60% to 70% oil)

1 large egg

1 large egg white

2 teaspoons vanilla extract

1¼ cups all-purpose flour

1 teaspoon baking soda

½ teaspoon salt

2½ cups old-fashioned or quick-cooking oats, uncooked

1 cup bittersweet (60% cacao) or semisweet chocolate chips (6 ounces)

1. Preheat oven to 350°F.

2. In large bowl, with mixer over medium heat-low speed, beat both sugars and vegetable spread until well blended, occasionally scraping bowl with rubber spatula. Add egg, egg white, and vanilla; beat until smooth. Beat in flour, baking soda, and salt until mixed. With spoon, stir in oats and chocolate chips until well combined.

3. Drop dough by rounded measuring tablespoons, 2 inches apart, on two ungreased large cookie sheets. Bake until golden, 12 to 13 minutes, rotating cookie sheets between upper and lower oven racks halfway through baking. With wide metal spatula, transfer cookies to wire rack to cool completely. Repeat with remaining dough.

4. Store cookies in airtight container up to 3 days, or freeze up to 1 month.

EACH COOKIE: About 80 calories, 1g protein, 11g carbohydrate, 4g total fat (1g saturated), 1g fiber, 4mg cholesterol, 70mg sodium

OATMEAL-RAISIN COOKIES

If you thought the words "delicious" and "low-fat" could never be used to describe the same cookie, think again. This one's chewy and sweet, yet it has only 2 grams of fat per cookie.

ACTIVE TIME: 15 minutes **TOTAL TIME:** 35 minutes

MAKES: about 4 dozen cookies

2	cups all-purpose flour
1	teaspoon baking soda
½	teaspoon salt
½	cup light (56% to 60% fat) corn-oil spread (1 stick)
¾	cup packed dark brown sugar
½	cup granulated sugar
2	large egg whites plus 1 large egg
2	teaspoons vanilla extract
1	cup quick-cooking oats
1	cup dark seedless raisins

1. Preheat oven to 375°F. Grease 2 large cookie sheets. In medium bowl, combine flour, baking soda, and salt.

2. In large bowl, with mixer at low speed, beat corn-oil spread, brown sugar, and granulated sugar until well combined. Increase speed to high; beat until mixture is light and fluffy. Add egg whites, whole egg, and vanilla; beat until blended. With wooden spoon, stir in flour mixture, oats, and raisins until combined.

3. Drop dough by level tablespoons, 2 inches apart, on prepared cookie sheets. Bake until golden, 10 to 12 minutes, rotating cookie sheets between upper and lower oven racks halfway through baking. With wide spatula, transfer cookies to wire racks to cool completely. Repeat with remaining dough.

EACH COOKIE: About 65 calories, 1g protein, 12g carbohydrate, 2g total fat (0g saturated), 0g fiber, 4mg cholesterol, 72mg sodium

VEGAN OATMEAL-RAISIN COOKIES

When making these cookies, be sure to use vegan stick margarine, not spread, or your cookie dough won't have the right consistency.

ACTIVE TIME: 35 minutes **TOTAL TIME:** 1 hour

MAKES: 3 dozen cookies

1	cup all-purpose flour
1	teaspoon ground cinnamon
½	teaspoon baking soda
½	teaspoon salt
¾	cup vegan stick margarine
¾	cup packed brown sugar
⅓	cup granulated sugar
½	cup plain soy milk
1	teaspoon vanilla extract
3	cups old-fashioned oats
1	cup raisins
1	cup walnuts, chopped

1. Preheat oven to 350°F. Spray 3 large baking sheets with nonstick cooking spray. In small bowl, whisk flour, cinnamon, baking soda, and salt.

2. In large bowl, beat margarine, brown sugar, and granulated sugar until smooth and fluffy. Beat in soy milk and vanilla (mixture will look curdled). Beat in flour mixture. Stir in oats, raisins, and walnuts.

3. Drop dough by heaping tablespoons onto prepared baking sheets, 2 inches apart. Bake one sheet at a time until cookies look dry and are browned at edges, 13 to 15 minutes. Let stand on baking sheet 1 minute before removing with wide spatula to wire rack to cool completely.

EACH COOKIE: About 135 calories, 2g protein, 18g carbohydrate, 6g total fat (2g saturated), 9g fiber, 0mg cholesterol, 93mg sodium

NUTRITIONAL NOTE: OATMEAL

One cup of cooked oats is high in bone-building manganese and cancer-fighting selenium. It is also a good source of fiber, protein, and vitamin B_{12}.

GRANOLA JUMBOS

Granola's great on its own but it also makes delicious, crunchy cookies like these great big treats.

ACTIVE TIME: 25 minutes **TOTAL TIME:** 35 minutes
MAKES: 2 dozen cookies

2 ¼ cups all-purpose flour
2   cups granola cereal with oats and raisins
¾   cup granulated sugar
½   cup packed light brown sugar
½   cup sweetened flaked coconut
1   teaspoon baking soda
1   teaspoon salt
2   large eggs, lightly beaten
½   cup vegetable oil
2   teaspoons vanilla extract

1. Preheat oven to 375°F. In large bowl, combine flour, cereal, granulated and brown sugars, coconut, baking soda, and salt. With fork, stir in eggs, oil, and vanilla. Knead dough with hands until thoroughly blended.

2. Drop dough by scant ¼ cups, 3 inches apart, on ungreased large cookie sheet. With hand, press dough to flatten slightly. Bake until cookies are lightly browned, 12 to 14 minutes. Transfer cookies to wire rack to cool completely. Repeat with remaining dough. Store cookies in tightly covered container up to 1 week.

EACH COOKIE: About 175 calories, 3g protein, 26g carbohydrate, 7g total fat (2g saturated), 1g fiber, 18mg cholesterol, 160mg sodium

WHOLE-GRAIN FIG BARS

Made with whole-wheat flour and dried figs (a fiber-packed miracle food in its own right), these soft, chewy goodies are good for you, too! For an additional whole-grain boost, sprinkle the batter with 2 tablespoons honey-crunch wheat germ before baking.

ACTIVE TIME: 15 minutes **TOTAL TIME:** 35 minutes

MAKES: 24 bars

4	ounces dried Calimyrna figs (¾ cup)
½	cup all-purpose flour
½	cup whole-wheat flour
⅓	cup packed dark brown sugar
1	teaspoon ground cinnamon
½	teaspoon ground ginger
½	teaspoon baking powder
¼	teaspoon salt
⅓	cup light (mild) molasses
2	tablespoons butter, melted
1	teaspoon vanilla extract
1	large egg white

1. Preheat oven to 350°F. Grease 8-inch square metal baking pan. Line pan with foil; grease foil.

2. With kitchen shears, cut stems from figs; cut figs into small pieces. In large bowl, with spoon, stir figs, all-purpose and whole-wheat flours, brown sugar, cinnamon, ginger, baking powder, and salt until mixed. Stir in molasses, melted butter, vanilla, and egg white just until blended and evenly moistened. With metal spatula, spread batter in pan (batter will be sticky).

3. Bake until toothpick inserted in center comes out clean, 20 to 25 minutes. Cool completely in pan on wire rack. When cool, transfer with foil to cutting board. Cut into 3 strips, then cut each strip crosswise into 4 pieces. Cut each rectangle diagonally in half to make 24 triangles. Store cookies between layers of waxed paper in a tightly covered container up to 3 days or freeze up to 3 months.

EACH BAR: About 65 calories, 1g protein, 13g carbohydrate, 1g total fat (0g saturated), 2g fiber, 0mg cholesterol, 45mg sodium

LEMON MERINGUE DROPS

These melt-in-your-mouth meringues are both crunchy and cloud-light—not to mention low in calories and fat-free.

ACTIVE TIME: 45 minutes plus standing **BAKE TIME:** 1 hour 30 minutes
MAKES: about 60 cookies

3   large egg whites
¼   teaspoon cream of tartar
⅛   teaspoon salt
½   cup sugar
2   teaspoons freshly grated lemon peel

1. Preheat oven to 200°F. Line two large cookie sheets with parchment paper.

2. In medium bowl, with mixer over high heatspeed, beat egg whites, cream of tartar, and salt until soft peaks form. With mixer running, sprinkle in sugar, 2 tablespoons at a time, beating until sugar dissolves and meringue stands in stiff, glossy peaks when beaters are lifted. Gently fold in lemon peel.

3. Spoon meringue into decorating bag fitted with ½-inch star tip. Pipe meringue into 1½-inch stars, about 1 inch apart, on prepared cookie sheets.

4. Bake meringues until crisp but not brown, about 1 hour 30 minutes, rotating cookie sheets between upper and lower racks halfway through baking. Turn oven off; leave meringues in oven until dry, about 1 hour.

5. Remove meringues from oven and cool completely. Remove from parchment with wide metal spatula. Store meringues in airtight container up to 1 month, or freeze up to 3 months.

EACH MERINGUE: About 5 calories, 0g protein, 2g carbohydrate, 0g total fat, 0g fiber, 0mg cholesterol, 10mg sodium

HEALTHY MAKEOVER BROWNIES

Decadent! Each square has only 95 calories and three grams of fat—compared to a regular brownie's doubly high calories and nearly quadrupled fat. Our cheat? Swapping nonfat cocoa for chocolate.

ACTIVE TIME: 15 minutes plus cooling **BAKE TIME:** 22 minutes
MAKES: 16 brownies

1	teaspoon instant coffee powder or granules
2	teaspoons vanilla extract
½	cup all-purpose flour
½	cup unsweetened cocoa
¼	teaspoon baking powder
1¼	teaspoons salt
1	cup sugar
¼	cup vegetable oil spread (60% to 70% oil)
3	large egg whites

1. Preheat oven to 350°F. Line 8-inch square metal baking pan with foil; grease foil. In cup, dissolve coffee in vanilla extract.

2. On waxed paper, combine flour, cocoa, baking powder, and salt.

3. In medium bowl, whisk together sugar, vegetable spread, egg whites, and coffee mixture; then blend in flour mixture. Spread evenly in prepared pan.

4. Bake 22 to 24 minutes, until toothpick inserted in brownies 2 inches from edge comes out almost clean. Cool completely in pan on wire rack, about 2 hours.

5. When cool, lift foil, with brownie, out of pan; peel foil away from sides. Cut brownies into 4 strips, then cut each strip crosswise into 4 squares. Refrigerate brownies in airtight container up to 3 days, or freeze up to 3 months.

EACH BROWNIE: About 95 calories, 2g protein, 17g carbohydrate, 3g total fat (1g saturated), 1g fiber, 0mg cholesterol, 75mg sodium

LOW-FAT BUTTERSCOTCH BLONDIES

These chewy bars prove that a low-fat dessert can be just as flavorful as its high-fat counterpart. With just three grams of fat per blondie, you can have your "cake" and eat a second piece, too.

ACTIVE TIME: 15 minutes **BAKE TIME:** 35 minutes

MAKES: 16 blondies

1   cup all-purpose flour
½   teaspoon baking powder
¼   teaspoon salt
3   tablespoons butter
¾   cup packed dark brown sugar
2   large egg whites
⅓   cup dark corn syrup
2   teaspoons vanilla extract
2   tablespoons finely chopped pecans

1. Preheat oven to 350°F. Line 8-inch square baking pan with foil; grease foil. In small bowl, with wire whisk, mix together flour, baking powder, and salt.

2. In large bowl, with mixer over medium heat speed, beat butter and brown sugar until well blended, about 2 minutes. Reduce speed to low; beat in egg whites, corn syrup, and vanilla until smooth. Beat in flour mixture just until combined. Spread batter evenly in prepared pan. Sprinkle with pecans.

3. Bake until toothpick inserted in center comes out clean and edges are lightly browned, 35 to 40 minutes. Cool completely in pan on wire rack.

4. When cool, lift foil, with blondie, out of pan; peel foil away from sides. Cut blondies into 4 strips, then cut each strip crosswise into 4 squares. Refrigerate blondies in airtight container up to 3 days, or freeze up to 3 months.

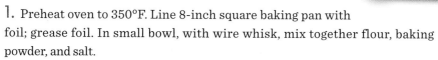

EACH BLONDIE: About 115 calories, 1g protein, 21g carbohydrate, 3g total fat (1g saturated), 0g fiber, 6mg cholesterol, 94mg sodium

HERMIT BARS

Originating in New England in clipper-ship days, these spicy bars got their name because they keep so well. Sailors would stow them "like hermits" for snacking on long voyages.

ACTIVE TIME: 20 minutes **TOTAL TIME:** 35 minutes plus cooling

MAKES: 32 bars

2	cups all-purpose flour
1	teaspoon ground cinnamon
½	teaspoon baking powder
½	teaspoon baking soda
½	teaspoon ground ginger
¼	teaspoon ground nutmeg
¼	teaspoon salt
⅛	teaspoon ground cloves
1	cup packed brown sugar
½	cup butter (1 stick), softened
⅓	cup dark molasses
1	large egg
1	cup dark seedless raisins
1	cup pecans (4 ounces), toasted and coarsely chopped (optional)

1. Preheat oven to 350°F. Grease and flour 2 large cookie sheets.

2. In large bowl, with wire whisk, mix flour, cinnamon, baking powder, baking soda, ginger, nutmeg, salt, and cloves.

3. In separate large bowl, with mixer at medium speed, beat brown sugar and butter until light and fluffy. Beat in molasses until well combined. Beat in egg. With mixer at low speed, beat in flour mixture just until blended, occasionally scraping bowl with rubber spatula. With spoon, stir in raisins and pecans, if using.

4. Divide dough into quarters. With lightly floured hands, shape each quarter into 12" by 1½" log. On each prepared cookie sheet, place 2 logs, leaving about 3 inches in between.

5. Bake until logs flatten and edges are firm, 13 to 15 minutes, rotating cookie sheets between upper and lower oven racks halfway through baking. Cool logs on cookie sheets on wire racks 15 minutes.

6. Transfer logs to cutting board. Slice each log crosswise into 8 bars. Transfer to wire racks to cool completely.

EACH BAR: About 105 calories, 1g protein, 19g carbohydrate, 3g total fat (2g saturated), 1g fiber, 15mg cholesterol, 80mg sodium

JAM CRUMBLE BARS

A food processor makes quick work of these delicious bars. For variety, use contrasting colors of jams and spread them in alternating stripes, or drop random spoonfuls and swirl them together for a marbled effect.

ACTIVE TIME: 15 minutes **BAKE TIME:** 40 minutes
MAKES: 16 bars

1¼ cups all-purpose flour
½ cup packed light brown sugar
¼ teaspoon baking soda
¼ teaspoon ground cinnamon
½ cup cold butter (1 stick), cut into pieces
¼ cup pecans, chopped
½ cup jam (such as raspberry or blackberry)

1. Preheat oven to 350°F. Line 9-inch square baking pan with foil. In food processor with knife blade attached, process flour, brown sugar, baking soda, and cinnamon until mixed. Add butter; process until mixture resembles coarse crumbs and, when pressed, holds together. Transfer ½ cup crumb mixture to small bowl; stir in pecans. Reserve for topping. Press remaining mixture firmly onto bottom of prepared pan.

2. With small metal spatula, spread jam evenly over dough, leaving ½-inch border all around. Crumble reserved topping mixture over jam.

3. Bake until top and edges are browned, 40 to 45 minutes. Cool completely in pan on wire rack.

4. When cool, lift foil, with pastry, out of pan; peel foil away from sides. Cut pastry into 4 strips, then cut each strip crosswise into 4 pieces. Store bars in airtight container up to 5 days, or freeze up to 3 months.

EACH BAR: About 150 calories, 1g protein, 21g carbohydrate, 6g total fat (2g saturated), 0g fiber, 16mg cholesterol, 85mg sodium

TIN ROOF PUFFED RICE TREATS

Just like their namesake sundae, these dressed-up cereal treats are topped with melted chocolate and salted, Spanish peanuts. Indulge—for just 135 calories and two grams of saturated fat per bar.

TOTAL TIME: 20 minutes plus chilling
MAKES: 16 bars

½   cup creamy peanut butter
24   large marshmallows
4   cups puffed rice cereal
⅔   cup semisweet chocolate chips
2   tablespoons roasted, salted Spanish peanuts, chopped

1. Line bottom of 8-inch square baking pan with foil; spray with nonstick cooking spray.

2. In microwave-safe 4-quart bowl, combine peanut butter and marshmallows. Cover bowl with vented plastic wrap and cook in microwave on High 1 minute, until melted. With rubber spatula, quickly stir in puffed rice until evenly coated. Evenly pat puffed rice mixture into prepared baking pan.

3. In microwave-safe cup, heat chocolate in microwave on High, 35 to 45 seconds or until soft; stir until smooth. With offset spatula, spread melted chocolate on top of puffed rice mixture. Sprinkle with peanuts; gently press so nuts adhere to chocolate.

4. Refrigerate until chocolate is set, about 30 minutes. Lift foil, with pastry, out of pan; peel foil away from sides. Cut lengthwise into 4 strips, then cut each strip crosswise into 4 pieces. With small metal spatula, separate treats. Refrigerate in airtight container up to 1 week.

EACH BAR: About 135 calories, 3g protein, 18g carbohydrate, 7g total fat (2g saturated), 1g fiber, 0mg cholesterol, 51mg sodium

LEMON-MAPLE ICEBOX CAKE

This icebox cake combines layers of whole-grain graham crackers with a lemon-maple filling for a quick and easy treat. The best part is, the creamy filling is made with nonfat Greek yogurt, so you can enjoy this dessert guilt-free!

TOTAL TIME: 10 minutes plus chilling

MAKES: 6 servings

2¼ cups nonfat plain Greek yogurt
1 tablespoon maple syrup
½ teaspoon grated lemon peel, plus additional for garnish
½ teaspoon vanilla extract
⅛ teaspoon no-calorie sweetener
6 full sheets of low-fat, whole-grain graham crackers, broken into halves

1. Line 8½" by 4½" loaf pan with plastic wrap, leaving overhang on the two long sides.

2. In a bowl, stir together the yogurt, syrup, ½ teaspoon lemon peel, vanilla, and sweetener.

3. Line the bottom of loaf pan with 3 graham cracker halves. Spread one-third of yogurt mixture over crackers. Repeat, layering twice. Top with remaining 3 graham cracker halves.

4. Using plastic overhang, wrap cake and refrigerate at least 2 hours, or up to 4 hours. Unwrap cake and, using overhanging plastic, pull cake out of pan. With serrated knife, gently cut cake into 6 slices. Garnish with lemon peel and serve.

EACH SERVING: About 115 calories, 9g protein, 18g carbohydrate, 1g total fat (0g saturated), 1g fiber, 0mg cholesterol, 127mg sodium

APPLE-PEAR CRISP WITH PEANUT BUTTER

We swapped in heart-smart peanut butter for the butter in this fruity oat crumble. You could use any nut butter in its place. For photo, see page 404.

ACTIVE TIME: 20 minutes **TOTAL TIME:** 45 minutes

MAKES: 6 servings

- ½ cup old-fashioned oats
- 3 small Gala or Empire apples, peeled and chopped
- 2 medium pears, peeled and chopped
- 1 tablespoon water
- 2 teaspoons light brown sugar
- ½ teaspoon ground cinnamon
- ½ teaspoon ground ginger
- ½ cup dried cranberries
- ⅓ cup chunky, sweetened peanut butter
- 3 tablespoons whole-wheat flour
- ⅜ cup fat-free whipped cream

1. Preheat oven to 375°F. Spread oats in single layer on jelly-roll pan. Toast 5 to 8 minutes, until golden brown, stirring once halfway through.

2. Meanwhile, in 4-quart saucepan, combine apples, pears, water, sugar, cinnamon, and ginger. Cook over medium heat, stirring occasionally, 10 to 12 minutes, until sugar dissolves and fruit softens. Remove from heat and stir in cranberries. Divide mixture among six shallow 12- to 16-ounce baking dishes.

3. In medium bowl, combine oats, peanut butter, and flour. Rub mixture between your fingers to form small clumps, then sprinkle over fruit mixture in baking dishes.

4. Bake 15 to 20 minutes, until browned and bubbling. To serve, top each crisp with 1 tablespoon whipped cream.

EACH SERVING: About 230 calories, 5g protein, 39g carbohydrate, 8g total fat (1g saturated), 6g fiber, 1mg cholesterol, 70mg sodium

TIP

If you don't have individual baking dishes, you can use one shallow 2-quart baking dish and bake for 20 to 25 minutes instead.

"BAKED" APPLES

Cooking these fruit-filled apples in the microwave oven saves time without sacrificing a bit of flavor—and provides a delicious, warm, low-fat dessert in the middle of winter.

ACTIVE TIME: 10 minutes **TOTAL TIME:** 20 minutes

MAKES: 4 servings

4   large Golden Delicious apples (8 ounces each)
¼   cup pitted prunes, chopped
2   tablespoons golden raisins
2   tablespoons brown sugar
2   teaspoons butter, softened
½   teaspoon ground cinnamon
Pinch salt

1. Core apples, cutting 1¼-inch-diameter cylinder in center of each, almost but not all the way through to bottom. Place apples in 8-inch square glass baking dish or shallow 1½-quart microwave-safe casserole dish.

2. In small bowl, combine prunes, raisins, brown sugar, butter, cinnamon, and salt. Fill each cored apple with equal amounts of prune mixture.

3. Cook apples, covered, in microwave oven over High heat about 8 minutes, until tender. Spoon any juices from baking dish over apples before serving.

EACH SERVING: About 185 calories, 1g protein, 44g carbohydrate, 3g total fat (0g saturated), 6g fiber, 0mg cholesterol, 65mg sodium

HEART-SMART INGREDIENT: APPLES

Apples contain antioxidant nutrients and heart-healthy dietary fiber. Low in calories (about 80 per apple) and portable, apples are a perfect on-the-go snack food and, of course, a favorite in apple crisps, pies, and cobblers.

STRAWBERRY-RHUBARB CRISP

This sweet-tart confection is just as tasty as Grandma's strawberry-rhubarb pie—but with one-fifth the calories. By replacing the butter-laden crust with a whole-grain crumble, we've eliminated more than 30 grams of total fat and slashed the saturated fat by almost 90 percent. Grab a spoon and dig in!

ACTIVE TIME: 15 minutes **TOTAL TIME:** 1 hour 5 minutes
MAKES: 8 servings

1   small orange
1   pound strawberries, hulled and cut in half, or into quarters if large
10   ounces rhubarb, trimmed and cut into ½-inch-thick slices
¼   cup granulated sugar
1   tablespoon cornstarch
⅓   cup old-fashioned oats
⅓   cup packed dark brown sugar
¼   cup whole-wheat flour
Pinch salt
3   tablespoons butter, slightly softened

1. Preheat oven to 375°F. From orange, grate peel and divide between 2 large bowls; squeeze ¼ cup orange juice into small bowl.

2. In one large bowl with peel, combine strawberries, rhubarb, and granulated sugar until well mixed. To small bowl with juice, add cornstarch; stir until well mixed. Stir juice mixture into fruit mixture to combine. Pour into 9-inch glass or ceramic pie plate; spread filling in an even layer.

3. In other large bowl with peel, combine oats, brown sugar, flour, and salt. With pastry blender or fingertips, blend in butter until mixture forms coarse crumbs with a few pea-size pieces.

4. Sprinkle oat mixture evenly over strawberry mixture. Place pie plate on foil-lined cookie sheet to catch any drips. Bake 45 minutes, or until topping is golden brown and fruit filling is hot and bubbling.

5. Cool crisp on wire rack until filling is set but still slightly warm, at least 1 hour. Serve warm.

EACH SERVING: About 155 calories, 2g protein, 27g carbohydrate, 5g total fat (3g saturated), 3g fiber, 12mg cholesterol, 70mg sodium

STOVE-TOP BLUEBERRY CRISPS

This dessert is homespun and delicious—and easy to stir up in a saucepan!

TOTAL TIME: 15 minutes

MAKES: 4 servings

1	lemon
2	tablespoons brown sugar
2	teaspoons cornstarch
2	teaspoons almond-flavor liqueur
½	cup cold water
1	tablespoon butter, softened
1	pint blueberries
10	amaretti cookies, coarsely crushed

Confectioners' sugar

1. From lemon, grate ¼ teaspoon peel and squeeze 1 teaspoon juice. In 2-quart saucepan, with spoon, stir lemon peel, lemon juice, brown sugar, cornstarch, almond liqueur, and water. Add butter and half of blueberries to mixture in saucepan; lightly crush blueberries with potato masher or side of spoon. Cook over medium heat, stirring constantly, until mixture boils. Stir in remaining blueberries and boil 2 minutes longer, stirring.

2. Spoon hot blueberry mixture into 4 dessert or custard cups; top with amaretti cookie crumbs and sprinkle with confectioners' sugar. Serve warm.

EACH SERVING: About 160 calories, 1g protein, 30g carbohydrate, 4g total fat (1g saturated), 2g fiber, 0mg cholesterol, 50mg sodium

HEALTHY MAKEOVER STRAWBERRY SHORTCAKE

Sun-kissed berries star in this luscious dessert. And our lean take has advantages of its own that the classic can't claim: The fruit's true sweetness stands out because we've cut down on the sugar, and the cakes are more flavorful because we've added fiber-rich oats.

ACTIVE TIME: 30 minutes **TOTAL TIME:** 45 minutes

MAKES: 8 servings

¾	cup old-fashioned oats, uncooked
1¼	cups all-purpose flour
1½	teaspoons baking powder
½	teaspoon baking soda
¼	teaspoon salt
7	tablespoons plus ½ teaspoon sugar
2	tablespoons cold butter, cut up
¾	cup buttermilk
2	large egg whites
2	pounds strawberries, hulled and cut in half
¼	teaspoon freshly grated lemon peel
1	cup plain fat-free Greek yogurt
½	cup reduced-fat sour cream
1	teaspoon vanilla extract

1. Preheat oven to 425°F. Line cookie sheet with parchment paper or foil.

2. In food processor with knife blade attached, pulse oats until coarsely ground. Add flour, baking powder, baking soda, salt, and 3 tablespoons sugar. Pulse until combined. Add butter; pulse until mixture resembles cornmeal. Add buttermilk and 1 egg white; pulse just until dry ingredients are evenly moistened.

3. With ¼-cup measuring cup, scoop mixture into mounds on prepared sheet, placing mounds 2 inches apart.

4. In small bowl, lightly beat remaining egg white. Brush on top of shortcakes, then sprinkle with ½ teaspoon sugar.

5. Bake 16 minutes or until shortcakes are golden brown. Place sheet on wire rack and let cakes cool completely. Cakes can be kept, tightly wrapped, at room temperature overnight. (Refresh in toaster oven or preheated conventional oven at 375°F for 5 minutes before serving.)

6. Meanwhile, in large bowl, combine strawberries, lemon peel, and 1 table-spoon sugar. Let stand. Can be refrigerated, covered, overnight.

7. In medium bowl, stir yogurt, sour cream, vanilla, and remaining 3 table-spoons sugar. Can be refrigerated, covered, up to overnight.

8. Split open shortcakes. Divide strawberries and filling among shortcakes.

EACH SERVING: About 255 calories, 8g protein, 43g carbohydrate, 6g total fat (2g saturated), 3g fiber, 9mg cholesterol, 335mg sodium

APPLE-BERRY HAND PIES

Priscilla Yee of Concord, California, began cooking heart-healthy after her dad survived a heart attack. Her salty, sweet, and yummy Apple-Berry Hand Pies won our hearts—and earned the grand prize at our second Cook Your Heart Out contest. Crisp, tart apples and sweet, juicy berries fill premade phyllo dough (which has 86 percent less fat than piecrust), and the nonfat yogurt and maple syrup topping helps keep this recipe light.

ACTIVE TIME: 30 minutes **TOTAL TIME:** 40 minutes plus cooling

MAKES: 15 hand pies

1½ cups peeled and chopped tart apples, such as Granny Smith
¾ cup blackberries
1 teaspoon fresh lemon juice
1 tablespoon all-purpose flour
¼ cup plus 2 teaspoons sugar
⅝ teaspoon apple pie spice
10 sheets (14" by 9" each) fresh or thawed frozen phyllo dough
Nonstick cooking spray
¼ teaspoon kosher salt or coarse sea salt
1 cup plain nonfat Greek yogurt
3 tablespoons maple syrup

1. In bowl, mix apples, berries, lemon juice, flour, ¼ cup sugar, and ½ teaspoon apple pie spice.

2. Cover stacked phyllo with slightly damp kitchen towel and place in work area. Transfer 1 phyllo sheet to work surface; lightly coat with cooking spray. Top with another sheet; spray top. Cut lengthwise into three 3-inch-wide strips. Mound 1 heaping tablespoon fruit filling at end of 1 strip, about 1 inch from corner. Fold 1 corner of phyllo diagonally across filling to opposite edge to form triangle. Continue to fold triangle onto itself to end of strip. Repeat with remaining phyllo sheets and filling.

3. Preheat oven to 400°F. Lightly coat cookie sheet with cooking spray. Place pies, seam sides down, on prepared sheet; spray tops with cooking spray. In small bowl, mix salt and remaining 2 teaspoons sugar and ⅛ teaspoon apple pie spice; sprinkle over pies.

4. Bake 10 to 12 minutes, until phyllo is golden brown. Place cookie sheet on wire rack and let pies cool slightly.

5. For topping, stir together yogurt and maple syrup. Serve pies warm with topping.

EACH ½ HAND PIE: About 170 calories, 4g protein, 34g carbohydrate, 2g total fat (0g saturated), 2g fiber, 0mg cholesterol, 200mg sodium

APRICOT UPSIDE-DOWN CAKE

Instead of the canned pineapple typically used in this homey dessert, this version takes full advantage of juicy apricots when they are in season. For image, see back cover, top center.

ACTIVE TIME: 25 minutes **TOTAL TIME:** 1 hour plus chilling

MAKES: 8 servings

½   cup packed brown sugar
8   ripe apricots, cut in half and pitted
1¼ cups all-purpose flour
½   cup granulated sugar
¼   cup cornmeal
1¼ teaspoons baking powder
½   teaspoon salt
½   teaspoon baking soda
¾   cup low-fat buttermilk
2   large eggs
2   tablespoons butter, melted
2   tablespoons canola oil
1   teaspoon freshly grated lemon peel
1   teaspoon vanilla extract

1. Preheat oven to 350°F. Spray 10-inch cast-iron or ovenproof skillet with non-stick cooking spray. Sprinkle brown sugar evenly over bottom of skillet. Arrange apricot halves, cut side down, over brown sugar.

2. In large bowl, whisk flour, granulated sugar, cornmeal, baking powder, salt, and baking soda until blended. In small bowl, whisk buttermilk, eggs, butter, oil, lemon peel, and vanilla. Add buttermilk mixture to dry ingredients and fold with a spatula until just blended. Pour batter over apricots and spread to cover evenly.

3. Bake 35 to 40 minutes, or until toothpick inserted in center of cake comes out clean. Let cool in skillet on wire rack 10 minutes. Run knife around side of skillet. Place platter on top of skillet and carefully invert cake onto platter. Remove skillet. Cool cake slightly, about 30 minutes, and serve warm.

EACH SERVING: About 290 calories, 5g protein, 49g carbohydrate, 8g total fat (1g saturated), 2g fiber, 62mg cholesterol, 365mg sodium

WARM CHOCOLATE BANANA CAKE

Chocolate lovers won't feel deprived when they dig into this low-fat, brownie-like cake with a fudgy texture. Serve with fat-free vanilla ice cream, if you like.

ACTIVE TIME: 15 minutes **TOTAL TIME:** 50 minutes

MAKES: 8 servings

1	cup all-purpose flour
1	cup unsweetened cocoa
½	cup granulated sugar
1	teaspoon baking powder
¼	teaspoon salt
¼	teaspoon ground cinnamon
1	ripe large banana, mashed (½ cup)
1	large egg, beaten
¼	cup cold water, plus 1¼ cups boiling water
2	tablespoons butter, melted
1	teaspoon vanilla extract
½	cup packed dark brown sugar

1. Preheat oven to 350°F. In large bowl, combine flour, ¾ cup cocoa, granulated sugar, baking powder, salt, and cinnamon.

2. In medium bowl, with wooden spoon, stir banana, egg, cold water, melted butter, and vanilla until blended.

3. Stir banana mixture into flour mixture just until blended (batter will be thick). Spoon into ungreased 8-inch square baking dish; spread evenly in pan.

4. In same large bowl, with wire whisk, beat brown sugar, remaining ¼ cup cocoa, and boiling water until blended. Pour over chocolate batter in baking dish; do not stir.

5. Bake 35 minutes (dessert should have some fudgy sauce on top). Cool in pan on wire rack 5 minutes. Serve warm.

EACH SERVING: About 235 calories, 5g protein, 47g carbohydrate, 5g total fat (3g saturated), 4g fiber, 35mg cholesterol, 240mg sodium

HEALTHY MAKEOVER CARROT CAKE

A dessert with a vegetable in its name sounds like it should be good for you, so we've made sure our version is exactly that—healthy as well as delicious. Here's our slimmed-down take on this classic, with just 210 calories and 1 gram of saturated fat per slice. For an even healthier treat, skip the icing altogether.

ACTIVE TIME: 20 minutes **TOTAL TIME:** 1 hour 5 minutes plus cooling

MAKES: 20 servings

CAKE

2¼ cups all-purpose flour

2   teaspoons baking soda

2   teaspoons ground cinnamon

1   teaspoon ground ginger

1   teaspoon baking powder

1   teaspoon salt

2   large eggs

2   large egg whites

1   cup granulated sugar

¾   cup packed dark brown sugar

1   can (8 to 8¼ ounces) crushed pineapple in juice

⅓   cup canola oil

1   tablespoon vanilla extract

1   bag (10 ounces) shredded carrots

½   cup dark seedless raisins

CREAM CHEESE ICING

2   ounces reduced-fat cream cheese

¾   cup confectioners' sugar

½   teaspoon low-fat (1%) milk

¼   teaspoon vanilla extract

1. Preheat oven to 350°F. Spray nonstick 12-cup Bundt-style pan with nonstick cooking spray with flour.

2. Prepare cake: Combine flour, baking soda, cinnamon, ginger, baking powder, and salt.

3. In large bowl, with mixer over medium heat speed, beat eggs and egg whites until blended. Beat in granulated and dark brown sugars; beat 2 minutes. On low speed, beat in pineapple with juice, oil, and vanilla. Add flour mixture; beat 1 minute. Stir in carrots and raisins.

4. Pour batter into pan. Bake 45 to 50 minutes, until toothpick inserted in center comes out clean. Cool in pan 10 minutes. Invert cake onto rack; cool completely.

5. Prepare icing: In bowl, stir cream cheese and ¼ cup confectioners' sugar until smooth. Add milk, vanilla, and remaining confectioners' sugar; stir to a syrupy consistency. Drizzle icing over cake.

EACH SERVING: About 210 calories, 3g protein, 40g carbohydrate, 5g total fat (1g saturated fat), 1g fiber, 23mg cholesterol, 295mg sodium

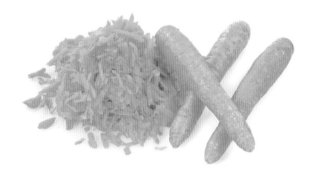

ANGEL FOOD CAKE

Beloved for its clean flavor and light texture, this classic cake has an added attraction—it's low in both calories and fat.

ACTIVE TIME: 30 minutes **TOTAL TIME:** 1 hour 5 minutes

MAKES: 16 servings

1   cup cake flour (not self-rising)
½   cup confectioners' sugar
1⅔ cups egg whites (from 12 to 14 large eggs; see Tip)
1½ teaspoons cream of tartar
½   teaspoon salt
1¼ cups granulated sugar
2   teaspoons vanilla extract
½   teaspoon almond extract

1. Preheat oven to 375°F. Sift flour and confectioners' sugar through sieve set over small bowl.

2. In large bowl, with mixer over medium heat speed, beat egg whites, cream of tartar, and salt until foamy. Increase speed to medium-high heat heat; beat until soft peaks form when beaters are lifted. Sprinkle in granulated sugar, 2 tablespoons at a time, beating until sugar has dissolved and egg whites stand in stiff, glossy peaks when beaters are lifted. Beat in both extracts.

3. Transfer egg-white mixture to larger bowl. Sift flour mixture, one-third at a time, over beaten egg whites; fold in with rubber spatula just until flour mixture is no longer visible. Do not overmix.

4. Scrape batter into ungreased 9- to 10-inch tube pan; spread evenly. Bake until cake springs back when lightly pressed, 35 to 40 minutes. Invert cake, in pan, onto large metal funnel or bottle so that it is suspended upside down; cool completely. Run thin knife around cake to loosen from side and center tube of pan. Remove from pan and place on cake plate.

EACH SERVING: About 115 calories, 3g protein, 25g carbohydrate, 0g total fat, 0g fiber, 0mg cholesterol, 114mg sodium

TIP
You can freeze the egg yolks for another use for up to one month, if you like.

BUTTERMILK PANNA COTTA WITH BLACKBERRY SAUCE

This smooth and creamy dessert features antioxidant-rich blackberries.

ACTIVE TIME: 15 minutes **TOTAL TIME:** 25 minutes plus chilling

MAKES: 8 servings

1	envelope unflavored gelatin
¼	cup plus 2 tablespoons water
2 ¾	cups buttermilk
½	cup plus 4 teaspoons sugar
10	ounces frozen blackberries, thawed
1	teaspoon fresh lemon juice

1. In cup, evenly sprinkle gelatin over ¼ cup water. Let stand 2 minutes to allow gelatin to absorb liquid and soften.

2. In 3-quart saucepan, heat ½ cup buttermilk and ½ cup sugar over medium heat, 2 to 3 minutes or until sugar dissolves, stirring occasionally. Reduce heat to low; whisk in gelatin. Cook 1 to 2 minutes or until gelatin dissolves, stirring. Remove saucepan from heat; stir in remaining 2 ¼ cups buttermilk.

3. Pour buttermilk mixture into eight 4-ounce ramekins or 6-ounce custard cups. Place ramekins in jelly-roll pan for easier handling. Cover pan with plastic wrap and refrigerate panna cotta at least 4 hours or overnight, until well chilled and set.

4. Reserve ⅓ cup blackberries for garnish. In blender, puree remaining blackberries with lemon juice, remaining 2 tablespoons water, and 4 teaspoons sugar. Pour puree through sieve set over small bowl, stirring to press out fruit sauce; discard seeds. Cover and refrigerate sauce if not serving right away.

5. To unmold panna cotta, run tip of small knife around edge of ramekins. With hand, sharply tap side of each ramekin to break seal; invert onto 8 dessert plates. Spoon sauce around each panna cotta. Garnish with reserved berries.

EACH SERVING: About 115 calories, 4g protein, 24g carbohydrate, 1g total fat (1g saturated), 1g fiber, 3mg cholesterol, 90mg sodium

BLUEBERRY-LEMON TIRAMISU

Impress your friends and family with this summery, low-fat take on tiramisu!

ACTIVE TIME: 20 minutes **TOTAL TIME:** 25 minutes plus chilling
MAKES: 9 servings

1 to 2 lemons
3¾ cups blueberries
¾ cup sugar
4 tablespoons water
1 container (17 to 18 ounces) nonfat Greek yogurt
1 package (3 ounces) ladyfingers (see Tip)
Mint sprig, for garnish

1. From lemons, grate 1½ teaspoons peel and squeeze ¼ cup juice.

2. In medium saucepan, combine 1½ cups blueberries, ¼ cup sugar, and 1 tablespoon water. Heat over medium heat 5 minutes or until blueberries soften and juices thicken, stirring occasionally. Transfer to medium bowl and stir in 1½ cups blueberries. Set aside.

3. In microwave-safe small bowl, combine ¼ cup sugar and remaining 3 tablespoons water. Microwave on High, 1 minute. Stir in 3 tablespoons lemon juice and 1 teaspoon lemon peel.

4. In medium bowl, stir together yogurt and remaining ¼ cup sugar, 1 tablespoon lemon juice, and ½ teaspoon lemon peel.

TIP
We tested this recipe with both soft and hard (Italian-style) ladyfingers (sometimes called savoiardi) and had good results with both.

5. In 8-inch square baking dish, arrange half of ladyfingers. Brush with half of lemon syrup. Spoon blueberry mixture evenly over ladyfingers. Arrange remaining ladyfingers over blueberries. Brush with remaining lemon syrup. Spoon yogurt mixture on top, spreading evenly. Cover and refrigerate overnight. To serve, top tiramisu with remaining ¾ cup blueberries and garnish with mint sprig.

EACH SERVING: About 165 calories, 7g protein, 34g carbohydrate, 1g total fat (0g saturated fat), 2g fiber, 23mg cholesterol, 90mg sodium

GRAPEFRUIT-MERINGUE NESTS WITH BERRIES

Grapefruit adds citrus appeal to these edible meringue berry baskets. Slices of other citrus and kiwi would also pair nicely with the grapefruit syrup.

ACTIVE TIME: 25 minutes **TOTAL TIME:** 3 hours 25 minutes

MAKES: 8 servings

MERINGUE NESTS

3   large egg whites

⅛   teaspoon cream of tartar

½   cup sugar

1   teaspoon freshly grated Ruby Red grapefruit peel

MIXED BERRIES

1   container (4.4 ounces) blueberries

1   container (4.4 ounces) raspberries

2   pounds strawberries, hulled and cut in half

¼   cup sugar

¼   cup fresh Ruby Red grapefruit juice

1. Prepare Meringue Nests: Preheat oven to 200°F. Line large cookie sheet with parchment paper or silicone baking mat. In large bowl, with mixer over high heatspeed, beat egg whites and cream of tartar until soft peaks form. Sprinkle in sugar, 2 tablespoons at a time, beating until sugar dissolves and meringue stands in stiff, glossy peaks when beaters are lifted. With large rubber spatula, gently fold grapefruit peel into meringue until well combined.

2. Divide mixture into 8 even mounds (by heaping ¼-cup measuring cup) on prepared sheet, spacing about 2 inches apart. Pressing back of spoon into center of each meringue, form mounds into 3-inch-round nests. Bake 2 hours or until firm. Turn off oven; leave meringues in oven 1 hour or overnight to dry. When meringues are dry, carefully remove from parchment. Meringues can be stored in tightly sealed container at room temperature up to 2 weeks.

3. Prepare Mixed Berries: In large bowl, combine blueberries, raspberries, and half of strawberries. In 12-inch skillet, combine sugar and grapefruit juice. Bring to a boil over medium heat, stirring occasionally. Boil 2 minutes or until sugar dissolves and mixture is clear pink. Add remaining strawberries and cook 1 to 3 minutes or until berries release their juices and have softened slightly. Pour mixture over uncooked berries. Stir gently until well combined.

4. Place meringue nests on serving plates. Divide berries among nests and drizzle grapefruit syrup all around. Serve immediately.

EACH SERVING: About 130 calories, 30g carbohydrate, 2g protein, 1g total fat (0g saturated), 4g fiber, 0mg cholesterol, 25mg sodium

WATERMELON SLUSHIE

We combined antioxidant-rich pomegranate juice with fresh watermelon and ice to create this ruby-red summer cooler.

TOTAL TIME: 5 minutes

MAKES: 1 serving

2   cups seedless watermelon, cut into 1-inch pieces
½   cup pomegranate juice
½   cup ice cubes

In blender, combine watermelon, pomegranate juice, and ice cubes. Blend until smooth. Pour into tall glass.

EACH SERVING: About 170 calories, 2g protein, 40g carbohydrate, 1g total fat (0g saturated), 2g fiber, 0mg cholesterol, 10mg sodium

CREAMY BANANA SORBET

Here's an all-natural frozen treat made with bananas, vanilla, and a touch of maple syrup. Fast, easy, and deliciously creamy, it'll be loved by kids and adults alike.

TOTAL TIME: 5 minutes

MAKES: 6 servings

4   medium very ripe bananas

⅓   cup maple syrup

1   teaspoon vanilla extract

Pinch salt

1. Peel bananas and place in large self-sealing plastic bag. Freeze overnight or until very firm.

2. Slice frozen bananas. In food processor with knife blade attached, blend bananas with maple syrup, vanilla, and salt until creamy but still frozen, about 2 minutes. Serve immediately.

EACH SERVING: About 115 calories, 1g protein, 29g carbohydrate, 0g total fat, 1g fiber, 0mg cholesterol, 25mg sodium

> **TIP**
> This is a great way to use up any extra, ripe bananas that you may have on hand. Before the bananas begin to brown, peel them and freeze in a large self-sealing bag for up to 1 week. Then, you'll have frozen bananas whenever you want to make this luscious dessert.

SUMMER SALSA WITH SWEET TORTILLA CHIPS

This salsa is best made just before serving, but the homemade chips can be baked up to one week ahead.

ACTIVE TIME: 25 minutes **TOTAL TIME:** 35 minutes

MAKES: about 3½ cups or 8 servings

SWEET TORTILLA CHIPS

4   (8-inch) flour tortillas

1   tablespoon butter, melted

1   tablespoon sugar

Pinch ground cinnamon

SUMMER SALSA

1   lime

1   tablespoon sugar

1   large ripe peach, pitted and chopped

1   large ripe red or purple plum, pitted and chopped

1   large ripe apricot, pitted and chopped

½   cup dark sweet cherries, pitted and chopped

½   cup seedless green grapes, chopped

1. Preheat oven to 375°F. Brush tortillas with melted butter. In cup, combine sugar and cinnamon. Sprinkle 1 side of each tortilla with cinnamon-sugar. Stack tortillas and cut into 6 wedges, making 24 wedges in total. Arrange wedges, sugar side up, in single layer on 2 large cookie sheets. Place on 2 oven racks and bake chips until golden, 10 to 12 minutes, rotating cookie sheets between upper and lower racks halfway through baking. Cool chips on cookie sheets on wire racks. Store chips in tightly covered container up to 1 week.

2. Just before serving, prepare Summer Salsa: From lime, grate ¼ teaspoon peel and squeeze 1 tablespoon juice. In medium bowl, stir lime peel, lime juice, sugar, and chopped fruit until combined.

3. To serve, spoon salsa into serving bowl. Use chips to scoop up salsa.

EACH SERVING: About 155 calories, 3g protein, 28g carbohydrate, 4g total fat (2g saturated), 2g fiber, 4mg cholesterol, 150mg sodium

SLICED CITRUS WITH LIME SYRUP

This versatile fruit dish can be eaten atop yogurt for breakfast or dessert.

ACTIVE TIME: 20 minutes **TOTAL TIME:** 25 minutes plus chilling
MAKES: 6 servings

1 to 2 lemons
1 lime
¼ cup sugar
2 navel oranges
2 clementines
2 red or white grapefruit

1. From lemons, grate 1 teaspoon peel and squeeze 3 tablespoons juice. From lime, grate ½ teaspoon peel and squeeze 1 tablespoon juice.

2. In 1-quart saucepan, combine lemon and lime juices with sugar; bring to boiling over medium-high heat. Reduce heat to low; simmer 1 minute. Stir in lemon and lime peels, cover, and refrigerate until cold.

3. Meanwhile, cut peel and white pith from navel oranges, clementines, and grapefruit. Slice all fruit crosswise into ¼-inch-thick rounds. Arrange slices on large, deep platter. Spoon syrup over fruit. Serve, or refrigerate up to 2 days.

EACH SERVING: About 95 calories, 1g protein, 24g carbohydrate, 0g total fat, 3g fiber, 0mg cholesterol, 1mg sodium

COOK'S TIP: CITRUS

Here's how to remove the peel and pith from citrus:

1. Using a sharp paring knife, trim off the top and bottom of the citrus fruit to create an even base; set the fruit cut side up on a cutting board.

2. Following the fruit's contour and working from top to bottom, slice between the peel and flesh to remove a strip of the peel and pith. Repeat, working around the fruit, until you've removed all of the peel.

3. Trim remaining pith, then slice the citrus as instructed in the recipe.

CARAMELIZED FRUIT PLATTER

A beautiful arrangement of sliced oranges and pineapple is topped with a drizzle of caramelized sugar.

ACTIVE TIME: 20 minutes **TOTAL TIME:** 30 minutes

MAKES: 8 servings

5 large navel oranges
1 pineapple, peeled, cored, and sliced into ¼-inch-thick rounds
1 cup sugar

1. From oranges, remove 3 strips peel, 3" by ¾" each. Cut strips lengthwise into very thin slivers. Cut remaining peel and white pith from oranges. Slice oranges into ¼-inch-thick rounds.

2. Arrange orange and pineapple slices, overlapping slightly, on deep platter. Sprinkle with orange-peel slivers; set aside.

3. In 10-inch skillet, cook sugar over medium heat about 10 minutes, swirling sugar in skillet when it begins to melt. Continue cooking and swirling until sugar melts completely and becomes deep amber in color. Remove skillet from heat. Drizzle caramelized sugar over fruit.

4. Serve fruit immediately for a crunchy, candylike topping, or cover and refrigerate until caramel melts, about 2 hours, or until ready to serve.

EACH SERVING: About 165 calories, 1g protein, 42g carbohydrate, 0g total fat, 3g fiber, 0mg cholesterol, 2mg sodium

NUTRITIONAL NOTE: ORANGES

A single orange delivers almost 120 percent of your daily dose of vitamin C. Oranges are also full of compounds called phytochemicals that can help to ward off cancer and other diseases.

RASPBERRY-PEACH DOME

This inexpensive dessert starts with store-bought pound cake.

TOTAL TIME: 30 minutes plus freezing

MAKES: 16 servings

1   frozen pound cake loaf (10 ¾ to 12 ounces), thawed
2   tablespoons seedless raspberry jam
2   pints raspberry sorbet
1   quart peach ice cream
Fresh raspberries, for garnish

1. With serrated knife, cut top crust from pound cake. Place cake on one long side; cut lengthwise into 3 equal slices. With spatula, spread 1 tablespoon jam on cut side of 1 cake slice. Top with another cake slice and spread with remaining 1 tablespoon jam. Top with remaining cake slice. Trim off remaining crusts along sides of cake and slice cake crosswise into ⅜-inch-thick slices.

2. Line deep 2½-quart bowl with plastic wrap, leaving about a 2-inch overhang. Arrange cake rectangles along bottom and up side of bowl (slices will extend slightly above rim) to make a decorative design. If necessary, cut some rectangles into triangles to fill in any open areas, gently pushing cake pieces together to get a tight fit. With knife or kitchen shears, trim off overhanging ends of cake to create an even rim around bowl. (If you like, save trimmings to use as ice cream topping another day.) Place in freezer to firm cake dome slightly, about 20 minutes. Meanwhile, soften the raspberry sorbet.

3. With back of spoon, working quickly, gently spread sorbet over cake layer to an even thickness. Place bowl in freezer 20 minutes to firm sorbet slightly. Meanwhile, soften the peach ice cream.

4. Spoon peach ice cream into center of bowl; spread evenly. Cover bowl with plastic wrap and freeze overnight to ensure dome is frozen throughout. If not serving same day, wrap and freeze up to 2 weeks.

5. To serve, uncover bowl and invert onto platter. Wrap towel dampened with warm water around entire bowl for about 20 seconds to soften dome slightly. Remove bowl and plastic wrap. Garnish dome with raspberries.

EACH SERVING: About 205 calories, 2g protein, 34g carbohydrate, 7g total fat (4g saturated), 2g fiber, 33mg cholesterol, 64mg sodium

PEACHY FROZEN YOGURT

Served as a fruity dessert or snack, this creamy treat delivers a double dose of peach flavor and only 1 gram of fat per serving. It's best made right before you serve it—if it sits in the freezer for longer than an hour, it will turn icy.

TOTAL TIME: 5 minutes

MAKES: 4 servings

1   bag (10 to 12 ounces) frozen sliced peaches
2   containers (6 ounces each) low-fat peach yogurt
1   tablespoon sugar

In food processor with knife blade attached, process peaches until finely shaved. Add yogurt and sugar. Process just until smooth. Serve immediately or pour into 9-inch square baking pan; cover and freeze no longer than 1 hour for best texture.

EACH SERVING: About 130 calories, 4g protein, 28g carbohydrate, 1g total fat (1g saturated), 2g fiber, 6mg cholesterol, 50mg sodium

COOK'S TIP:
PEELING PEACHES

If you have a lot of peaches, our favorite way to peel them is to submerge a few at a time in boiling water for about 20 seconds (no longer or they will start to cook). Remove them with a slotted spoon and plunge them immediately into a large bowl of ice water. The skins should slip right off. Another method, if the peaches are perfectly ripe, is to insert the tip of a paring knife into the stem end and peel away the skin in strips. Whatever you do, don't peel a ripe peach with a vegetable peeler—you'll bruise the delicate flesh.

BOLD BERRY GRANITA

Frosty, fruity, and fat-free, this mix of pureed raspberries and strawberries is the ultimate summer dessert.

TOTAL TIME: 20 minutes plus freezing
MAKES: 5 servings

1   cup water
½   cup sugar
1 to 2 lemons
1   pound strawberries, hulled and cut in half
1½ cups raspberries

1. In 2-quart saucepan, bring water and sugar to a boil over high heat, stirring until sugar dissolves. Reduce heat to low and simmer, uncovered, 5 minutes. Set aside to cool slightly, about 5 minutes.

2. Meanwhile, from lemons, grate 2 teaspoons peel and squeeze ¼ cup juice. In food processor with knife blade attached, blend strawberries and raspberries until pureed. With back of spoon, press puree through sieve into medium bowl; discard seeds.

3. Stir sugar syrup and lemon juice and peel into berry puree. Pour into 9-inch square metal baking pan. Cover and freeze granita mixture until partially frozen, about 2 hours, then stir with a fork to break up the chunks. Cover and freeze until completely frozen, at least 3 hours or overnight.

4. To serve: Use a metal spoon to scrape across the surface of the granita, transferring the ice shards to chilled dessert dishes or wine goblets without packing them.

EACH SERVING: About 60 calories, 1g protein, 15g carbohydrate, 0g total fat, 2g fiber, 0mg cholesterol, 0mg sodium

HEALTHY MAKEOVER STRAWBERRY ICE CREAM

This delectable treat calls for a mere ten minutes of your time and freezes into scoopable sweetness in an hour—no fancy machine required. A serving of custard-based strawberry ice cream has 282 calories and 12 grams of saturated fat, compared to the 70 calories and 0 grams saturated fat in our luscious dessert. So go ahead: Spoon up some more.

ACTIVE TIME: 10 minutes **TOTAL TIME:** 1 hour 10 minutes

MAKES: 7 servings

1   pound frozen strawberries
1   cup 2% plain Greek yogurt (see Tip)
¼   cup sugar
½   teaspoon vanilla extract
Fresh strawberries, for garnish

1. In food processor with knife blade attached, pulse 1 cup strawberries until finely chopped. Transfer to large metal bowl.

2. In food processor, puree yogurt, sugar, vanilla, and remaining strawberries until smooth. Transfer to bowl with strawberries; stir until well combined.

3. Cover and freeze about 1 hour, until firm but not hard. Garnish with fresh strawberries.

EACH ½-CUP SERVING: About 70 calories, 3g protein, 14g carbohydrate, 1g total fat (0g saturated), 1g fiber, 1mg cholesterol, 10mg sodium

TIP

You can substitute plain low-fat yogurt for the Greek yogurt. When testing this recipe, we found both worked well, but we preferred Greek yogurt's creamier texture. We also tested this in three different freezers and found that the freezing time varied, depending on freezer make and model. Begin checking your ice cream at one hour, and continue freezing if you prefer a firmer texture.

TROPICAL SORBET LOAF

A slice of this dessert looks like a summer sunset. The best part is, it's really easy; just scoop and freeze. Your kids can help.

TOTAL TIME: 20 minutes plus freezing
MAKES: 16 servings

1   pint raspberry or strawberry sorbet, softened
1   pint mango or passion fruit sorbet, softened
1   pint coconut sorbet, softened
1   pint orange or peach sorbet, softened
Shaved coconut, fresh raspberries, and fresh mint leaves, for garnish

1. Spray 9" by 5" loaf pan with nonstick cooking spray. Line pan with plastic wrap.

2. Using 2-inch (¼-cup) ice cream scoop, arrange 8 alternating scoops of sorbet (2 scoops of each flavor) in single layer in pan. Place plastic wrap on sorbet scoops and press mixture down to flatten and eliminate air pockets; remove plastic. Repeat to make 2 more layers in same way, alternating sorbets within each layer and from layer to layer, making sure to press mixture down each time. Cover and freeze until firm, at least 6 hours.

3. To serve, uncover pan and invert onto platter. Wrap towels dampened with warm water on bottom and sides of pan for about 20 seconds to slightly soften sorbet. Remove pan and plastic wrap. Garnish loaf with coconut, raspberries, and mint.

EACH SERVING: About 125 calories, 0g protein, 26g carbohydrate, 1g total fat (1g saturated), 1g fiber, 0mg cholesterol, 15mg sodium

TROPICAL BANANA SPLITS

The king of soda-shop desserts is even better made with sorbets and coconut.

TOTAL TIME: 15 minutes

MAKES: 4 servings

¼   cup sweetened flaked coconut
2   ripe medium bananas, peeled and cut lengthwise in half, then crosswise into quarters
1   cup fat-free passion fruit sorbet, slightly softened
1   cup fat-free raspberry sorbet, slightly softened
2   medium kiwifruit, peeled and cut crosswise into 8 slices

1. In small nonstick skillet, toast coconut over medium heat, stirring frequently.

2. To serve, on each of 4 dessert plates (oval if possible), arrange 2 banana quarters, cut sides up, on opposite sides of plate. Place ¼-cup scoop each of passion fruit and raspberry sorbets between banana quarters.

3. Top with 4 slices kiwifruit and sprinkle with 1 tablespoon toasted coconut.

EACH SERVING: About 230 calories, 1g protein, 45g carbohydrate, 3g total fat (2g saturated), 4g fiber, 0mg cholesterol, 20mg sodium

FROZEN FRUIT YOGURT

It's so simple: In just 10 minutes you can make delicious frozen yogurt by blending your favorite frozen fruit with plain yogurt. And it's low-fat!

TOTAL TIME: 10 minutes

MAKES: about 2½ cups

12	ounces (2¾ cups) frozen strawberries, cherries, or peaches
10	ounces (2⅓ cups) frozen raspberries or other fruit
1	cup plain low-fat yogurt
½	cup sugar
1	tablespoon fresh lemon juice
⅛	teaspoon almond extract

1. In food processor with knife blade attached, blend frozen fruit until it resembles finely shaved ice, stopping processor occasionally to scrape down bowl. If fruit is not finely shaved, dessert will not be smooth.

2. Add yogurt, sugar, lemon juice, and almond extract, and process just until mixture is smooth and creamy, scraping down bowl occasionally. Serve immediately. Or spoon into freezer-safe containers and freeze to serve later; let stand at room temperature 10 minutes to soften slightly before serving.

EACH SERVING: About 130 calories, 3g protein, 29g carbohydrate, 1g total fat (1g saturated), 1g fiber, 3mg cholesterol, 35mg sodium

STRAWBERRY FLOATS

This is a creative and colorful twist on the ice cream soda.

TOTAL TIME: 10 minutes

MAKES: 5 sodas

1½ cups milk

1   package (10 ounces) frozen sliced strawberries, partially thawed

1   pint strawberry ice cream, slightly softened

1   bottle (16 ounces) club soda or strawberry soft drink, chilled

1. In blender at high speed, blend milk and strawberries 15 seconds; pour into five 12-ounce glasses.

2. Add a scoop of strawberry ice cream to each; slowly add soda to fill almost to the top.

EACH SERVING (1 SODA): About 203 calories, 4g protein, 32g carbohydrate, 7g total fat (5g saturated), 1g fiber, 26mg cholesterol, 77mg sodium

NUTRITIONAL NOTE: STRAWBERRIES

A single serving of strawberries (1 cup) is a powerhouse of vitamin C and a very good source of bone-building magnesium, dietary fiber, and iodine, which is vital to healthy thyroid function.

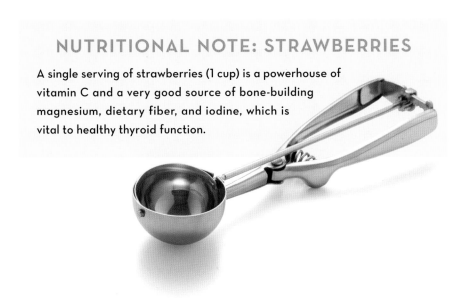

SGROPPINO SORBET WITH PROSECCO AND MINT

Sgroppino is a classic after-dinner beverage from the Veneto region in northern Italy. It's usually made by whipping up lemon sorbet and Prosecco; a splash of vodka is sometimes added. Here we've left the sorbet intact as a light and refreshing float—a luscious and low-cal end to dinner.

TOTAL TIME: 5 minutes

MAKES: 6 servings

1   pint lemon sorbet
2   cups Prosecco (Italian sparkling wine)
Fresh mint sprigs, for garnish

Evenly scoop sorbet into 6 wineglasses or dessert bowls. Pour ⅓ cup Prosecco into each glass; garnish with mint. Serve immediately.

EACH SERVING: About 135 calories, 0g protein, 22g carbohydrate, 0g total fat, 0g fiber, 0mg cholesterol, 10mg sodium

METRIC EQUIVALENT CHARTS

The recipes that appear in this cookbook use the standard United States method for measuring liquid and dry or solid ingredients (teaspoons, tablespoons, and cups). The information on this chart is provided to help cooks outside the United States successfully use these recipes. All equivalents are approximate.

METRIC EQUIVALENTS FOR DIFFERENT TYPES OF INGREDIENTS

A standard cup measure of a dry or solid ingredient will vary in weight depending on the type of ingredient. A standard cup of liquid is the same volume for any type of liquid. Use the following chart when converting standard cup measures to grams (weight) or milliliters (volume).

Standard Cup	Fine Powder (e.g. flour)	Grain (e.g. rice)	Granular (e.g. sugar)	Liquid Solids (e.g. butter)	Liquid (e.g. milk)
1	140 g	150 g	190 g	200 g	240 ml
¾	105 g	113 g	143 g	150 g	180 ml
⅔	93 g	100 g	125 g	133 g	160 ml
½	70 g	75 g	95 g	100 g	120 ml
⅓	47 g	50 g	63 g	67 g	80 ml
¼	35 g	38 g	48 g	50 g	60 ml
⅛	18 g	19 g	24 g	25 g	30 ml

USEFUL EQUIVALENTS FOR LIQUID INGREDIENTS BY VOLUME

¼ tsp=					1 ml
½ tsp=					2 ml
1 tsp =					5 ml
3 tsp =	1 tbls =		½ fl oz =	15 ml
	2 tbls =	⅛ cup =	1 fl oz =	30 ml
	4 tbls =	¼ cup =	2 fl oz =	60 ml
	5⅓ tbls =	⅓ cup =	3 fl oz =	80 ml
	8 tbls =	½ cup =	4 fl oz =	120 ml
	10⅔ tbls =	⅔ cup =	5 fl oz =	160 ml
	12 tbls =	¾ cup =	6 fl oz =	180 ml
	16 tbls =	1 cup =	8 fl oz =	240 ml
	1 pt =	2 cups =	16 fl oz =	480 ml
	1 qt =	4 cups =	32 fl oz =	960 ml
			33 fl oz =	1000 ml = 1 L

USEFUL EQUIVALENTS FOR DRY INGREDIENTS BY WEIGHT

(To convert ounces to grams, multiply the number of ounces by 30.)

1 oz	=	¹⁄₁₆ lb	=	30g
4 oz	=	¼ lb	=	120g
8 oz	=	½ lb	=	240g
12 oz	=	¾ lb	=	360g
16 oz	=	1 lb	=	480g

USEFUL EQUIVALENTS LENGTH

(To convert inches to centimeters, multiply the number of inches by 2.5.)

1 in	=		2.5cm
6 in	= ½ ft =		15cm
12 in	= 1 ft =		30cm
36 in	= 3 ft = 1 yd	=	90cm
40 in	=		100cm = 1 m

USEFUL EQUIVALENTS FOR COOKING/OVEN TEMPERATURES

	Fahrenheit	Celsius	Gas Mark
Freeze Water	32°F	0° C	
Room Temperature	68°F	20° C	
Boil Water	212°F	100° C	
Bake	325°F	160° C	3
	350°F	180° C	4
	375°F	190° C	5
	400°F	200° C	6
	425°F	220° C	7
	450°F	230° C	8
Broil			Grill

PHOTOGRAPHY CREDITS

Cover: ©Johnny Miller

Back cover, clockwise from top left: © Emily Kate Roemer/Studio D;
    James Baigrie (2); Kate Mathis; Anna Williams; Alan Richardson

©Antonis Achilleos: 101, 322
©James Baigrie: 20, 35, 57, 105, 108, 138, 213, 215, 299, 350, 371, 378, 388, 433, 443
Depositphotos: ©indigolotos: 361; ©lenyvavsha: 19
©Tara Donne: 98, 377, 380, 398
Chris Eckert/Studio D: 15
Philip Friedman/Studio D: 7
©Brian Hagiwara: 113 (x3), 187, 205, 217, 219 (x5), 257, 260, 325, 358, 428, 449
iStock:
©4kodiak: 289; ©AK2: 23; ©anna1311: 65; ©Mehmet Hilmi Barcin: 437; ©bluestocking: 431;
    ©bonchan: 157; ©OliverChilds: 79; ©cobraphoto: 103: ©Creativeye99: 92; ©didyk: 16;
    ©Dole08: 175, 366; ©egal: 123, 313; ©Floortje: 107, 399; ©MarkGillow: 342; ©Grafissimo:
    301; ©Ermin Gutenberger: 13, 247; ©Oliver Hoffmann: 126; ©hudiemm: 85; ©iSailorr:
    151; ©ChristianJung: 319; ©mashabuba: 12; ©James McQuillan: 408; ©Marek Mnich:
    425; ©Spetnitskaya Nadva: 27; ©Natikka: 74; ©PaulPaladin; ©photovideostock: 8; ©Judd
    Pilossof: 412; ©Sintez: 203; ©small_frog: 183; ©Oksana Struk: 281; ©Kajdi Szabolcs: 111;
    ©Jarek Szymanski: 386; ©Diana Talium: 29; ©tchara: 381; ©Thammasak_Chuenchom: 461;
    ©unalozmen: 191 (dried tomatoes); ©MargarytaVakhterova: 191 (cheese): ©victoriya89:
    68, 191 (lemons); ©Viktar: 227; ©Suprun Vitaly: 71; ©Yasonya: 364, 459; ©Yin Yang: 51
©Yunhee Kim: 63
©Robert Linton: 415
©Rita Maas: 96, 143, 309
©Kate Mathis: 25, 36, 45, 49, 80, 83, 86, 117, 119, 140, 168, 168, 189, 211, 220, 224, 269, 273,
    295, 314, 329, 336, 349, 360, 383, 391,397, 414, 418, 421, 427, 441, 445, 446, 454, 456
©Ellie Miller: 90
©Johnny Miller: 3, 137
©Con Poulos: 55, 66, 95, 114, 135, 184, 208, 234, 275, 302, 404, 422
©Alan Richardson: 317
©Emily Kate Roemer: 158
©Kate Sears: 11, 89, 124, 133, 173, 195, 200, 229, 230, 253, 255, 264, 287, 321, 384, 463
Shutterstock:
38, 160 (x3), 161(x3), 368; ©Bienchen-s: 46, 145, 334; ©Dionisvera: 341; ©Elena
    Elisseeva: 31; ©MShev: 345; Joshua Resnick: 363; ©Yuliya Rusyayeva: 279
©Amy Kalyn Sims: 43
StockFood:
©Keller & Keller: 438
©Ann Stratton: 401, 417
©Mark Thomas: 72, 167, 181
Kristen Somody Whelan: 53
©Anna Williams: 6, 121, 131, 163, 249, 284, 306

INDEX

Note: Page numbers in *italics* indicate photos of recipes located apart from recipe.

THE GOOD HOUSEKEEPING TRIPLE-TEST PROMISE

At Good Housekeeping, we want to make sure that every recipe we print works in any oven, with any brand of ingredient, no matter what. That's why, in our test kitchens at the **Good Housekeeping Research Institute**, we go all out: We test each recipe at least three times—and, often, several more times after that.

When a recipe is first developed, one member of our team prepares the dish and we judge it on these criteria: it must be **delicious, family-friendly, healthy**, and **easy to make**.

1. The recipe is then tested several more times to fine-tune the flavor and ease of preparation, always by the same team member, using the same equipment.

2. Next, another team member follows the recipe as written, **varying the brands of ingredients** and **kinds of equipment**. Even the types of stoves we use are changed.

3. A third team member repeats the whole process **using yet another set of equipment** and **alternative ingredients**.

By the time the recipes appear on these pages, they are guaranteed to work in any kitchen, including yours. WE PROMISE.